◆

*Critical Essays on*
# JAMES MERRILL

◆

# CRITICAL ESSAYS
# ON
# AMERICAN LITERATURE

James Nagel, General Editor
*University of Georgia, Athens*

◆

# *Critical Essays on*
# JAMES MERRILL

◆

*edited by*

## GUY ROTELLA

*G. K. Hall & Co.*
*An Imprint of Simon & Schuster Macmillan*
*New York*

*Prentice Hall International*
London • Mexico City • New Delhi • Singapore • Sydney • Toronto

For permission to quote from the copyrighted poems of James Merrill, the editor and contributors are especially grateful to Alfred A. Knopf, Inc. for excerpts from *Selected Poems* © 1992 and *The Changing Light at Sandover* © 1980, 1982 by James Merrill. Reprinted by permission.

G. K. Hall & Co.
An Imprint of Simon & Schuster Macmillan
1633 Broadway
New York, New York 10019

---

Library of Congress Cataloging-in-Publication Data

Critical essays on James Merrill / [edited by] Guy Rotella.
   p.   cm.—(Critical essays on American literature)
   Includes bibliographical references (p.      ) and index.
   ISBN 0-7838-0031-2
   1. Merrill, James Ingram—Criticism and interpretation.
I. Rotella, Guy L.   II. Series.
PS3525.E6645Z63   1996
811'.54—dc20                                                      95-43252
                                                                      CIP

---

The paper used in this publication meets the minimum requirements of American National Standard for Information Sciences—Permanence of Paper for Printed Library Materials. ANSI Z3948–1984. ⊚ ™

10   9   8   7   6   5   4   3   2   1

Printed in the United States of America

# Contents

◆

General Editor's Note     vii
Publisher's Note     ix
Introduction     1
     GUY ROTELLA


REVIEWS

The Country of a Thousand Years of Peace
     "Sunbursts, Garlands, Creatures, Men"     27
       MONA VAN DUYN

Nights and Days
     Merrill     31
       DAVID KALSTONE

The Fire Screen     36
       JOHN HOLLANDER

Braving the Elements
     Feux d'Artifice     38
       STEPHEN YENSER

Divine Comedies
     Evenings at the Ouija Board     44
       DAVID KALSTONE

Mirabell
     Answer, Heavenly Muse, Yes or No     50
       DAVID BROMWICH

Late Settings
     Fears and Farewells     57
       HELEN VENDLER

*A Scattering of Salts*
    The End of More Than Just a Book           70
        W. S. MERWIN


ESSAYS

    [On "Lost in Translation"]           77
        STEPHEN YENSER

    Rethinking Models of Literary Change:
    The Case of James Merrill           99
        MUTLU KONUK BLASING

    'I knew // That life was fiction in disguise':
    Merrill's Divergence from Auden and Modernism       116
        LYNN KELLER

    James Merrill's Masks of Eros, Masques of Love       145
        ERIC MURPHY SELINGER

    Against Apocalypse: Politics and James Merrill's
    *The Changing Light at Sandover*           175
        LEE ZIMMERMAN

    From Polylinguism to Metalinguism: Dante's Language
    in Merrill's Trilogy           190
        ANDREA MARIANI
        (Translated by Guy Rotella)

    Writing on the (Sur)face of the Past: Convival Visions and
    Revisions in the Poetry of James Merrill       215
        JEFF WESTOVER

    Braving the Elements           231
        J. D. McCLATCHY

*Index*           245

# General Editor's Note

◆

This series seeks to anthologize the most important criticism on a wide variety of topics and writers in American literature. Our readers will find in various volumes not only a generous selection of reprinted articles and reviews but original essays, bibliographies, manuscript sections, and other materials brought to public attention for the first time. This volume, *Critical Essays on James Merrill*, is the most comprehensive collection of essays ever published on this important modern poet. It contains both a sizable gathering of early reviews and a broad selection of current scholarship as well. Among the authors of reprinted articles and reviews are Helen Vendler, Lee Zimmerman, John Hollander, Stephen Yenser, Eric Murphy Selinger, W. S. Merwin, and J. D. McClatchy. In addition to a substantial introduction by Guy Rotella, there is an original essay by Jeff Westover commissioned specifically for publication in this volume and an article by Andrea Mariani newly translated from Italian. We are confident that this book will make a permanent and significant contribution to the study of American literature.

JAMES NAGEL
*University of Georgia, Athens*

# Publisher's Note

◆

Producing a volume that contains both newly commissioned and reprinted material presents the publisher with the challenge of balancing the desire to achieve stylistic consistency with the need to preserve the integrity of works first published elsewhere. In the Critical Essays series, essays commissioned especially for a particular volume are edited to be consistent with G. K. Hall's house style; reprinted essays appear in the style in which they were first published, with only typographical errors corrected. Consequently, shifts in style from one essay to another are the result of our efforts to be faithful to each text as it was originally published.

# Introduction

♦

GUY ROTELLA

James Merrill was born on March 3, 1926, in New York City, to Charles
E. Merrill, cofounder of the Merrill Lynch brokerage firm, and his second
wife, Hellen Ingram. He was raised in a New York brownstone and a
Southampton mansion, with vacations in Palm Beach. Although his companions were more often the household servants than his parents, it was a life
of comfort and privilege; and yet, as the phrasing may suggest, it could
laminate curses and blessings. In any case, a trust established by his father
would give him financial independence when he came of age. As Merrill
bluntly put it, "at five years old I was rich."[1] Merrill was precocious in
other ways as well, writing and performing puppet shows, for instance: a
fondness for masked display stayed with him, and later forays into drama
and fiction bear on his verse.

In 1939, when Merrill was thirteen, his parents divorced. The event's
echoes are a frequent subject of Merrill's work, in which autobiographical
treatment of displacement and reconciliation is often connected to the culture's archetypes of wholeness and division. Reversibility is one of its features.

After preparation at Lawrenceville, Merrill attended Amherst College.
He took a year off for military service and graduated in 1947, having
completed an honors essay on metaphor in Proust. He then taught briefly
at Bard and elsewhere. In the early 1950s, Merrill spent two and a half years
in Europe. This was a period of distressing, bracing, and transforming
encounters with his mother and father, with art and opera, with mentors,
psychoanalysts, and homosexual lovers. Merrill recounts those years in the
memoir *A Different Person*, which reveals cunningly framed vignettes of much
of his earlier and later life. In the mid-1950s, Merrill and his lover and
long-time companion, David Jackson, moved to a house in the seacoast
village of Stonington, Connecticut. The couple more or less lived there
together thereafter, punctuating their time at Water Street with extended
yearly stays at other homes in New York, Greece, and, later, Key West,

1

and with travel to Europe, Asia, and the American Southwest, as well as with lovers' quarrels and separations. Settled and unsettled domesticity, faith and infidelity, and travel's trails and trouvées are also important Merrill subjects, with their own versions of reunion and divorce.

Merrill reports that he began writing poetry during his second year at Lawrenceville. Elinor Wylie was an early model, but he was soon aware of Rilke, Ransom, Stevens, and Yeats as he developed his polished early style.[2] His first publication was *Jim's Book*, printed in 1942 as a surprise from his father. In 1946 came an appearance in *Poetry*, and the twelve privately printed poems of *The Black Swan*. Their period style is stiffly winged, but these early poems fledge Merrill's principal themes, among them "the necessity and impossibility of love" and its passage "into memory and art."[3] As his style eased toward a formal mastery that is flexible and free but never loose, Merrill's treatment of those matters persisted. His poetry grew more autobiographically direct (although it is never simple nor "confessionally" urgent), and it expanded to include the epic concerns for human survival of *The Changing Light at Sandover* (1982), in which the achievements and failures of love are related to the largest cultural patterns: poetry, politics, and language; history, ideology, and belief. For Merrill, those patterns are themselves necessary and impossible; their passing into memory and art is a loss and gain that joins and divides, injures and sustains.

James Merrill died of a sudden heart attack on February 6, 1995, in Arizona. A month later his final book was published. The dust jacket of *A Scattering of Salts* shifts the tense of the author's note in the text from present to past, a dissonant consonance of a nearly Merrillian sort.

James Merrill may have been our most honored contemporary poet; he received two National Book Awards, the Bollingen and Pulitzer Prizes, and most of the other distinctions offered to American poets. Yet Merrill's literary reputation remains unsettled, perhaps because his poetry and its critical reception reflect developments, divisions, and debates that have marked American culture, poetry, and scholarship since 1950.

At least in retrospect, the American 1950s have seemed to many a period of consensus; what followed has seemed an era of dissent. In one version of the cultural situation of Merrill's age, in the early 1950s, continuing effects of the unified effort required to fight the Second World War joined with fears of a return to prewar economic difficulties and encouraged a conformity of appearance, thought, and behavior that briefly concealed serious divisions of race, class, and social and political opinion. In poetry, an orthodox academic style obtained, based on the New Critics' elevation of "high modernist" poetry to a set of rules requiring that poems reflect such qualities as impersonality, allusiveness to high cultural traditions, the containment of conflicting ideas by means of linguistic and figurative tensions, especially irony, and a conception of the poem as a perfected, self-referential object. While it enforced high-modernist models, the academic style also rejected other modernist modes and even the experimentalism of high modernism itself, encouraging in its place a return to formal rigor and the regularities of meter, rhyme, and stanza pattern. Recourse to models from the past as a means to restore or retain a supposedly threatened cultural unity was an important feature of the time, in poetry and beyond it. Critical practice in those years focused on the literary work, often apart from and at the expense of its relations to the culturally imbedded artist who made it and to the world it might be thought to address.

Conformity can both produce and conceal anxiety; to many, what looked like consensus masked differences and disagreements and repressed alternative possibilities for living, for writing poems, and for reading them. To some, literature and scholarship seemed complicitous with cultural forces censoring the individualism often equated with the American self. Uniformity would soon be challenged from several sides. The debates define the age.

Since the 1950s, such factors as the civil rights movement, various forms of youth rebellion, the political and social crisis of the Vietnam War, movements for women's and gay and lesbian liberation, the shocks of a series of assassinations, an intensifying distrust of institutions, and various demands for a society more responsive to multicultural differences all mark the failure or erosion of whatever consensus actually existed. They can also signify that Merrill's is a period in which no single version of literary practice, purpose, or attainment is likely to earn collective consent.

Poetry, too, in these years was, and remains, an arena of debate. The academic style has been challenged by multiple alternatives. First, the poetry and poetics of beat, projectivist, confessional, and neosurrealist poets challenged the academic claim to present universal truths by impersonal and formalist means. These poets insist instead on the authority of personal experience and thus on autobiographical presentation, or they emphasize the relativism and artificiality of artistic acts. They insist, too, that perfected "closed" forms are mechanistic constraints out of step with the natural and human or with the recognition by biology and physics that everything is a relational event. Traditional forms are therefore judged inferior to experimental, "open," and provisional or contingent organic shapes. Other poets, whose work is rooted in ethnic, racial, class, gender, sexual, and even regional identities, also challenge consensus views. They question the priority and propriety of high cultural models, insisting on their relativity or irrelevance. To them, the literary and cultural past, once seen as a resource for repairing rupture or resisting debilitating change, may seem instead the site of repression or an obstacle to desirable transformation. More recently, poets influenced by ideas related to literary theory have further complicated and enriched the scene. Such writers doubt the existence, coherence, and authenticity of the self, assert the constructed rather than essential or necessary nature of all human systems (including poetry), suspect that we are more produced by language than producing it, and insist that art conspires with power even when it seeks to chastize it. Such views contest not only the academic model but many of the alternatives to it as well. At the same time, current neo-formalist poets are reinscribing some of the claims of the tradition. It is a stimulating situation, but more amenable to contestation than consensus.

Similar changes have marked literary criticism since the 1950s. Competing approaches, first psychoanalytical and archetypal ones, then structuralism and semiotics, then feminism and various versions of poststructuralism, have worked to restore the poem to its relations to the writer's self and world, at times in ways that faithfully encourage art's engagement of private and public realms, at times in ways that distrust its relationships to established authority and power. In a period when poets and critics can disagree about something so fundamental as whether art upholds or holds down what we value, an artist's critical reception is apt to be unsettled. The critical response to Merrill's work reflects the situation.

Merrill's *First Poems* was published in 1951. Reviewers in *Poetry*, the *New York Times Book Review*, and the *New Yorker* respected its youthful mastery of difficult forms, its polish and poise. They also noted its evasively impersonal voice, its emphasis on objects and abstractions rather than on people, emotions, or felt ideas, and its achievement of or acquiescence to a period style. Most evaluations are frankly mixed. Rolfe Humphries admires Merrill's proficiency but finds that he lacks "ardor." Howard Nemerov is crisp: "The poems are slight but fully accomplished." James Dickey seems irritated: Merrill is one of the "agreeable craftsmen of the forties and fifties who promised most and delivered least."[4]

Audible in this is the stress and strain of the academic consensus breaking up well before Ginsberg's *Howl* (1956) or Lowell's *Life Studies* (1959) certified its collapse. Louise Bogan put the matter clearly in a manner Merrill took to heart. Poetry has become a formula that considers experience vulgar and feelings suspect; it values the surface texture of a work over its connection to actual life. Merrill, Bogan thinks, has the formula down pat: his poems "are impeccably written, but everything about them smells of the lamp; they are as frigid and dry as diagrams."[5] Years later, Merrill includes a formulaic diagram within a poem and boldly redefines his lamp,[6] not so much to counter Bogan's stricture as to show what he learned from it.

Between *First Poems* and his next collection of poetry eight years later, Merrill published a novel, *The Seraglio*, in 1957. This Jamesian narrative—the tale of an American innocent who is damaged by a rich, promiscuous, and domineering father, retreats from love and sex in elegant international surroundings, and then, after a nearly suicidal attempt at self-emasculation, finds a serene inheritance—was praised for its dense symbolic texture, its "genuine intimation" of decadent sophistication, and its wry humor. Those who delivered the praise also judged the book a badly focused failure. Whitney Balliett called it nonsense.[7] The partly autobiographical subject and themes remained with Merrill to appear in poems that combine lyric with narrative modes and make a sense including nonsense.

The Country of a Thousand Years of Peace came out in 1959, the year of Lowell's Life Studies, with its frankly autobiographical treatment of madness, suicide, and the starker forms of the family romance. To some reviewers Merrill's continuing formal reserve seemed tame. One expresses hope that Merrill will someday escape from the sculpture museum. But other reviewers redefine Merrill's obliquity as a mode of self-expression. For William Meredith, the poems show that things appearing "precious in the false sense may be precious in the true."[8] The most important review of The Country of a Thousand Years of Peace is by Mona Van Duyn. She avoids the characteristic divisions of the day and their praise or condemnation of poems for being impersonal or personal, formally closed or open, of the intellect or the body, and describes Merrill's poems as an "intellectual treat" and "warm and deeply moving." They work "with and against traditional forms." And they treat passion and restraint not as terms of a neatly balanced tension or a resolvable dialectic but as the extremes of a continuous process of growth.[9] This begins to define Merrill's place in his time's debates, his sense that art is part and parcel of what ails and heals us, that the private and public are of a piece and in pieces. Other readers will be a while catching up.

Although it was not so widely reviewed as the preceding books, responses to Merrill's next collection, Water Street (1962), named for his Stonington address, indicate that the new directions Van Duyn had perceived were intensifying in Merrill's work, as perhaps they were in wider literary and critical realms as well. Writing in 1962, Peter Davison says that while Lowell's distinction between "cooked" and "raw" poetry had been a just metaphor for poetry's situation five years earlier, it now seemed insufficient: the "raw" poets were "finding forms and styles for shaping naked experience," and the "cooked" poets were breaking down academic forms "to suit the kicking, shoving demands of the world around them." Davison implies that Merrill, if hardly "raw," was taking his cooking more rare. X. J. Kennedy agrees: Merrill's earlier poems are "terribly aloof, involved in their own artifice"; now, in his third book, the "skill remains evident," but there is "a deeper compassion, a kind of humility, a capacity for bitter amusement at his own expense."[10] The scene was set for a breakthrough in Merrill's work and its evaluation.

First, though, comes the detour of another experiment in fiction; it helped Merrill continue to expand and challenge his lyric mode and his confidence in and doubts about "well-made" art. The (Diblos) Notebook was published in 1965. Its palimpsest of visible revisions indicates the arbitrariness and contingency of literary and other organizing acts. Its sense of the difficulties and discoveries attendant upon the translation of experience into art, of the interpenetrations of fact and fiction, is vital to Merrill's emerging style and vision. Reviewers who weren't merely impatient with the novel's layered self-consciousness observed those features.[11]

Merrill's fourth collection of poems, *Nights and Days*, appeared in 1966. In length and ambition, in the inclusion of unresolved personal and public disruptions, and in narrative and dramatic range (one result of Merrill's efforts in novels and plays is a multiplication of genres, voices, scenes, perspectives, and styles in his verse), these new poems breach the confines of the well-made academic lyric. Although not beat, confessional, projectivist, nor neosurrealist, they are experimental.

So far, Merrill's volumes had typically been discussed in omnibus reviews. This practice continues in responses to *Nights and Days*, but two extended reviews devoted entirely to it indicate an increasing sense of Merrill's importance. And even brief comments notice changes in the quality and qualities of Merrill's work, often in terms Van Duyn initiated. For instance, Anthony Hecht writes that Merrill's early poems "were beautifully executed but somewhat frail"; in *Nights and Days*, as in *Water Street*, however, without "sacrificing any of their technical skill, his poems have become more openly dramatic." Hecht also notes the scope of Merrill's poetic ambition; for example, he dares to risk (and survives) comparison to Yeats. Gene Baro describes similar developments in terms that will be central both to discussions of Merrill's work and of postmodernism: his "disposition to question a convention while working within it"; his view of life as "either an illusion of actions and purposes or the explanation we choose to make of them."

The longer critical statements have room to support their assertions. David Kalstone writes that *Nights and Days* consolidates attainments begun in *Water Street*. Poems now "invite the imagination and dismiss it." The yearning of the early poems for solution, resolution, mastery, and release persists but is now "a passion unfulfilled, deferred, glimpsed in its relation to the nagging voices of everyday." Richard Howard notes a new certainty in the presentation of "place and circumstance" and a greater freedom in "erotic gestures." He adds that in these poems "nothing is trivial because everything is interpreted, mediated." Still, no interpretation resolves or persists, as shown by Merrill's "self-conscious suspicion" of his mediations and by his disruptive pleasure "in novelistic complication (breaking up the narrative by interpolated quotations, discrepant verse forms, conversation)."[12]

Merrill published *The Fire Screen* in 1969; it extends the developments of *Nights and Days*. Merrill's increasingly implicated views of aesthetic and social hierarchies, of their virtues and vices, emerge in poems that vary in everything from genre and length to degrees of autobiographical utterance and generalizing cultural comment. Something of their dense, serious, and playful variety can be suggested by a passage describing audience reaction to the opening moments of a performance of *Das Rheingold*: the river is present in a "rippling azure scrim," and sopranos move on "invisible strings,"

"Until with pulsing wealth the house is filled, / No one believing, everybody thrilled." The puns set out—without settling them—many and conflicting valuations (to name a few, art as a delusory fraud, the preserve of money and power; or art as a source of transport, a force for transformation). The earnest play both credits and erodes the power of language to keep us eccentric and set us straight. Even when dazed or baffled, reviewers were generally respectful. William Pritchard's conclusion is characteristic: "at his best James Merrill seems to me a matchless poet, no more adequately understood as an aesthete than as a romantic, or a poet of the dark dream, a farceur, a classicist of technique."

The most important reviews of *The Fire Screen* are by F. D. Reeve and John Hollander. Reeve shows how Merrill, knowing that only "the staged life can be examined," creates fresh forms by mocking conventions he also employs. Reeve also notes Merrill's emphasis on social change. Hollander offers summation: "How to make use of memory and dream, of experiences of the interstitial, is a question that total human sanity, rather than its usual frenzied simulacrum, must always pursue. Here, in scenes that embody recurrent phases in the rhythms of vacation and return, of performance and post-mortem . . ., the subtlety and potent sensitivity of Merrill's earlier poetry has moved into deeper and brighter regions."[13]

As quotations from laudatory reviews of Merrill's work pile up, the claim that Merrill's reputation even now remains unsettled may seem false. After all, he is widely reviewed in the mainstream journals and praised as a major poet by distinguished poets and critics. But for others, especially those who speak for aspects of the American poetry scene less represented by the establishment reviews and reviewers, Merrill seems either irrelevant or a proper object of attack, whether for formalism, social or aesthetic elitism, or something else. In 1987, Marjorie Perloff reported that although Merrill is "celebrated on the East Coast as *the* . . . ultimate poet," he is often unread elsewhere. Also, if by the time of *Nights and Days* and *The Fire Screen* Merrill was seriously discussed, serious discussion would renew old questions and open new debates.

In 1971, the revolutionary group known as the Weathermen accidentally blew up the house at 18 West 11th Street where Merrill had been born; one of the would-be bombers was Cathy Wilkerson, whose family owned the house at the time. Like Merrill, she was the child of a wealthy financier; she was injured in the blast and disappeared. The supposedly disengaged and apolitical Merrill reacted in a poem named for the address. In it, the explosive public event joined some of his more private themes. The poem was first printed in the politically committed *New York Review of Books*, and again in *Braving the Elements*, Merrill's sixth collection of verse, in 1972. Perhaps the highly charged political climate of the day helps explain the mixed response the book received.

When *Braving the Elements* won the Bollingen Poetry Prize, a *New York*

*Times* editorial criticized the committee for honoring in troubled times a genteel and private poet. Demanding political commitment, the *New Leader*'s reviewer condemned Merrill in this way: "Merrill's intellectual game . . . is to write brilliantly, without ever revealing where he stands." John Vernon finds tortured language without a proportionately serious subject. Stephen Spender admires much but considers Merrill's world merely private. New versions of old accusations: artificial, finicky, inconsequent. The most potent attack is Richard Pevear's. He charges that Merrill lacks the radical artistic spirit that would expose his own ethos as a limited and changeable construction. In fact, Merrill may be radical in just those terms. Nonetheless, Pevear's brief indicates the new version of an old debate about the quality and value of Merrill's work.[14]

Other reviews affirm. Stephen Yenser praises Merrill's "furiously patient attempt to frame the fiction of life," an effort out of phase with demands for *immediate* commitment or engagement. Helen Vendler says Merrill has overcome the secrecy and obliquity that were his besetting vices and begun to present the vagaries of self and love in ways "masked and unmasked at once." The fullest response to *Braving the Elements* is a twenty-five page review essay by Richard Sáez. This amounts to the first extensive critical article on Merrill's poetry; it brings together the political and private terms of earlier condemnation and praise. Sáez concludes that the work of this allegedly private poet has come to deal "more memorably and more incisively" with such public issues as "liberation, radical violence, kidnapping, space travel, the assassination of political leaders, and the effect of mass-media on the English language than any poetry written in America today." It was the most thoroughly argued response to Merrill's work to date.[15]

Sáez's article marks a new phase in Merrill scholarship. It had antecedents. In 1968, interviews with Merrill appeared in *Contemporary Literature* and *Shenandoah*; a third was printed in *Saturday Review* a few years later. Those interviews are signs of increasing scholarly attention to Merrill in the early 1970s, as are Morris Eaves's essay on decision and revision in *The (Diblos) Notebook* and Judith Moffett's important review essay on masking and unmasking in *Braving the Elements*. Moffett shows how unspoken and sublimated elements in Merrill's poems return to demand expression; what they have to say is made more complicated and more lucid by their having been, as it were, away. For inner and outer travel, it is one of Merrill's patterns.[16]

The shift in emphasis from book reviews to academic scholarship on Merrill occurs in the late 1970s and early 1980s, concurrently with the poems that became Merrill's epic counter-epic, *The Changing Light at Sandover* (1982). Remarkable for its length, complexity, and ambition, *Sandover* reflects Merrill's ravelings of private and public strands (love affairs and world affairs) and his mixed views of the value of art and other organizing systems. That last feature is encoded in the startling choice as muse of a choir of dead or divine informants who dictate much of the poem through a Ouija board. This decision (whether Merrill chose or was chosen) recalls and troubles an array of hierarchical divisions, say, those between reality and imagination, poetry and science, high and low culture, the natural and supernatural, and the idea that truth is a discovered or revealed and permanent absolute and the idea that it is invented or constructed, contingent, provisional, and always changing in relation to time and place, class or race, gender, sexual orientation, and other less easily codified conditions. Opinions aside, Merrill's themes are those of his age.

Sandover's three major sections, The Book of Ephraim (included in Divine Comedies [1976], along with a group of non-Sandover poems), Mirabell (1978), and Scripts for the Pageant (1980), received unusually many and long reviews. Most expend significant energy and space describing aspects of Merrill's emerging epic. Their dominant note (such a poem from such a poet at such a time!) is surprise. As Harold Bloom says, Emerson called surprise "the essential American trope of power." However that may be, Divine Comedies closes one phase of Merrill's career and opens another. "Lost in Translation" is the hinge. As David Kalstone's review presents it, this lyric and narrative poem revisits the conflicts of the broken home and its attendant passions (matters which characterize the earlier poems) and absorbs them "into a more spacious and generous perspective where nothing, finally, is lost."

Many reviewers praise the shorter poems of Divine Comedies as perfecting Merrill's style so far but disapprove of The Book of Ephraim. Calvin Bedient's strictures are stringent: Merrill has misunderstood his gifts; the "epic size is too coarse and ambitious for him"; he has "written a poem neither imposingly public nor poignantly personal"; his "musings twist and preen themselves into defeating abstraction." If Merrill's reputation had briefly seemed secure, his new, ambitious work unsettled it again. Stanley Poss sees Ephraim as style without substance. Bloom's praise is apocalyptic: Ephraim's "occult splendor" "dares everything"; "nothing since the greatest writers of our century equals it in daemonic force." Other critics are more restrained. For instance, Willard Spiegelman emphasizes the poem's novelistic feel for society and characterization, Judith Moffett's fourteen-page review gives a helpful introduction, and Phoebe Pettingell concludes that even "comic poets cannot be sure whether poetry is what heals us, or only a method of measuring our despair."[17]

Reviewers of Mirabell are often puzzled or uncertain. David Bromwich wonders if his doubts about the work result from a "peevish empiric" and suggests that the epic form may offer the private Merrill a way to engage public events and issues. Joseph Parisi notes the volume's "daring and extraordinary accomplishment" yet has doubts about its "camp" or "high tea" atmosphere. Robert B. Shaw sees "beauties and perplexities." Others offer surer praise or damnation. Stephen Yenser calls Mirabell "absorbing, ambitious, and richly varied"; Peter Stitt stacks dispraises: the book is an "intellectual sham"; its poetry "is as inartisitic as the content is fatuous; the structure is haphazard; the lyricism virtually mute." Meanwhile, Calvin Bedient, who disliked *Ephraim*, is persuaded by *Mirabell* that Merrill is at work on "a great modern poem of affection."

Especially helpful reviews are Helen Vendler's and Phoebe Pettingell's, the latter of which includes these observations: "*Mirabell* holds a mirror up to our deepest fears: that our actions are impelled not chosen; that we cannot assimilate the increasingly complex way in which our world must be viewed; that we have lost religion and morality; that our race is doomed to extinction. But at the same time . . ., the poem offers numinous reassurance that we can be saved by 'the life raft of language'." This exaggerates Merrill's faith in language but identifies the epic's terms.[18]

Reviews of *Scripts for the Pageant* also reach mixed judgments: Denis Donoghue finds "heart-breaking" and "compelling" passages yet feels it is "wretched to have to cross such a dismal terrain to reach them"; Walter Clemons notes "confounding weirdness and extraordinary beauty." Other reviews are frankly negative. William Harmon treats the poem at length and helpfully names several of its intellectual and literary traditions; then he writes, "without a shaping sense of good and evil, Merrill's verse-novel spends most of its time floundering in chit-chat and mumbo-jumbo." "Monumentally boring" is Richard Tillinghast's verdict. Charles Molesworth is constructive. He explores Merrill's reasons for attempting an epic in a time inimical to the long poem and marks just those issues and positions Merrill makes dramatic but will not or cannot resolve: " 'Yes & No': taken serially these three words form irreducible language acts, namely assertion, qualification, and denial. Taken all together they form the essence of equivocation, which can be seen as the fullest sort of language act or the very subversion of language." Other worthwhile reviews are by Mary Jo Salter and Vernon Shetley, who describes the poem as the "expression of an almost perfectly solipsistic will, structured in such a way that it refuses to admit to being a product of will at all." Judith Moffett's essay review of *Scripts* is valuable as "a summary with critical asides."[19]

In 1982 Merrill published *The Changing Light at Sandover* and *From the First Nine*, a selection of poems from the earlier works, some of them revised. Those volumes occasioned overviews of his career; the number of them indicates Merrill's assumed if not always honored place of significance on the literary scene. Speaking of *Sandover* only, Dana Yeaton says, "there's so little of our own lives in these books that it's hard to care about them. Ultimately we don't." But most reviewers do. Vernon Shetley prefers the lyric to the epic achievement and says Merrill's body of work places him "among our two or three finest poets." To Dean Flower, in "escaping his own ego, Merrill found a way to join the world," a view refuting persistent charges of preciously private inconsequence. John Hollander calls the two books "monumental." Other reviews are respectful. The longest and most important of them are by R. W. Flint, Robert Mazzocco, and James Richardson (whose review is of the 1992 reissue of *Sandover* and its companion *Selected Poems*). Notable, too, is Michael Harrington's autobiographical consideration of the poem in its relation to his own subject, "the effective decline of religious belief in Western society."[20]

In 1983, David Lehman and Charles Berger edited *James Merrill: Critical Essays*. This collection of newly written pieces surpasses most of the scholarly work on Merrill until then. Still, some significant scholarship immediately preceded the Lehman and Berger volume. Until the late 1970s, scholarly attention to Merrill was limited to interviews, review essays, and a lone article on his second novel. In the late 1970s that trickle began to swell. Four or five items from those years are especially important. Applying Susan Sontag's thoughts on "camp," Robert K. Martin briefly considers Merrill's poetry in the context of a "gay sensibility." An interview appears in the *New York Review of Books*. And J. D. McClatchy's conversation with Merrill's partner at the Ouija board, David Jackson, provides background on the sources and composition of *Sandover*. McClatchy's fine essay, "Lost Paradises," ostensibly a review of *Divine Comedies*, offers an illuminating version of Merrill's career to date, including this attractive summation: Merrill's poems are a "demanding, occasionally oblique and spare series of evocations of 'meaning relieved of sense,' and achieve their force as telling meditations on Merrill's most consistent concerns, the flows and flaws of time as it constitutes, intersects, undoes, and fulfills a life and its relationships. Such distinguishing tactics and themes have accustomed us . . . to appreciate . . . the enduring individuality of a Merrill poem which, under its art's own spell, effects its disenchantments, the antiromantic transformation of experience into self-revelation by means of recognition and acceptance."[21]

The most important scholarly treatments of Merrill in the late 1970s are by David Kalstone and Henry Sloss. Kalstone's *Five Temperaments* examines versions of autobiographical writing in the poetry of Merrill and four of his contemporaries. It demonstrates the insufficiency of critical judgments based on sharp divisions of impersonal from personal presentation, of "high" from colloquial style, of formalist from experimental versification. As are many contemporary poets, Kalstone says, "Merrill is writing a kind of autobiography in verse," however much it is sometimes veiled or indirect. He is not, though, "engaged in capturing the raw momentary feel of experience in the present tense," the goal of some autobiographical poets. Merrill's poems "come close to day-to-day living by discovering the fantasies behind our civilized arrangements, our secret links to fiction." Merrill also joins his contemporaries in absorbing into poetry "the resources of daily conversation and prose," yet he does so with unusual vigilance "to the meanings which lurk in apparently casual words and phrases." This distinguishes him from poets more straightforwardly committed to the virtues of the demotic. Merrill's attitude toward "poetic closure and the composed self" also confounds critical categories. He brings to those things a conviction that many contemporary poets "suspect as artificial, false to the provisional nature of things." Yet it is precisely at moments of closure or self-composition that Merrill's works unfold new and contingent perspectives.

Where Kalstone addresses the body of Merrill's work, Sloss explores *Ephraim*, offering an essential treatment of that initial section of Merrill's so-called trilogy or epic. The essay's elaborate arguments are elegantly sustained. For Sloss, *Ephraim* dramatizes Merrill's growing commitment to the "other" and to culture's traditional task: not to create an alternative, escapist reality in the work of art, but to assist survival in the world itself. The poem's strategy "is Romantic, the recreation of experience and its recollection in relative tranquillity, but the terms of the enchantment are distinctly modern: what is asked of the reader, as it is exemplified by the poet, is both submersion in and resistance to the other-worldly revelation in the poem."[22]

Merrill received increasing scholarly attention in the early 1980s. For example, in the years before the Lehman and Berger collection, three more interviews with the poet appeared, a bibliographical checklist of his publications was compiled, and he was the subject of an entry, later supplemented, in the *Dictionary of Literary Biography* (this overview by Willard Spiegelman remains valuable, not least for its observation that in Merrill's universe as in Freud's nothing is lost or wasted: "there is only displacement and shifting"). All these pieces signal Merrill's installation as an important poet.[23] So, too, do six critical essays and the first book devoted to his work.

Edmund White considers homosexuality as a theme in Merrill's "prophetic books." Stephen Yenser analyzes *The Book of Ephraim* in an article subsumed in his full-length critical study of Merrill, which will be discussed more fully below. An essay by Judith Moffett takes up the issue of deliberate obscurity in poetry, illustrating its arguments with passages from Merrill's verse and locating Merrill within contemporary debates about difficulty, accessibility, and audience. Robert von Hallberg extends Kalstone's effort to place Merrill in relation to the autobiographical modes of the 1960s and 1970s and also attends to issues of class. John Hollander considers Merrill among poets who have resisted the modernist distrust of the didactic and preferred to explore the "moral consequences of myth-making poetry"; he includes a detailed discussion of the poem "Mirror." "Mirror" is also a subject of J. D. McClatchy's essay on Merrill's second book, *The Country of a Thousand Years of Peace*. McClatchy points out that travel and the move to Stonington expanded Merrill's subject matter and his "recognition of a world outside the boundaries of verse and the self." This amounts to a recognition of history, "of significance emerging from process rather than embodied in a product." That remark (about his second book) shows how quickly Merrill moved beyond the assumptions of the academic style without abandoning formalism; so, too, does McClatchy's concluding point, that it is characteristic of Merrill "to work not with a set of opposites but with a series of dissolves."[24]

The first book on Merrill, Ross Labrie's *James Merrill*, appeared in 1982 in Twayne's United States Authors series. It has an introductory chapter on Merrill's life and art, treatments of all of his collections of poems through *Scripts*, and discussions of the plays, short stories, and novels. Its analyses are generally cogent and its conclusions sometimes suggestive: for instance, the insight that for Merrill "the gratuitous play of the mind . . . is the surest sign of its value in a world that otherwise seems shadowed by calculation and acquisitiveness."[25]

If Labrie's book is further indication of Merrill's establishment as an important contemporary poet, Lehman and Berger's 1983 collection, *James Merrill: Essays in Criticism*, seems a culmination. Published by Cornell University Press, it comprises an introduction and eleven original essays, most by distinguished scholars and critics. Although less systematic than Labrie's study, it covers the poetry through *Sandover* and is less restricted by the demand to be introductory. David Lehman discusses the unity of Merrill's verse, denominating Merrill's diverse texts as a singular school where "an education of the feelings takes place under the tutorship of language," a place where "breakdown leads eventually to breakthrough." This comic outlook is both subverted and reinforced by the fact that for Merrill "the impulse to bring order out of wreckage seems ever accompanied by the desire to reverse the process, to crack the well-wrought urn."

Other essays focus more closely on one or another aspect of Merrill's poetry. Attending to precedents in Proust, J. D. McClatchy discusses *Water Street* and shows that Merrill's poems question their own assumptions, temper "headstrong convictions with heartfelt reservations," and maintain "a revisionary attitude" toward both experience and feelings about experience. The effect is "emotional honesty, an openness that belies the very artistry used to achieve it." Thus, certain debates about Merrill's work dissolve.

Samuel E. Schulman reads *The Fire Screen* and *Braving the Elements* as volumes in which Merrill "lets go the consolations of self and style" and "abandons the search for domesticity and contact, which characterize his earlier lyrics." Those changes can be seen in Merrill's new resistance to art's ordering consolations and in his refiguring of such images as houses and clothes. On his way to the trilogy's exposure of the self to otherness, Merrill finds ways to "relinquish knowledge," "diffuse identity," and "yield to the power of other voices and names." The formalist will to control and contain is displaced.

David Kalstone examines "persisting figures" in Merrill's work; they are repeated but always reworked: disassembled, recomposed. Rachel Jacoff compares and contrasts Merrill's trilogy with Dante's, reaching this illuminating verdict: "The trilogy attempts what no other poem of our time has dared: to acknowledge the fragmentary, provisional, kaleidoscopic nature of contemporary knowledge and belief and to incorporate such awareness in a poetic structure that does justice to 'the pressure of reality' . . . without succumbing to it. And it does so on a scale that invites comparison with the very grandest poems of our tradition." Peter Sacks interprets the trilogy as a poem of mourning and consolation in the elegiac tradition, while Willard Spiegelman studies its device of "interruption," which demonstrates the "inevitable presence of the unseen" and confirms "the continuity that, far from being disturbed by breakings, is paradoxically strengthened and assured by them."

Richard Sáez places *Sandover* alongside other versions of apocalypse and articulates Merrill's revolutionary reaching for a vision of paradise that recognizes transience and the inextricability of foul from fair, Stephen Yenser examines the trilogy's modulations of unity and division and diversity, and Charles Berger distinguishes between orthodox and schismatic modernisms (revising the falsely chronological modernist/postmodernist divide). He classes Merrill with the blessed heretics who refuse to "mythologize history" and instead create literary forms "open to transformation and flux"; "they convey the pathos of endings without any rancor." In a grace note, David Jackson discusses his and Merrill's Ouija board encounters and their translation into the trilogy's verse. This book is indispensable to Merrill studies.[26]

*James Merrill: Essays in Criticism* seals Merrill's stature as an artist who earns and rewards sustained attention, a major poet (however uneasy we have become about the term). The bulk of scholarship that follows on it verifies the claim. But there are dissenters, and their arguments have weight. For instance, most readers take the odder and more unpleasant aspects and ideas of the trilogy not as thematic or political positions but instead as marks of Merrill's textual and textural participation in (without surrender to) a postmodernist scene of floating signifiers. For them, the poem's free play of information and interpretation precludes finality and coercion; its provisional techniques preserve it from charges of elitism. Not everyone agrees. Marking what he sees as Merrill's "almost abnormal aloofness from the world around him," Bruce Bawer judges Merrill's doubtful or alarmed reaction to such "received" ideas in the trilogy as homosexual superiority in the arts or the animal state of the masses to be only rhetorical gestures. Perhaps thinking any expression "merely rhetorical" is an encumbrance to reading poems, but Bawer's honest discomfort before the trilogy's less happy implications deserves a response. Poststructuralist reassurances that everything is constructed may not be sufficient. An interpretation of Merrill's antitotalizing strategies of inclusion and evasion might fare better.[27]

The mid-1980s saw international attention to Merrill's achievements. For instance, in 1984 the Italian scholar Andrea Mariani extended his earlier work as a critic and translator of Merrill with a learned study of the ways in which the trilogy records, repays, and cancels its debts to Dante. Another monograph on Merrill also appeared in 1984, Judith Moffett's *James Merrill*:

*An Introduction to the Poetry.* Moffett covers all the poems through *Sandover* and provides extensive background information. Although the book is frankly introductory, Moffett brings a poet's eye and ear to interpretation.[28]

A second collection of essays on Merrill was published in Harold Bloom's Modern Critical Views series in 1985. It reprints materials on Merrill discussed above. In addition, Bloom's introduction notes that Merrill (like and unlike Proust) "studies the nostalgias" in wonder rather than elegy; Bloom also makes an aptly uneasy effort at canonical placement. There are two new essays as well. Charles Berger shows how Merrill's purgatorial *Mirabell* swerves away from the modernist near equation of apocalypse with catastrophic violence and toward an alternative emphasis on the term's association with comic cosmic revelations, while Leslie Brisman tracks another swerving: this one away from Yeats's midcareer desire to transcend earthly passion and toward the "knowledge that death is common, and life less impossible to mend than to replace."[29]

The late 1980s were productive years for Merrill commentary; Merrill was productive, too. After the epic exertions of *Sandover*, he returned to "CHRONICLES OF LOVE & LOSS" in the new collections of 1985 and 1988, *Late Settings* and *The Inner Room*. Reviews tend to assume Merrill's importance and to reflect on his career as well as the work at hand.

Vernon Shetley describes *Late Settings* as autumnal but not mellow; it adds "further lustre to an oeuvre already among the most powerful and significant of our time." Ashley Brown places Merrill in the tradition of Byron and Pope, who see life as "a comedy to be observed, not a tragedy to be endured," but adds that Merrill's situation differs from theirs: his age does not provide him with a stylistic center but with dozens of them, many "decidedly impure or worn out." Merrill uses all strands and also admits "more and more data from popular culture." Peter Stitt makes the related point that Merrill's poems are "at once relaxed and elevated, ill kempt and elegant, mundane and cosmological." And D. W. Hartnett observes in these poems "a new sense of historical actuality that owes much to the trilogy." The most important reviews of *Late Settings* are by Brad Leithauser and Helen Vendler. Leithauser concentrates on Merrill's prosody, with particular attention to slant rhyme. Vendler also examines Merrill's technique, commenting on his use of rhyme and on his concision, which she says does not drive toward the aphoristic or epigramatic but rather toward "the complex and dense image that will be perceptual, personal, social, and philosophical at once." Vendler also notes Merrill's thematic concern with the self's extinction and his revision of solacing traditions in a way that records their erosion and pays tribute to their bedrock persistence.[30]

Reviews of *The Inner Room* also give praiseful attention, yet Merrill's reputation is not so settled as to preclude demurral altogether. To Dennis Sampson, Merrill's work reveals "someone throroughly committed to his craft and yet maddeningly unable to render experience." Sampson complains of "contrivance," "overingenuity of language," and disengagement. He regards as a "bad habit" the self-interruptions and questionings that other critics read as expressing Merrill's sense of contingency. Moreover, Sampson thinks Merrill is "afflicted with grandiose gestures and an achingly shallow interpretation" of life. More typical reviews outline attainments. Phoebe Pettingell says Merrill strives "to reach beyond nostalgia and memorial." J. D. McClatchy explores the inclusion *as poems* of dramatic and narrative forms in this volume. Helen Vendler observes that the external marks of Merrill's style are now imitated by younger poets, although usually without the inner life that motivates them. She then asks how Merrill's "inferred interior" generates the Merrill surface. Her answer is definitive.[31]

Merrill scholarship from 1986 through 1994 includes two noteworthy essays by D. L. Macdonald. One is an intertextual exploration of orientalism and eroticism in Merrill and Byron; the other invokes Freud and argues that *Sandover* "uses the psychopathology of eternal life" (perhaps a term for any totalizing system) "in an attempt to recapture a nonpathological relation to everyday life." It may be just such features of Merrill's epic that give David Perkins pause in the magisterial assessment of Merrill's achievement that concludes his history of modern poetry; it is required reading for anyone seeking to measure Merrill's reputation.[32]

The two most important contributions on Merrill in the late 1980s are by Lynn Keller and Stephen Yenser. Keller's *Re-making It New* uses paired chapters to locate contemporary or postmodernist poets in relation to their modernist precursors. The Merrill chapters compare him with Auden. While "Auden tries to hold side by side two seemingly contradictory aspects of actuality," "Merrill's double focus takes in the fictional and the 'actual.' " Merrill's postmodern sense of the belated, always already represented constructedness of human signifying systems is especially strong in *Sandover*, where it results not in apocalyptic despair or stoical acceptance of limits but in a chastened and comic liberation.

Stephen Yenser's *The Consuming Myth: The Work of James Merrill* is the most significant study of Merrill so far. It discusses all the poetry, prose, and drama through *Late Settings* and "The Image Maker," and Yenser's interpretations are extensive, subtle, learned, and revealing. Yenser is more committed to local acts of attentive and difficult elucidation than to an "argument," but these are his main themes. Because Merrill is "committed to duality," he "has been sharply aware of the divergent demands that art and life make." Because he is "dedicated to unity," he has "devoted himself to confounding the dichotomy." Merrill's poetry does not resolve or contain the contraries it treats: life and art, poetry and prose, lyric and epic, faith and betrayal, private and public, good and evil. Instead, as in field work or field theory, it reports transactions between and among them, including the indeterminate effects of the reporter's presence and portrayal.[33]

Other important work on Merrill in the late 1980s includes a Merrill number of the magazine *Verse*, with appreciations by fellow poets. Several scholarly essays appeared as well, along with three chapters in books. Even the slighter pieces are useful: an explication of the poem "Bronze" and a treatment of Merrill's "language and music." Other essays are more substantial. Jefferson Humphries considers Merrill's poststructuralist progress toward a poetry that undoes or dissolves both the writing self and its writing, and Jeffery Donaldson compares Richard Howard's and Merrill's sense of history. Like those two essays, most of this period's Merrill work addresses the epic. Timothy Materer examines alchemical references in *Sandover*. Lee Zimmerman looks at the anti-apocalyptic politics of Merrill's long poem. And Philip Kuberski suggests that Merrill's trilogy creates a metaphysics of postmodern death, which transforms existentialist and formalist views of life as tragic by means of a communion with the dead.[34]

Three books with chapters on Merrill came out in 1989. Each addresses large issues in contemporary American poetry, and Merrill's inclusion in each makes its own statement about his importance. Again, the epic provides their focus. Thomas Gardner places *Sandover* in the Whitmanian tradition he believes undergirds the contemporary American long poem. Although Merrill's poem does not mention Whitman, Merrill acknowledges Whitman's sense that a "poetics of self-translation" involves an effacement of the self, and he shares, along with other contemporary poets, Whitman's view that the artist's anxiety about art's medium is just what enables its use.

Willard Spiegelman considers *Sandover* as a particularly postmodern or metadidactic version of the traditional didactic poem that modernism so preachily claimed to reject. He emphasizes such features as the poem's dissolution of the self, its fiction of collaborative authorship, its "nominal theses," and its consideration of the distinctively human qualities of "affection, appearance, language, and time." Among the poem's lessons are these: one can be at home in the past, unity is plural (composed at least of singularity and mutuality, independence and relationship), all truths are metaphorical, and learning is "a process of absorption, forgetting, and reminiscence." In the end, but without "conclusion," Merrill transforms the lamentation of elegy into affirmation: nothing is lost, all is converted to good, even the dead return.

Spiegelman's summary sounds humanistic notes, however modified or muted. Considering the "social text" in contemporary American poetry, Walter Kalaidjian accents less solacing or compensatory tones in Merrill's poem: its "anxious sense of belatedness," its awareness of the disturbed status of "traditional genres in the face of postmodern mass culture," its sense that a self-cancelling "constituting fiction" is the only acceptable source of poetic or other "authority," and its knowing that no discourse is original, independent, or transparent. *Sandover* overturns "hierarchies among literary genres" and subverts "the wider hegemony of cultural discourses." "Like much poststructuralist writing, Merrill's ludic textuality is designed to baffle and disperse the windy platitudes of the Western humanist tradition." This emphasis on Merrill as a corrosive writer defines one response to what may be a central question of Merrill scholarship for some time to come: does he offer ways to retain the tradition by remaking it, however ruinous his necessary deconstructions, or does he intone the funeral oration; can culture continue its ancient effort to define and preserve what we value when we know our fictions are fictions, or must it produce hegemony, exclusion, and oppression? Perhaps the terms and their either/or configuration are insufficient.[35]

Merrill scholarship in the early 1990s consists mostly of essays. One of the most important is Mutlu Konuk Blasing's "Rethinking Models of Literary Change: The Case of James Merrill." Blasing says that the tendency to equate experimental forms with liberation and traditional forms with reactionary repression (so frequent a feature of the more simplistic modes of praising or blaming Merrill and of representing the history of contemporary verse) implies an evolutionary or technological model of artistic change, which fails to represent what actually happens in literature and literary history. As replacement, she offers Tynianov's model of literary change, in which forms and functions do not die or become obsolete but alter in relation to one another: forms change functions and functions change forms. Only such a model can account for "Merrill's project, which is rhetorically and functionally discontinuous with the canonical tradition his forms invoke." Comments on Merrill's poems and their critics accompany Blasing's metacritical discussion, which seems a proleptic rejoinder to Mary Karr's complaint that as a "decorative" formal poet Merrill must lack clarity and emotion.[36]

Other Merrill materials from the early 1990s are various. C. A. Buckley discusses *Sandover* in an interview with Merrill. Jeffrey Mehlman offers suggestive commentary on Merrill's erotics of translation, the eloquence of misconstrual in his life and work. Timothy Materer examines Merrill's glossings of "error," which include its place in the generative wandering of revelation. And J. D. McClatchy's "literary biography" offers the best brief introduction to Merrill's career to date.[37]

In other Merrill essays of the 1990s, Alan Nadel implicitly objects to postmodernist accounts of Merrill and argues that "Lost in Translation" represents a movement away from high modernism toward a poetics of transcendence, while C. A. Buckley connects the holistic world view of *Sandover* to developments in quantum physics and their "popularization." Writing in Italian, Andrea Mariani discusses Merrill's version of Yeats and— in English—his relations to the postmodern. A chapter in Vernon Shetley's *After the Death of Poetry* considers Merrill's sense of audience, suggesting that his development "is informed by a tension between public and private modes of expression."[38]

The most recent work on Merrill includes a glib piece on Merrill's father and his heirs in *GQ* and four significant essays. Helen Sword continues the recent emphasis on *Sandover* in her discussion of Merrill, Sylvia Plath, and the poetics of Ouija. Implicitly rejecting the notion that Merrill seeks transcendent authority, she concludes that he and Plath use " 'this absurd, flimsy contraption, creaking along' " in order to move beyond modernist antipathy toward popular culture and "to transport the age-old prophetic mode toward the cynical, subversive, ludic realm of the postmodern." Eric Murphy Selinger studies a wider swatch of Merrill's work amid the conventions of love poetry, tracing its course "from unease through reconciliation to a new, deeper despair" which then gives rise to a "consoling, chastened vision." This trajectory follows the patterns of crisis that Roland Barthes and Julia Kristeva chart in "postmodern amorous discourse" and makes Merrill one of the finest American poets of love. Jeff Westover's essay on Merrill's convivial revision, published here for the first time, has a similarly grateful and gracious scope. Jeffery Donaldson explores matters of allusion, echo, and audience in Merrill and Auden. In addition, the University of Michigan Press has recently published Robert Polito's remarkable *A Reader's Guide to James Merrill's* The Changing Light at Sandover. A "handbook and alphabetical index," this volume aims to ease a reader's participation in Merrill's "self-revising pageant"; it is supplemented by nearly one hundred pages of reprinted reviews, includes a foreword by Merrill, and is framed by Polito's instructive introduction and afterword.[39]

James Merrill's recent death and the subsequent publication of *A Scattering of Salts* have occasioned a number of valedictory reviews and comments. Alison Lurie recalls Merrill as "a ringmaster of language: alert to every possible twitch and roar." Helen Vendler concludes that he offers us what he said once he found in Rilke: "help with suffering." Apt terms: mastery and solace, neither final nor complete. Two of the most moving responses to Merrill's death and ultimate work, W. S. Merwin's review of *Salts* and J. D. McClatchy's "postscript" on Merrill's life and career, conclude, respectively, the review and essay sections of this book.[40]

The present collection supplements and does not repeat materials in the collections edited by Lehman and Berger and by Bloom. The more recent of those is now ten years old, and much of the material gathered here has been written since. Reviews of some of Merrill's major books of poems illuminate his work and offer snapshots of his emerging reputation, while the essays (one available here for the first time in English, another written specifically for this collection) are arranged in order to make a case, if not an argument. Yenser's essay outlines Merrill's life and career by treating a culminating poem. Along with Blasing's statement of method, it constitutes an introduction. Subsequent pieces treat the range of Merrill's career from a variety of critical approaches and perspectives. Those are followed by essays that focus on *The Changing Light at Sandover*. Then the collection moves outward to breadth again before concluding in McClatchy's tender recollection.

Merrill scholarship is at an early stage; much remains to be done. The time will come—perhaps has come—for the standard scholarly projects: a full-dress biography, collected and variorum editions of the poems, a complete edition of the prose, a full descriptive bibliography of Merrill's publications, and the like. In the meantime, additional practical and theoretical commentary on individual poems and volumes is needed, as are considerations of Merrill's career in its own terms and in relation to its cultural, poetic, and literary historical contexts. Merrill's place within the welter of modernist and postmodernist positions remains to be defined. Studies of Merrill's fiction and plays and of their relationships to the poetry would be welcome, as would studies of his influences, his prosody, his intertextuality, his use and revision of genres, and the roles of science and popular culture and of sexual orientation and class in his work. Given the terms of current critical debate, discussions of Merrill's humanist or posthumanist views, of his sense of the artist as producing or being produced by language and culture, of his understanding of the self as coherent or discontinuous would also be useful. Given the tendency of contemporary literary criticism to combine radical skepticism with overweening righteousness, such studies might invoke the humble words that open Merrill's most ambitious poem: "Admittedly I err."

James Merrill's great theme is the incarnation and withdrawal of a god: parent, lover, muse, the glory and grief of language, that translation. He honors comings and goings, substantiations and dispersals, and he acknowledges the sorrow and relief that none of them is final. In "Processional," urged by inherited burdens "(LOAD, GOAD)," the ludic poet (three strokes at word golf, better than par, a birdie) turns LOAD to GOLD. Cheap trick and magical transformation, it traps and confirms our aspirations.

## Notes

1. James Merrill, *A Different Person: A Memoir* (New York: Knopf, 1993), 5.
2. Merrill, *A Different Person*, 13–19.
3. J. D. McClatchy, "James Merrill," in *American Writers: A Collection of Literary Biographies*, supp. 3, pt. 1, ed. Lea Baechler and A. Walton Litz (New York: Scribner's, 1991), 317.
4. Rolfe Humphries, "Verse Chronicle," *Nation*, 10 February 1951, 138; Howard Nemerov, "The Careful Poets and the Reckless Ones," *Sewanee Review* 60 (1952), 196; James Dickey, "James Merrill," in his *Babel to Byzantium* (New York: Farrar, Straus & Giroux, 1968), 97.
5. Louise Bogan, "Verse," *New Yorker*, 9 June 1951, 109–10.
6. See "Syrinx," in *Braving the Elements* (1972) and "From the Cupola," in *Nights and Days* (1966).
7. Whitney Balliett, "Content and Form," *New Yorker*, 30 March 1957, 134–35;

Jerome Stone, "Forlorn Eunuch," *Saturday Review*, 16 March 1957, 19, 30; Richard Sullivan, "Tycoon's Harem," *New York Times Book Review*, 21 April 1957, 18–19.

8.  James Dickey, "James Merrill," in his *Babel to Byzantium*, 100; William Meredith, "Images and Reality," *New York Times Book Review*, 3 May 1959, 26.

9.  Mona Van Duyn, " 'Sunbursts, Garlands, Creatures, Men'," *Poetry* 94 (1959), 199–202.

10.  Peter Davison, "New Poetry," *Atlantic* 212 (December 1963), 84, 86; X. J. Kennedy, "Four Fashions in Contemporary Verse," *New York Times Book Review*, 25 November 1962, 42.

11.  The most useful reviews are: Mona Van Duyn, "The Poet as Novelist," *Poetry* 109 (1967), 335–36; Naomi Bliven, "Nothing But the Truth," *New Yorker*, 11 September 1965, 221–24; and F. D. Reeve, "An Island of Form," *Hudson Review* 18 (1965), 290–92.

12.  Anthony Hecht, "Poetry Chronicle," *Hudson Review* 19 (1966), 331–32; Gene Baro, "Varied Quintet," *New York Times Book Review*, 26 June 1966, 12, 14; David Kalstone, "Merrill," *Partisan Review* 34 (1967), 146–50; Richard Howard, "Illusion Wedded to Simple Need," *Poetry* 108 (1966), 329–35.

13.  William H. Pritchard, "Shags and Poets," *Hudson Review* 23 (1970), 275–77; F. D. Reeve, "Through the Fire Screen," *Poetry* 117 (1971), 388–91; John Hollander, on Merrill's *The Fire Screen*, *Harper's* 239 (October 1969), 136.

14.  Selden Rodman, "Petrified by Gorgon Egos," *New Leader*, 22 January 1973, 20; John Vernon, "A Gathering of Poets," *Western Humanities Review* 27 (1973), 107–9; Stephen Spender, "Can Poetry Be Reviewed?," *New York Review of Books*, 20 September 1973, 8–10; Richard Pevear, "Poetry Chronicle," *Hudson Review* 26 (1973), 201–3.

15.  Stephen Yenser, "Feux d'Artifice," *Poetry* 122 (1973), 163–68; Helen Vendler, *"Braving the Elements,"* *New York Times Book Review*, 24 September 1972, 5, 14, 16, 18; Richard Sáez, "James Merrill's Oedipal Fire," *Parnassus* 3 (1974), 159–84.

16.  Donald Sheehan, "An Interview with James Merrill," *Contemporary Literature* 9 (1968), [1]–14; Ashley Brown, "An Interview with James Merrill," *Shenandoah* 19 (1968), 3–15; David Kalstone, "The Poet: Private," *Saturday Review*, 2 December 1972, 43–45; Morris Eaves, "Decision and Revision in James Merrill's *The (Diblos) Notebook*," *Contemporary Literature* 12 (1971), 156–65; Judith Moffett, "Masked More and Less Than Ever: James Merrill's *Braving the Elements*," *Hollins Critic* 10 (1973), 1–12.

17.  David Kalstone, "Evenings at the Ouija Board," *Times Literary Supplement*, 28 October 1977, 1267; Calvin Bedient, "Books Considered," *New Republic*, 5 June 1976, 22–23; Stanley Poss, " 'What Underlies These Odd / Inseminations by Psycho-Roulette'," *Western Humanities Review* 30 (1976), 354–58; Harold Bloom, "Harold Bloom on Poetry," *New Republic*, 20 November 1976, 20–21; Willard Spiegelman, on *Divine Comedies*, *Southwest Review* 61 (1976), 333–34; Judith Moffett, "The Other World and the Real," *Poetry* 129 (1976), 40–53; Phoebe Pettingell, "The Comic Stance," *New Leader*, 24 May 1976, 17.

18.  David Bromwich, "Answer, Heavenly Muse, Yes or No," *Hudson Review* 32 (1979), 456–60; Joseph Parisi, "Ghostwriting," *Poetry* 135 (1979), 161–73; Robert B. Shaw, "James Merrill and the Ouija Board," *New York Times Book Review*, 29 April 1979, 15, 53; Stephen Yenser, "New Books in Review," *Yale Review* 68 (1979), 557–66; Peter Stitt, "Knowledge, Belief, and Bubblegum," *Georgia Review* 33 (1979), 699–700, 704–7; Calvin Bedient, "New Confessions," *Sewanee Review* 88 (1980), 487–88; Helen Vendler, "V Work," *New Yorker*, 3 September 1979, 95–105; Phoebe Pettingell, "Voices from the Atom," *New Leader*, 4 December 1978, 14–15.

19.  Denis Donoghue, "What the Ouija Board Said," *New York Times Book Review*, 15 June 1980, 11, 20; Walter Clemons, "A Modern Divine Comedy," *Newsweek*, 16 June 1980, 84–86; William Harmon, "The Metaphors and Metamorphoses of M," *Parnassus* 8 (1980), 29–41; Richard Tillinghast, "Scattered Nebulae," *Sewanee Review* 90 (1982), 292, 295–97;

Charles Molesworth, "Scripts for the Pageant," *New Republic*, 26 July 1980, 34–36; Mary Jo Salter, "YES & NO: The Vision of James Merrill," *Atlantic* 246 (October 1980), 96–98; Vernon Shetley, "Take But Degree Away," *Poetry* 137 (1981), 301–2; Judith Moffett, "'I HAVE RECEIVED FROM WHOM I DO NOT KNOW / THESE LETTERS. SHOW ME, LIGHT, IF THEY MAKE SENSE'," *Shenandoah* 31 (Summer 1980), [35]–74.

20. Dana Yeaton, "Beyond All Criticism," *New England Review* 4 (1981), 330–33; Vernon Shetley, "This World and the Other," *Poetry* 143 (1983), 101–7; Dean Flower, "James Merrill's Voices," *Hudson Review* 36 (1983), 724–33; John Hollander, "Poetry in Review," *Yale Review* 73 (1983), R9; R. W. Flint, "Metamorphic Magician," *New York Times Book Review*, 13 March 1983, 6, 14–16; Robert Mazzocco, "The Right Stuff," *New York Review of Books*, 16 June 1983, 41–46; James Richardson, "James Merrill: Rooms Within Rooms," *Poetry* 167 (1993), 282–97; Michael Harrington, "Paradise or Disintegration," *Commonweal*, 4 November 1983, 585–89.

21. Robert K. Martin, "James Merrill," in his *The Homosexual Tradition in American Poetry* (Austin: Univ. of Texas Press, 1979), 202–9; Helen Vendler, "James Merrill's Myth: An Interview," *New York Review of Books*, 3 May 1979, 12–13; J. D. McClatchy, "DJ: A Conversation with David Jackson," *Shenandoah* 30 (1979), 23–44; J. D. McClatchy, "Lost Paradises," *Parnassus* 5 (1977), 305–20.

22. David Kalstone, "James Merrill: Transparent Things," in his *Five Temperaments* (New York: Oxford Univ. Press, 1977), 77–128; Henry Sloss, "James Merrill's *The Book of Ephraim*." Parts 1 and 2. *Shenandoah* 27; 28 (1976), 63–91; 83–110.

23. Jean Lunn, "A Conversation with James Merrill," *Sandscript* 6 (1982), 2–23; J. D. McClatchy, "The Art of Poetry XXXI: James Merrill," *Paris Review* 24 (1982), 184–219; Ross Labrie, "James Merrill at Home: An Interview," *Arizona Quarterly* 38 (1982), 19–36; Jack W. C. Hagstrom and George Bixby, "James Merrill: A Bibliographical Checklist," *American Book Collector*, N.S. 4 (November–December 1983), 34–47; Willard Spiegelman, "James Merrill," in *American Poets since World War II*, pt. 2 of vol. 5 of *Dictionary of Literary Biography*, ed. Donald J. Greiner (Detroit: Gale Research, 1980), 53–65; Stephen Sandy, "James Merrill," in *DLB Yearbook: 1985*, ed. Jean W. Ross (Detroit: Gale Research, 1986), 292–302.

24. Edmund White, "The Inverted Type: Homosexuality as a Theme in James Merrill's Prophetic Books," in *Literary Visions of Homosexuality*, ed. Stuart Kellogg (New York: Haworth Press, 1983), 47–52; Stephen Yenser, "The Fullness of Time: James Merrill's *Book of Ephraim*," *Canto* 3 (1980), 130–59; Judith Moffett, "Sound without Sense: Willful Obscurity in Poetry," *New England Review* 3 (1980), 294–312; Robert von Hallberg, "James Merrill: 'Revealing by Obscuring'," *Contemporary Literature* 21 (1980), 549–71; John Hollander, "A Poetry of Restitution," *Yale Review* 70 (1981), 161–86, esp. 165–71; J. D. McClatchy, "Monsters Wrapped in Silk: *The Country of a Thousand Years of Peace*," *Contemporary Poetry* 4 (1982), 1–30.

25. Ross Labrie, *James Merrill* (Boston: Twayne, 1982).

26. *James Merrill: Essays in Criticism* ed. David Lehman and Charles Berger (Ithaca: Cornell Univ. Press, 1983).

27. Bruce Bawer, "A Summoning of Spirits: James Merrill and *Sandover*," *New Criterion* 2 (June 1984), 35–42.

28. Andrea Mariani, "Dal Polilinguismo al Metalinguismo: Il Linguaggio Dantesco nella Trilogia di James Merrill," *Letterature d'America* 5 (1984), 127–60; Judith Moffett, *James Merrill* (New York: Columbia Univ. Press, 1984).

29. *James Merrill*, ed. Harold Bloom (New York: Chelsea House, 1985), 198.

30. Vernon Shetley, review of *Late Settings*, *Poetry* 147 (1986), 301–3; Ashley Brown, review of *Late Settings*, *World Literature Today* 60 (1986), 109; Peter Stitt, "Poets Witty and Elegaic," *New York Times Book Review*, 1 September 1985, 11; D. W. Hartnett, "Innocence and Destruction," *Times Literary Supplement*, 7 February 1986, 138; Brad Leithauser, "Playing

with Fire," *New York Review of Books*, 26 September 1985, 11–13; Helen Vendler, "Fears and Farewells," *New Republic*, 5 August 1985, 34–39.

31.   Dennis Sampson, "Poetry Chronicle," *Hudson Review* 42 (1989), 510–11; Phoebe Pettingell, "Fabulists for Our Time," *New Leader* 9 January 1989, 16–17; J. D. McClatchy, "Masks and Passions," *Poetry* 154 (1989), 43–48; Helen Vendler, "In Praise of Perfume," *New Republic*, 3 April 1989, 35–38.

32.   D. L. Macdonald, "Orientalism and Eroticism in Byron and Merrill," *Pacific Coast Philology* 21 (1986), 60–64; D. L. Macdonald, "Merrill and Freud: The Psychopathology of Eternal Life," *Mosaic* 14 (1986), 159–72; David Perkins, "The Achievement of James Merrill," in his *A History of Modern Poetry: Modernism and After* (Cambridge: Harvard Univ. Press, 1987), 638–59.

33.   Lynn Keller, " 'Those who love illusion / And know it': The Continuity between Auden and Merrill," and " 'I knew / / That life was fiction in disguise': Merrill's Divergence from Auden and Modernism," in her *Re-making It New* (New York: Cambridge Univ. Press, 1987), 184–225 and 226–53; Stephen Yenser, *The Consuming Myth* (Cambridge: Harvard Univ. Press, 1987).

34.   *Verse* 5 (1988), 21–67; Ruth Thompson, "Merrill's 'Bronze'," *Explicator* 47 (1988), 48–50; James Baird, "James Merrill's Sound and Feeling: Language and Music," *Southwest Review* 74 (1989), 361–77; Jefferson Humphries, "The Voice within the Mirror: The Haunted Poetry of James Merrill," *Boundary 2* 15 (1988), 173–94; Jeffery Donaldson, "Going Down in History: Richard Howard's *Untitled Subjects* and James Merrill's *The Changing Light at Sandover*," *Salmagundi* 76–77 (1987–88), 175–202; Timothy Materer, "Death and Alchemical Transformation in James Merrill's *The Changing Light at Sandover*," *Contemporary Literature* 29 (1988), [82]–104; Lee Zimmerman, "Against Apocalypse: Politics and James Merrill's *The Changing Light at Sandover*," *Contemporary Literature* 30 (1989), [370]–86; Philip Kuberski, "The Metaphysics of Postmodern Death: Mailer's *Ancient Evenings* and Merrill's *The Changing Light at Sandover*," *ELH* 56 (1989), 229–55.

35.   Thomas Gardner, "Imbued with Otherness: James Merrill's *The Changing Light at Sandover*," in his *Discovering Ourselves in Whitman* (Champaign: Univ. of Illinois Press, 1989), [170]–204; Willard Spiegelman, "The Sacred Books of James Merrill," in his *The Didactic Muse* (Princeton: Princeton Univ. Press, 1989), 192–246; Walter Kalaidjian, "A Poetics of Errancy: James Merrill's *The Changing Light at Sandover*," in his *Languages of Liberation* (New York: Columbia Univ. Press, 1989), 93–119.

36.   Mutlu Konuk Blasing, "Rethinking Models of Literary Change: The Case of James Merrill," *American Literary History* 2 (1990), [299]–317; Mary Karr, "Against Decoration," *Parnassus* 16 (1991), 227–300.

37.   C. A. Buckley, "Exploring *The Changing Light at Sandover*: An Interview with James Merrill," *Twentieth Century Literature* 38 (1992), 415–35; Jeffrey Mehlman, "Merrill's Valéry: An Erotics of Translation," in *Rethinking Translation*, ed. Lawrence Venuti (London: Routledge, 1992), 86–105; Timothy Materer, "The Error of His Ways: James Merrill and the Fall into Myth," *American Poetry* 7 (1990), 64–86; J. D. McClatchy, "James Merrill," *American Writers: A Collection of Literary Biographies*, suppl. 3, pt. 1, ed. Lea Baechler and A. Walton Litz (New York: Scribner's, 1991), 317–38.

38.   Alan Nadel, "Replacing the Waste Land: James Merrill's Quest for Transcendent Authority," *College Literature* 20 (1993), 154–76; C. A. Buckley, "Quantum Physics and the Ouija Board: James Merrill's Holistic World View," *Mosaic* 26 (1993), 39–61; Andrea Mariani, "Yeats in Merrill: maschera e figura," in *Yeats oggi*, 89–105; Andrea Mariani, "James Merrill: A Postmodern Poet? Yes & No," *RSA Journal* 4 (1993), 31–56; Vernon Shetley, "Public and Private in James Merrill's Work," in his *After the Death of Poetry* (Durham: Duke Univ. Press, 1993), [65]–101.

39.   Joseph Nocera, "Charlie Merrill and His Stock," *GQ*, October 1994, 222–29, 269–78; Helen Sword, "James Merrill, Sylvia Plath, and the Poetics of Ouija," *American*

*Literature* 66 (1994), [553]–72; Eric Murphy Selinger, "James Merrill's Masks of Eros, Masques of Love," *Contemporary Literature* 35 (1994), [30]–65; Jeffery Donaldson, "The Company Poets Keep: Allusion, Echo, and the Question of Who is Listening in W. H. Auden and James Merrill," *Contemporary Literature* 36 (1995), 35–57; Robert Polito, *A Reader's Guide to James Merrill's* The Changing Light at Sandover (Ann Arbor: Univ. of Michigan Press, 1994).

40.   Alison Lurie, "On James Merrill (1926–1995)," *New York Review of Books*, 23 March 1995, 9; Helen Vendler, "Chronicles of Love and Loss," *New York Review of Books*, 11 May 1995, 46–51; W. S. Merwin, "The End of More Than a Book," *New York Times Book Review*, 26 March 1995, 3; J. D. McClatchy, "Braving the Elements," *New Yorker*, 27 March 1995, 49–61.

# REVIEWS

◆

# The Country of a Thousand Years of Peace

◆

## "Sunbursts, Garlands, Creatures, Men"

### MONA VAN DUYN

Surely there are few new books of poems that cause one to feel real dissatisfaction with anything less than an Ideal Condition of reading and reviewing. James Merrill's second book does exactly this. For reading, the collection should be bound in at least four volumes. When poems are as demanding and rewarding as these, and when one is the kind of reader to whom an unturned page constitutes an irresistible invitation to keep going, the riches of a forty-poem volume are an intellectual and emotional embarrassment. For reviewing, space should be available to give each poem a separate essay. Each entices to a considerable depth of immersion, and the process of coming up for critical air between poems gives one some sort of reader's equivalent of "the bends." Because Mr. Merrill's technical and imaginative resources are great, each of his poems is a genuinely individual experience of form, sound, movement, tone, and metaphoric statement. (This is not to say that he has not found his own recognizable voice; he has. But it happens to be one with an unusual range of expression.) To talk about the book as a whole, to generalize and sum up, requires strenuous simplifications of these experiences which one would like to avoid.

However, as Mr. Merrill well knows, the strenuous disciplines have their function, mediating as they do between the ideal and the actual, so we may as well proceed to generalizations.

His most consistent method of statement is the conceit, sometimes extended only through a sestet, sometimes running for fifty or more lines. The *explicit* end of the metaphor is developed into a full-bodied narrative or anecdote, rich in perceptions, sharp with visual details, witty and delightful in itself. It may be "about" hayfever, an octopus, telephone-pad doodling, Greek statuary, or greenhouse plants, for this poet has ingratiating variety in his occasions for meaning. The *implicit* end, sometimes cued for the reader in a phrase or two, sometimes left to his own reading, operates simultaneously, detail by detail, and with increasing revelation. It is "about" the great constants of human experience and thus engages the feelings, which are so incessantly preoccupied with them. Probably it is this manner of operation that makes for a quality I find particularly gratifying. The poems are an intellectual treat—one's mind is busy with wit that ranges from puns (Europa is "no longer chaste but continent") to the most profound and freshly discovered resemblances—and they are at the same time warm and deeply moving.

Handling of line movement and musical patterns amply communicates Mr. Merrill's pleasure in working with and against traditional forms. *Marsyas*, *A Survival*, and *At the Bullfight*, for example, experiment with rhyme schemes for the sonnet, the last-mentioned also clipping all but its eighth and fourteenth lines to a four-foot length. In some of the forms one can see an extra challenge or two taken on out of sheer exuberance, a sense of mastery which lets him play with his art. The five quatrains of *Olive Grove* are made up of one non-stop sentence. *The Dunes*, whose four-line stanzas rhyme their first and last lines, uses the same end-sound for the second line of each of its stanzas. *The Charioteer of Delphi* has a complicated pattern of rhyme and line-length which is too long to map out here. This virtuosity does not call attention to itself, indeed is often uncovered with surprise in an attempt to find the source of a poem's effect.

Of all the technical resources he employs, only alliteration seems to tempt him occasionally into display or excess. Observing an octopus through aquarium glass, he tells us that "the writher / Advances in a godlike wreath / Of its own wrath." Since the image of the multiple-armed god is used in the poem, "wrath" is perfectly operative. "Writher" is both visually effective and points toward the "volutions of a Hindu dance" later on. But the "wreath" image seems present only by virtue of the word's initial sound. On the other hand, each word in the line "The rare bird bedded at the heart of harm" (*Fire Poem*) is justified by the rest of the poem, in both sound and sense, as kenning for the phoenix in the fire.

The most recurrent concern in this group of poems is with the difficult tension, in life, love, and art, between passion and restraint. Passion appears as a fire that consumes form, form as a drug that deadens feeling. Since no

achievement of a golden center is described, but only excesses in one direction
or the other, I would assume that Mr. Merrill shares with E. M. Forster
the notion of growth as a continuous series of excursions back and forth
between the claims of each. The risks of such "flights between ardor and
ashes" (*The Phoenix*) are dramatized: the burnt child learns a fear of "ardent
things" (*Fire Poem*) or craftsmen in brocade "belittle" real monsters and
nightmares into souvenirs for tourists (*The Cruise*). A museum statue (*Charioteer of Delphi*) of which only the driver holding fragments of reins has been
preserved suggests that the "killing horses" have broken away from restraint,
and serves as a reminder of what can go racing "uncurbed in us . . . upon
the taste of a sweet licence . . . when fires are fanned."

Love, shown in several hard-won final stanzas as achieved communion,
is most heavily represented by its terrible vulnerabilities. There is *A Narrow
Escape* from the vampire, whose

> nightly
> Drainings of one's life, the blood, the laugh,
> The cries for pardon, the indifferences . . .

are hidden behind her bland face; Salome, "sinuous on a string of motives
all her own / Summons the executioner"; a mad dog, in *Salome II*, demonstrates that animality can explode into violence from "too much of human
love" with its meeknesses and sweet subduings. And there is a hair-raising
poem about the woman as scientist (*Laboratory Poem*). She cuts out turtle
hearts, causing them to pound or to stop in her solutions, and

> What the heart bore, she noted on a chart,
> For work did not stop only with the heart,

while the man, gagging, watches and thinks

> of certain human hearts, their climb
> Through violence into exquisite disciplines
> Of which, as it now appeared, they all expired.

Yet "Soon she would fetch another and start over / Easy in the presence of
her lover."

Well, any criticisms I have of the poems are truly minor. In two of
them John Crowe Ransom's voice, rather than Mr. Merrill's, speaks out.
The sestet of *At the Bullfight* is the clearer ventriloquism:

> In a fringed shawl of blood the bull
> Moans and kneels down. His huge eye glazes
> On the confusing candor of her gauzes

> Who called, who of her own young will
> Hung him with garlands, tickled his nostril
> And urged him into the foam with gentle phrases.

A *Timepiece* is the other, but it is so beautiful and ceremonious a play upon "partial fullnesses" of shape and time—the pregnant woman in a hammock with her feet up like the pendulum of a clock, the pecked damsons on the ground, her half-grown daughters at play around her, the half-formed life within her—one would be really ungrateful to complain about its echo. The metaphorical pyrotechnics in the sestet of *Marsyas* seem to me too purely verbal. *A Renewal*, whose idea evokes Drayton's "Since there's no help, come let us kiss and part," is too slight to bear the comparison. The rest is fully satisfied silence.

I am supposing that readers of this magazine are familiar with at least some of Mr. Merrill's poems, and that I need not break into them for samples to prove how good a poet he is. Especially I would dislike representing my own favorites by a few quoted lines or stanzas. I hope, though, that no one misses *Mirror*, *Upon a Second Marriage*, *The Doodler*, and *Dream* (*Escape from the Sculpture Museum*) *and Waking*, and that "sunbursts, garlands, creatures, men" will continue to emerge for this thirty-three-year-old poet, playwright, and novelist "Ever more lifelike out of the white void."

# Nights and Days

◆

## Merrill

### David Kalstone

James Merrill's last volume of poems, *Water Street*, appeared in 1962; *Nights and Days* is its remarkable successor. There are lines in the earlier book that might well prepare us for the tone of this new collection:

> *back into my imagination*
> *The city glides, like cities seen from the air,*
> *Mere smoke and sparkle to the passenger*
> *Having in mind another destination*
>
> *Which now is not that honey-slow descent*
> *Of the Champs-Elysees, her hand in his,*
> *But the dull need to make some kind of house*
> *Out of the life lived, out of the love spent.*

His recent poems often—as these lines do—both invite the imagination and dismiss it. Readers of *Water Street* will remember it as marking a change, new powers expressed in poems that release the force of the coiled past, a personal past, "earth held up, a text not wholly undermined / By fluent passages of metaphor." The sly bows to his own richness of style are part of Merrill's strength. There is no pretense that the poet is shedding his skin;

"Merrill" by David Kalstone first appeared in *Partisan Review*, vol. 34, 1967, 146–50. Reprinted by permission.

he keeps all the playful and rewarding complication that marked his earlier poems, but gains a psychological intensity and authority that is new. American poetry in the past ten years—quite unpredictably, quite wonderfully—has come to include voices once heard primarily in our fiction, in novels of the inner life. The gain in force has been in some cases inseparable from a crude confessional style that finally lacks any interest as *poetry*. But the real craftsmen have assimilated these energies slowly, with great certainty, and with astonishing results. I am thinking not only of Robert Lowell, but of Merrill and John Berryman and Adrienne Rich, all of whom have transformed their already distinctive and mastered styles.

*Nights and Days* contains poems as supple as those of *Water Street* and continues its surprising liberties. But it includes something further, two important long poems, "From the Cupola" and "The Thousand and Second Night," the latter of which seems to me Merrill's best work. It is amusing and rapid, slips quite easily into prose interludes and a mocking verse analysis of itself, all this without sacrificing formal intensity. It would be hard to represent accurately the tone of this poem: on one hand the poet's surfacing memories and angular self-questioning (he is sometimes "I," sometimes distantly "you"); on the other, the rich settings of Istanbul and Greece and the background allusions to the *Arabian Nights*. They are there, these tempting frameworks, to remind us of the expectations and demands of our fantasy lives—Yeats's Byzantium, Scheherazade's inexhaustible inventions. But they are also there as mocking possibilities; the poem's sinewy movement forces us to see the connection between our privileged, detached fantasies and harsh facts. It begins, almost comically, in Istanbul with "an absurd complaint. The whole right half / Of my face refuses to move." That sharp disorientation is one of many in a poem whose traveler's extravagances are there finally to remind him of time and change: "Three good friends in as many months have complained, / 'You were nice, James, before your trip. Or so / I thought. But you have changed.' " This sailing to Byzantium has led to an unexpected goal:

> *Among the dancers on the pier*
> *Glides one figure in a suit of bones,*
> *Whose savage grace alerts the chaperones.*
>
> *He picks you out from thousands. He intends*
> *Perhaps no mischief. Yet the dog-brown eyes*
> *In the chalk face that stiffens as it dries*
> *Pierce you with the eyes of those three friends.*
> *The mask begins to melt upon your face.*

Inviting landscapes become landscapes of the mind, self confrontation in the thousand and one nights of one's remembered past. The titles of the poem's opening sections are in themselves revealing: *Rigor Vitae*, *The Cure* and, particularly, *Carnivals*, used here to mean more than celebrations— quite properly "sumptuous farewells to flesh," rich awakenings to mortality.

Merrill's poems are some of the most convincing expressions we have of the pressure of fantasy, and of the abiding, unavoidable connections between fantasy and the commonplace. So, "Time," the best of the book's short poems, incorporates fragments of daily demands, for one thing, the way a son hears a feeble father:

> *He grasped your pulse in his big gray-haired hand,*
> *Crevasses opening, numb azure.* Wait
> *He breathed and glittered*: You'll regret
> You want to Read my will first Don't
> Your old father All he has Be yours

But these voices are part of an already complicated vision whose initial picture of Time is more seductive: "Ever that Everest / Among concepts." That promise of adventure transforms games of Patience into "fifty-two chromosomes permitting / Trillions of 'lives.' "

> *You could inquire beneath*
> *The snowfield, the vine-monogram, the pattern*
> *Of winged cyclists, to where the flaw lay*
> *Crocus-clean, a trail inching between*
> *Sheer heights and drops, and reach what might have been.*

Against these fantasies play the voices of the possible—the feeble father, the postponing son. The emerging vision—still cards, still mountain-climbing—is now tempered, informed by the long littleness of life. Rich imaginings about time have been tested against neglect and procrastination:

> *You take up your worn pack.*
>
> *Above their gay crusaders' dress*
> *The monarchs' mouths are pinched and bleak.*
> *Staggering forth in ranks of less and less*
> *Related cards, condemned to the mystique*
>
> *Of a redeeming One,*
> *An Ace to lead them home, sword, stave, and axe,*
> *Power, Riches, Love, a place to lay them down*
> *In dreamless heaps, the reds, the blacks,*

> *Old Adams and gray Eves*
> *Escort you still.*

The technique, here as elsewhere, is one of bold transformations; the "worn pack" of eternal games of cards merges with the mountain-climber's burden. And here one comes to the special strangeness of Merrill's style, its taut alertness to meanings that lurk in words and phrases one casually comes upon. One finds this in all good poets, but here raised to a habit of vigilance, a quickened control and poise, sometimes bravado, that he clearly believes in as a source of power. The phrase "on the rocks" springs unexpectedly to life in this section from "The Broken Home":

> *When my parents were younger this was a popular act:*
> *A veiled woman would leap from an electric wine-dark car*
> *To the steps of no matter what—the Senate or the Ritz Bar—*
> *And bodily, at newsreel speed, attack*
>
> *No matter whom—Al Smith or José Maria Sert*
> *Or Clemenceau—veins standing out on her throat*
> *As she yelled* War mongerer! Pig! Give us the vote!,
> *And would have to be hauled away in her hobble skirt.*
>
> *What had the man done? Oh, made history.*
> *Her business (he had implied) was giving birth,*
> *Tending the house, mending the socks.*
>
> *Always that same old story—*
> *Father Time and Mother Earth,*
> *A marriage on the rocks.*

All conversational ease and finally outrageous humor, the wit allows us momentary relaxation and then plants its sting. The newsreel proves more than quaint, is charged with meaning in the context of a long poem whose speaker is exorcizing the ghosts of a broken home. Beneath amused glimpses of twenties bravado, the verse penetrates to parents' energies (both envied and resented) that shape and cripple a child's. "The Broken Home" is a splendid example of both the poise and the psychological intensity which distinguish these poems, and like "The Thousand and Second Night" it gives us a sense of dangerous mastery. The wit is exhilarating precisely because it is exercised in the shadow of brooding enemies honestly faced— one's past, out of one's control; and time.

It would be misleading to suggest that all the poems in this volume are cut from the same cloth; if anything the book has less unity than *Water Street*. There is an exuberant "Violent Pastoral" which brings Death back into Arcadia in a surprising way. There are also several fine love poems, particularly "Days of 1964," recalling Cavafy, which concludes the book. And the volume includes a second very long poem, "From the Cupola." It plays out the tale of Cupid and Psyche in modern instances, its heroine a New England spinster with a haunted attachment to an unknown stranger, mocked by sisters named, mischievously, Alice and Gertrude. Though as interesting an experiment in extended form as "The Thousand and Second Night," its protagonist is less dramatically recognizable, perhaps less a "psyche" than the speaker of the other long poem.

Finally, what marks off *Nights and Days* as a distinct collection is its strong sense of how Time shadows a life. Time's presence is stronger and more troubling than it was in *Water Street*. An inverse measure of the control and poise mustered against it are those moments when figures do "let go," like the speaker at the end of the poem "Time," who catches sight of something "not unlike / Meaning relieved of sense," or the man whose resisted temptation in "A Carpet Not Bought" cannot save him from "that morning . . . When sons with shears / Should set the pattern free / To ripple air's long floors / And bear him safe / Over a small waved sea." Or the splendid moment at the end of "The Thousand and Second Night" when the captivity of fantasy and flesh is finally ended and Scheherezade takes her leave of the Sultan. These visions are the most gifted passages in the poems, often occurring powerfully in their last lines. But they are measured, guarded by "an old distrust of imaginary scenes." The passion for release haunts *Nights and Days*, though it remains, now, wisely, a passion unfulfilled, deferred, glimpsed in its relation to the nagging voices of everyday.

# The Fire Screen

◆

## [Review of *The Fire Screen*]

### JOHN HOLLANDER

Each of James Merrill's books of poetry has been better than the previous one, and such a spectacle, in the case of one of our very best poets, is more than refreshing. *The Fire Screen* is an extraordinarily beautiful book in its total organization, as well as in its individual poems. It takes its title from the image of an embroidered fire screen, in a poem of fire-revery, that becomes as imaginatively radiant, as generative of meditation, as the very sheet of flames to what Gaston Bachelard called "the Prometheus complex." It is a fire screen that dissolves into the visionary (as a footnote, troped in as an apparent afterthought suggests: "All framework & embroidery rather than any deeper looking into words. Fire screen— screen *of* fire. The Valkyrie's baffle, pulsing at trance pitch, godgiven, elemental . . ."), and that leads out into the book's major theme. How to make use of memory and dream, of experiences of the interstitial, is a question that total human sanity, rather than its usual frenzied simulacrum, must always pursue. Here, in scenes that embody recurrent phases in the rhythms of vacation and return, of performance and post-mortem, of opera as drama and as part of one's own past, the subtlety and potent sensitivity of Merrill's earlier poetry has moved into deeper, but brighter regions. He is too fine and important a poet to have been bogged down in the Slough of Confession in which so many writers still struggle (to escape? or for exercise?), and in this book his fictions achieve the true generality of poetry that lies beyond fancy.

# Braving the Elements

◆

## Feux d'Artifice

STEPHEN YENSER

No rhinestone now, no dilute amethyst, But of the first water, linking star to pang, Teardrop to fire . . .

Because it was once the fashion to regard James Merrill as the Fabergé of contemporary poetry, one hesitates to begin a review of his new volume by applying to it his description (in *Up and Down*) of a bracelet. One hesitates—thinking that if this poet ever was handcuffed by artificiality, he long ago slipped those particular bracelets, and no one should be led to think otherwise—and then censures the impulse. If these lines define the quality of Merrill's recent work, it is fitting that they remind us of the integrity of career without which we could not have that work.

Twenty years ago, a reviewer of Merrill's first volume, while noting its precocious technique, complained that one could smell in its pages the well-wrought lamp of poetic learning. What looks to be a rejoinder came years later near the end of *From the Cupola* (*Nights and Days*), where Merrill took up one of that poem's recurrent symbols, "The lamp I smell in every other line," and went on with less brass than polish, less learning than magic, to ask:

"Feux d'Artifice" first appeared in *Poetry* 122 (1973), 163–68. Copyright © 1973 by the Modern Poetry Association. Reprinted by permission of Stephen Yenser and the Editor of *Poetry*.

Do you smell mine? From its rubbed brass a moth
Hurtles in motes and tatters of itself
—Be careful, tiny sister, drabbest sylph!—
Against the hot glare, the consuming myth,

Drops, and is still.

The dialectical process—the sublation of the elegant fiction of *First Poems*
and the rude reality of the criticism in a poem based on the Psyche-Eros
relationship—is characteristic. Everything is fuel for "the consuming myth."
The phrase could not have displeased the man who wrote of "Dying into a
dance"; and perhaps no poet since Yeats has seen as much by the flickering
light of that paradox.

    The corresponding image in *Up and Down* is of an emerald, offered by
his twice-widowed mother to the poet:

                               "He gave
Me this when you were born. Here, take it for—

For when you marry. For your bride. It's yours."
A den of greenest light, it grows, shrinks, glows,
Hermetic stanza buried in the prose
Of the last thirty semi-precious years.

I do not tell her, it would sound theatrical,
*Indeed this green room's mine, my very life.*
*We are each other's; there will be no wife;*
*The little feet that patter here are metrical.*

Every detail, from his birth to his "descendants," is a facet of the idea, more
true as it becomes more crucial in Merrill's writing, that the art—the stone
that this poem's hermetic philosopher has used to reduce his elements to
their etymological essence in "stanza"—is the life. That the idea is crucial,
the wit convinces us, for the passion is edged, armed with irony (the wry
turn on "theatrical," the self-conscious pathos of "the little feet"); and I
think that we are convinced as well that in braving these elements, Merrill
is in his own.

    His title comes from *Dreams about Clothes*, a poem which mocks its art
(its dreams and clothes) as quickly as it makes it and thereby exemplifies its
subject: the frustrating power possessed by and possessing dreamers like
Prospero and Proust. "The tempest used to be my cup of tea," says the
disciple who has so often taken himself to the cleaners that he must plead
for help from the proprietor of that establishment:

Tell me something, Art.
You know what it's like

> Awake in your dry hell
> Of volatile synthetic solvents.
> Won't you help us brave the elements
> Once more, of terror, anger, love?

Art's task, it appears, is to clean and press the poet's various suits, to help him brave the elements in style. Although the clothes will still, will *therefore* turn up with "holes made by the myth," it does not follow that "there's more enterprise / In walking naked." Yeats, like the old strippers, knew that nakedness was the end of disclosure, that one would be well-advised to put such lines at the conclusion of a volume, that the lights go off with the last article of apparel. And so does Merrill:

> Seeing there's no end to wear and tear
> Upon the lawless heart,
> Won't you as well forgive
> Whoever settles for the immaterial?
> Don't you care how we live?

The counterpoint insists that we all settle soon enough. Meanwhile, the "heart," worn on the sleeve or not, is a material concern, so it rhymes with "Art," "solvents" with "elements." Willy-nilly, then, "life [is] fiction in disguise."

*Days of 1935* is a fabling of that discovery in the form of a narrative of a kidnapping that has less the horror than the high color of *Bonnie and Clyde* and less the folktale basis than the fairy tale bias of Elizabeth Bishop's *Burglar of Babylon*. Early in the ballad, the artist remembers the boy who shuddered, hardly with fear alone, at the thought that it was "entirely plausible" for him to be abducted like the Lindbergh child:

> Lithe as a tiger, light as a moth,
> For a masked and crouching form
> Lithe as a tiger, light as a moth,
> To glide towards me, clap a firm
> Hand across my mouth,
>
> Then sheer imagination ride
> Off with us in its old jalopy,
> Trailing bedclothes like a bride
> Timorous but happy.

Because this is "sheer imagination," it must happen; and by means of verbs which are modulated into the present tense as the past materializes, before we know that it is happening, the boy is in a "hovel . . . Hidden from the world," under the control of Jean, "A lady out of *Silver Screen*," and Floyd, a "lean, sallow, lantern-jawed" gangster who sports a cartridge belt. Thereafter, light, iridescent stanzas float past, a string of soap bubbles, as the boy sleeps on a "rag rug, a rainbow threadbare," tells Jean tales within the tale, avoids rescue, but finally loses his captors to the Law and returns home, to "reality," where his parents await visits from "Tel & Tel executives, / Heads of Cellophane or Tin, / With their animated wives."

One of the most important of Merrill's elements, one that often fuses life and fiction, is fire, as readers of his preceding volume know from the footnote that glossed its title: "Fire screen—screen *of* fire. The Valkyrie's baffle, pulsing at trance pitch, god-given, elemental. Flames masking that cast-iron plaque—'contrecoeur' in French—which backs the hearth with charred Loves & Graces." Like a baffle-plate, the title phrase turned both ways, uniting the inner and the outer, passion and artifice, flames and framework; and so does this volume's first poem, a burning *Log* in two senses, even as it serves as a prologue to *After the Fire.* A quasi-autobiographical narrative that connects the partial burning of a house in Greece with the end of a love affair, the latter concludes with this encounter with a native "grandmother," who has been ill with a fever:

> I mean to ask whose feast it is today
> But the room brightens, the yiayia shrieks my name—
> *It's Tzimi! He's returned!*
> —And with that she returns to human form,
> The snuffed-out candle-ends grow tall and shine,
> Dead flames encircle us, which cannot harm,
> The table's spread, she croons, and I
> Am kneeling pressed to her old burning frame.

"Everything changes; nothing does," the opening line has reminded us; and what is the burning frame if not the screen of fire, the consuming myth? Today is love's feast, and the guest is celebrant and communicant, consumer and consumed.

This firm grasp of the knot, the slipknot of contrariety that is the self, is one with Merrill's ability to slide, as though from the real into the fictive, from the lyric into the dramatic; and this ability is one reason that he can get so much of his experience into his poetry. *"Ze ne suis plus voleur, seulement volaze!,"* exclaims the character suspected of starting the fire. One wants to respond, on the one hand, with Rimbaud and a latent sense of the title in mind, *"Donc le poète est vraiment voleur de feu";* and, on the other, that if Panayioti is fickle, it is because he is the poet, who has donned that disguise as surely as he has that of the yiayia.

The "old burning frame" is refurbished in *18 West 11th Street*, a meditation on the coincidence that the poet once lived in the New York dwelling demolished by the Weathermen's accidentally suicidal bomb blast in 1970. In a marvellously sustained passage, Merrill reels off a reconstruction of that disaster in terms of a news film of it, a "dry film" that is, however, "Run backwards, parching, scorching to consume / Whatever filled you to the brim," so that the progression of the poem coincides with the retrogression of the film, the creation of the vision with the vision of the destruction, to extend that point located in *Flèche d'Or* in the "heart of hearts" where "the parallels / Meet and nothing lasts and nothing ends."

The attempt at every juncture at such completeness and compression makes one fear that this poem, along with *Under Libra: Weights and Measures* and *Komboloi*, might not receive immediately the attention it rewards. It is to a dedication to completeness, however, that we owe the mandala-like clarity of *Flèche d'Or*, *Willowware Cup*, and *Syrinx*. *Syrinx* opens as "Bug, flower, bird on slipware fired and fluted, / The summer day breaks everywhere at once," as it dawns on the speaker that what the day demands expression of is its conjunction of nature and artifice, division and unity; and the poem proceeds, distich after distich of unalterable cadence and exact phrasing, the whole so amazingly laced together that "punning" misrepresents the means, to discover that all it can know of language suggests that what Keats located in art is true in nature. Indeed, the poem exploits language to the extent that it justifies its efforts to escape from it. Merrill is not merely ingenious when he makes us hear a muffled solmization in the last of these lines: "Who puts his mouth to me / Draws out the scale of love and dread— / O ramify, sole antidote!" Improvised on and by this scion of Pascal's "thinking reed," the poem ascends the scale of means of expression until it is teased out of thought, until there seems no place for it to go unless it translates itself into that condition to which all art is said to aspire. Or into mathematics:

> Some formula not relevant any more
> To flower children might express it yet
>
> Like
>
> $$\sqrt{\left(\frac{x}{y}\right)^{n}} = 1$$
> —Or equals zero, one forgets
> . . .

As the "zero" replaces the "I" that is the root of the multiple, only to be replaced by the "one" who "forgets," the dialectic is taken as far as it can go in words, in whatever numbers. So the poem moves through a breathtaking decrescendo of delicate *frissons* to affirm with a flourish its initial insight, as "Syrinx" envisions the moment when:

he reaches for me, then

Leaves me cold, the great god Pain,
Letting me slide back into my scarred case,

Whose silvery, breath-tarnished tones
No longer rivet bone and star in place

Or keep from shrivelling, leather round a stone,
The sunbather's precocious apricot

Or stop the four winds racing overhead

Nought
Waste        Eased
Sought

This volume ends with that squaring of the circle, a startling emblem of Merrill's furiously patient attempt to frame the fiction of a life. The results of that attempt have put him, in the middle of his career, in that awesome position of being incapable of writing less than some of the best poetry of his time.

# Divine Comedies

◆

## Evenings at the Ouija Board

### David Kalstone

With *Divine Comedies*, his seventh book of verse, James Merrill's poetry modulates into a new key and refigures everything he has written so far. The most engaging member of the gifted generation of American poets who emerged in the 1950s, Merrill has always known how to sustain and redirect his energies, how not to burn himself out or repeat himself, how to survive his gift as many American poets have not. It is a happy irony that though he has been praised for his inventiveness, his technical agility, and for a richness just barely reined in by witty narrative, these qualities have seldom distracted him as much as they have his reviewers. Merrill, with increasing awareness, courage and delight, has been developing an autobiography: "developing" as from a photographic negative which becomes increasingly clear. He has not led that kind of outwardly dramatic life which would make external changes the centre of his poetry. Instead, poetry itself has been one of the changes, something which continually happens to him, and Merrill's subject proves to be the subject of the great Romantics: the constant revisions of the self that come through writing verse. Each book seems more spacious because of the one which has come before.

Still, nothing could have exactly prepared readers for the deep focus of *The Book of Ephraim*, the wild, funny, mysterious long poem which makes up two-thirds of Merrill's *Divine Comedies*. Set against his shorter poems,

Reprinted from *Times Literary Supplement*, 28 October 1977, 1267. Reprinted by permission.

*The Book of Ephraim* accomplishes something of a transformation scene—as if on a darkened stage where we are accustomed to spotlit figures, suddenly in a blaze of light everyone is in place against a long and deepening perspective. The poem recapitulates much of Merrill's writing career and draws many of its principal characters back on stage. But with them this time taking bows is the director-choreographer, the beguiling muse and Eros of Merrill's last twenty years.

He is called Ephraim. He invaded Merrill's life in 1955 in what comes to seem, as the poem goes on, a less and less unorthodox manner; for this poem is "The Book of a Thousand and One Evenings Spent with David Jackson at the Ouija Board In Touch with Ephraim Our Familiar Spirit." Ephraim is identified (complete with the occasional upper case letters which indicate direct quotation from the board) as "A Greek Jew/Born AD 8 at XANTHOS . . . In Greece WHEN WOLVES & RAVENS WERE IN ROME / . . . Later a favorite of TIBERIUS Died / AD 36 on CAPRI throttled / By the imperial guard for having LOVED / THE MONSTERS NEPHEW [sic] CALIGULA." The bittersweet worldliness with which Ephraim addresses his two earthly charges DJ and JM is a clear cousin to Merrill's poised poetic voice. (Both of them it turns out come from broken homes.) "TAKE our teacher told us / FROM SENSUAL PLEASURE ONLY WHAT WILL NOT / DURING IT BE EVEN PARTLY SPOILED / BY FEAR OF LOSING TOO MUCH." More important, Ephraim incarnates Merrill's dedication—nurtured on Proust and Freud—to certain sacred encounters in his life which expose its deeper configurations.

Merrill's best poetry from *Water Street* (1962) on has been autobiographical in more than accidental and local detail. He has written plump, witty narratives in which the exterior order of events, however seductive, plays only a secondary or supporting role, like the timely progress of a love affair behind a sonnet sequence. The figures who appear and reappear in Merrill's poems have more substance than the legendary heroines who were muses to the sonneteers, but they have the same mesmerizing force. He has depicted them over and over in Proustian and Freudian constellations, each time with a greater sense of liberation and understanding, recalling himself as a child with a divorced mother and father, as in "The Broken Home," one of his best poems; or holding those figures in tension against his adult self in a landscape with a lover, as in the powerful diptych "Up and Down." Merrill's poems have used the objects and stages of daily life, the arrangements of civilized behaviour, almost as if he expected to awaken sleeping presences and take by surprise the myths he lives by.

It is the human ability to do so that Ephraim serio-comically confirms and guarantees for JM and DJ, whose shared life—away from and seated at the ouija board—conjures him up. Ephraim is the patient and genial custodian of an attractive system of reincarnation and second sight. It involves supervisory heavenly patrons, free at last of the annoying necessity to be reborn, and their earthly representatives, whose eventual progress guarantees the patron's promotion to some higher level of nine stages in the upper world. Ephraim often touches on outrageous possibilities, such as the precarious moment when a spirit finally severs itself from the bodily cycle:

> At least a century goes by before
> One night comes when the soul, revisiting
> Its deathplace here below, locates and enters
> On the spot a sleeping form its own
> Age and sex (easier said than done
> In rural or depopulated areas:
> E treats us here to the hilarious
> Upshot of a Sioux brave's having chosen
> By mistake a hibernating bear).

However comic some of the machinery, the details are valued as a way of explaining some of our premonitory glimpses and ecstasies, whether in dreams or poetry. For while the soul is busy severing its last earthly ties, the dislodged sleeper's spirit "replaces it in Heaven." So: a dream given to Merrill's friend, Maya Deren, an experimental filmmaker, and recounted in the poet's richest vein. In a roomful of people in evening dress, chandeliers ablaze, with an unknown admirer.

> She is a girl again, his fire-clear eyes
> Turning her beautiful, limber, wise,
> Except that she alone wears mourning weeds
> That weigh unbearably until he leads
> Her to a spring, or source, oh wonder! in
> Whose shining depths her gown turns white, her jet
> To diamonds, and black veil to bridal snow.
> Her features are unchanged, yet her pale skin
> Is black, with glowing nostrils—a not yet
> Printed self. . . . Then it is time to go.
> Long trials, his eyes convey, must intervene
> Before they meet again. A first, last kiss
> And fadeout. Dream? She wakes from it in bliss.

In a passage which illuminates the entire poem, Ephraim goes on to interpret the dream; which

> he blandly adds, is a low-budget
> Remake—imagine—of the *Paradiso*.
> Not otherwise its poet toured the spheres
> While Someone very highly placed up there,
> Donning his bonnet, in and out through that
> Now famous nose haled the cool Tuscan night.
> The resulting masterpiece takes years to write;

> More, since the dogma of its day
> Calls for a Purgatory, for a Hell,
> Both of which Dante thereupon, from footage
> Too dim or private to expose, invents.
> His Heaven, though, as one cannot but sense,
> Tercet by tercet, is pure Show and Tell.

The fable ranges past comedy to rapture and tells a lot about the initial allure of poetry for Merrill. His *First Poems*, in the vein of the *Paradiso* he here describes, reflect a young solitary's desire to witness and escape to an ideal world. When he turned to narrative and social comedy, it was always with the sense—Proust's sense—that the world discerned is not quite real, that in its flashing action he might catch glimpses of patterns activated by charged moments of his life.

What the young Merrill could not have foreseen was that the future ideal world he was working towards was not an empty evacuated space, but instead a rich experience of *déjà vu*. For him it was to be full of the past, of luminous figures, the living and the dead, all of whom coexist in *The Book of Ephraim* by virtue of the attention Merrill has given them throughout his work and the value he has come to attach to them. *The Book of Ephraim* includes figures resonant from earlier poems now almost icons of love, affection, authority or creative energy: his mother; his dead father, founder of a large American brokerage; David Jackson, who has shared his life in Stonington and Athens; Hans Lodeizen, the young Dutch poet whose death Merrill elegized in "The Country of a Thousand Years of Peace"; Strato, the Greek subject of Merrill's Cavafy-like sequence in *The Fire Screen*; Maria Mitsotáki, an Athenian Garbo and gardener; Kyria Kleo, his Greek maid; as well as literary masters such as Wallace Stevens and W. H. Auden. They make a community, according to Ephraim, "WITHIN SIGHT OF + ALL CONNECTED TO EACH OTHER DEAD OR ALIVE NOW DO U UNDERSTAND WHAT HEAVEN IS IT IS THE SURROUND OF THE LIVING". Of these figures, Ephraim says, "IT IS EASY TO CALL THEM BRING THEM AS FIRES WITHIN SIGHT OF EACH OTHER ON HILLS".

This last wonderful metaphor for the board's powers of convocation is typical of Merrill's tantalizing use of ouija throughout. No one leaves the poem thinking of the board in any simple way—and certainly not as either a fortune-telling trinket or as an excuse à la Victor Hugo for a transcendental salon. Merrill quotes Heinrich Zimmer at one point: "The powers have to be consulted again directly—again, again and again. Our primary task is to learn, not so much what they are said to have said, as how to approach them, evoke fresh speech from them, and understand that speech." The board allows Merrill to "evoke fresh speech" and to face in two directions: to deny the boundaries between the conscious and unconscious, the living and the dead, but also to make a counter assertion. It is the poet who brings figures together "as fires within sight of each other on hills." The board is *his* theatre of memory, its arc of letters an extension of the typewriter's amphitheatre of keys. For Dante's brightening circles, he has substituted the incandescent and irreducible alphabet and the fragile connections it allows him to make. (The book is set out in twenty-six consecutively lettered sections.)

Though Merrill's extravagant *ars poetica* is one dimension of the poem, the *ars vitae* and *ars amoris* are equally important. *The Book of Ephraim* explores the poet's relation to friends and lovers. If the poem reaps the rewards and transfusions of memory it also gives a sense of intimacies—taken and forgone. It explores the curious paradox—Petrarch brought up to date—that luminous figures to whom one is drawn because they expose certain patterns in one's life become themselves most available in memory and writing, in the deepening, even dwarfing power of the pattern. Ephraim and his transcendental system result from the loving collaboration of JM and DJ. Yet the poem registers this satisfaction against the potent erosions of time and the isolating force of Merrill's own art. The poem records the separations of JM and DJ, their less and less frequent meetings over the board, the twilight comedies of DJ's aged parents, the physical deterioration of the shared house in Connecticut where Ephraim first appeared. At the end he acknowledges the sense of depletion to which Ephraim is the beguiling guide:

> And here was I, or what was left of me.
> Feared and rejoiced in, chafed against, held cheap,
> A strangeness that was us, and was not, had
> All the same allowed for its description,
> And so brought at least me these spells of odd,
> Self-effacing balance.

In these contradictions Merrill concentrates the struggles of the poem, the sharp full sense of relinquishment at its close, and the almost involuntary access to another world ("A strangeness . . . had . . . allowed for its description"). It is precisely at the moments when writing penetrates beyond memory and renders transparent a familiar social or domestic scene that the poet is most aware of depletion ("what was left of me"). His house at the end of the poem is cold and empty. A mysterious and unidentified thief has been and gone. At moments Merrill all too completely shares the feelings of one of the characters in his poem:

> Sleep overtakes him clasping what he loathes
> And loves, the dead self dressed in his own clothes.

Yet the surface of this poem is as worldly as its insights are visionary. Everything is grist for Merrill's mill. He pays a call on chimpanzees being taught human language in Oklahoma. He interlaces the poem with the plot of a lost novel taking place near Los Alamos. He receives critiques of the poem in progress from Alexander Pope and Wallace Stevens. In the midst of a climactic encounter in Venice he pauses for what proves not at all a digression to explain what X-rays have revealed about Giorgione's "Tempesta." Behind Merrill's gusto and comic appetite is a surprised certainty that the apparently random materials of our lives and reading, history and gossip—the rational and irrational bombardments—are somehow selected and absorbed for our experience.

The Book of Ephraim could well have appeared alone. It stands in even higher relief beside the poems which precede it in Divine Comedies and which constitute an extended farewell to some of Merrill's cherished themes. "Yánnina" and "Lost in Translation" are among the most beautiful poems Merrill has ever written. "Yánnina"—a meditation on the town in northern Greece where the amorous and tyrannical legend of Ali Pasha is still alive— is also a poem in which Merrill completes a loving reidentification with his father. "Lost in Translation" revisits the world of "The Broken Home"— absorbing its tensions and conflicts into a more spacious and generous perspective where nothing, finally, is lost; the poem, like Valéry's "Palme", to which it pays homage, "Rustling with its angel, turns the waste / To shade and fiber, milk and memory." Transmuting childhood mysteries into the saddened versatility of adult performance, the poem is a long and grateful farewell to Proust whose doctrine of time recaptured has long been an article of faith for Merrill, but not until now so triumphantly realized in his work. He had after all, twenty years ago in a novel, The Seraglio, placed his family at some saving ironic distance. It is precisely Merrill's surprise at his enlarged, nourished and idiosyncratic relation to his past—rare in American poetry— that Divine Comedies records.

# Mirabell

◆

## Answer, Heavenly Muse, Yes or No

### David Bromwich

"Give me *tact*," said James Merrill, at a very young age, to the enchantress who shared the servants' quarters with a cook, a governess, and a tutor. (The enchantress was a one-time guest; the others were regulars, and had been instructed to provide their charge with "local color" from the streets of Istanbul or any of the rich, too rich Eastern cities over whose fallen glamour the poems he wrote as a grown-up would hover comically, elegiacally.) "And—isn't it the same thing—give me a *perfect ear*." The enchantress hesitated a moment, sensing in the faintly ridiculous expression a not quite distinct opportunity for a joke or a lesson; but she thought better of it, glanced doubtfully at a list of her other petitioners, and with a sigh, whose meaning none of the servants could possibly have interpreted, granted him both wishes. Since then, the joke she never made has lingered in the poet's mind, side by side with puzzles and puppies; and it is his fate to gaze long at the disappearing Cheshire Cat's grin of all questionable phrases, including his own, and show a half-raised eyebrow as a pledge of his self-consciousness. It is a minor wit's habit, the only such habit in Merrill's possession. He knows this very well, but loyalty to the enchantress forbids him from altering any detail of what he takes to be her legacy. Besides, he might observe (were he at all inclined to argue), certain of his poems have moved a generation

Reprinted by permission from *The Hudson Review*, vol. 32, no. 3 (Autumn 1979), 455–60. Copyright © 1979 by The Hudson Review, Inc.

of readers by making it hard to draw the line between manner and mannerism—with their calm deflections, their articulate wish to make something "Out of the life lived, out of the love spent," their brilliant and serious assurance that every claim they permit themselves is justified, because depths last longer than heights.

Merrill finds all images of himself absorbing: to be lost in the endless refinements of speculation is a destiny full of charm, which he firmly rejects. But the received styles of our period are autobiographical, or "confessional," and this is the poet in whom the more durable of those styles were unified. Lowell and Jarrell hardly touch the perfect surface of "The Broken Home" or "Lost in Translation"; their first steps seem the relics of an earlier and obsolete technology. In general, Merrill is undervalued by readers who care too much about the obvious fact that he is himself an inventor with a following. His poems are strangely adaptable. They abolish the debts they incur, and shrug off their burdens lightly in the only place where it ought to be done, between the first line and the last. Indeed, his poems do everything lightly; most disputes about them would center on this. He chose, as a mythological subject, not Faustus and Helen but Cupid and Psyche, for whom action cannot go beyond velleity. His sensibility appears to have formed itself wholly on the pains of *curiosa felicitas*, and he is happy to have it appear so.

Our sense of an achieved composure at the center of Merrill's work has tended to divert attention from the occasionally insensitive passages in which he seeks, in the record of his own memories, some reflection of the public life of his age. Sudden glimpses, of the Kennedy funeral train in "In Nine Sleep Valley" or of a newspaper photo in "An Urban Convalescence," have come near to ruining at least two fine poems. What Merrill needed was a way to house his public meditations in a sufficiently grand private vehicle. With *The Book of Ephraim* he seemed to have found it, and now we have the sequel, *Mirabell*, and still a third volume is promised to complete the long poem that borrows its scheme of ascent from Dante. This review is accordingly an interim report. It assumes that there is such a thing as poetic character (a different thing from *the* poetic character); that as Merrill looms larger for us it is to this element in him that we are chiefly drawn; and that his character is not, like Stevens', a journeying from strength to strength, or like Hart Crane's, a kind of human miracle that we would prefer not to see "in perspective" even if we could, but rather the compound we recognize in the best of our contemporaries, of weaknesses we can easily ignore with a single emphatic strength we can never forget.

*Ephraim* and *Mirabell* are about the structure of the universe, and answer the questions Whence? Whither? and How? Two generic voices dominate each of the two parts of the poem. Their names, we feel, ought to be Here and There, but at this point Merrill subdivides. Here may be JM (James Merrill) or DJ (David Jackson, friend and house-mate). There was originally Ephraim, a Greek Jew born in A.D. 8 "a favorite of TIBE-RIUS." It may now be Mirabell, or Maria Mitsotaki, or W. H. Auden, but with no strict rule against Chester Kallman, Marius Bewley, and any number of others. The truth is that as soon as a friend of the poet's has parked his car to the side of *our* busy thoroughfare, he knocks on the table at Stonington and is affectionately recycled into the poem: all are clubbable. The characters are sufficiently differentiated as to humor but not as to idiom, so that a few simple theatrical cues have to identify them: Auden says "MY DEARS," Maria "MES ENFANTS." Whether the spirits or "patrons," as Merrill calls them, actually used these eminently decipherable salutations, we are never told, but the result is convenient for following the story and only a little tiresome. There appears to be exactly one line of communication from There to Here, and Merrill's interlocutors now and then have the frantic air of collegiate disk jockeys wrestling for a microphone. This, however, is his only *donnée*.

The poetry is of two sorts. First, news of the universe, set up entirely in upper-case lettering, spoken by the voices There. Then, Merrill's observations on the bearing of all this upon his own life. In *Ephraim* the latter predominated, but in *Mirabell* the news itself has become all-important, at the confessed sacrifice of what we would ordinarily call poetry. Most of the book is written in telegraphic capitals which bear the mark not so much of Merrill's poetry as—with many Yr's and U's and Wd's and Shd's—of an accidental effusion by a ticker-tape, a crazed linotypist, several traffic signs, and Ezra Pound in one of the more imposing phases of his correspondence. Twenty or thirty pages into the poem, the eye grows accustomed to its new habitat, and we come to feel that the wits There are as sure-footed as Here, though more wearing. But granting *Mirabell* its typographical liberties, and reserving all our disappointment at having so much made of Mirabell's turning himself into a peacock out of infatuation with his new friends, which is something everyone has seen happen at a party, we may still suspect that the powers now divide almost too neatly into fancy and imagination. Maria, Auden, Mirabell, perhaps even DJ, who is too dimly seen for us to believe that he subsists entirely on this side of the ouija board, all are clever beyond our abilities and our needs, but none could have written the little poem beginning "No, no! Set in our ways / As in a garden's," the crown jewel of *Ephraim*. Nor could they have imagined the sonnet about Avebury from the notably this-worldly first book of *Mirabell*.

> Within a "greater circle" (the whole myth
> Dwarfed by its grass-green skyline) stand
> Two lesser, not quite tangent O's
> Plotted monolith by monolith.
>
> Two lenses now, whose once outrippling arcs
> Draw things back into focus. Round each stone

(As earth revolves, or a sheepdog barks)
Rumination turns the green to white.

It's both a holy and a homely site
Slowlier perfused than eye can see
(Whenever the stones blink a century
Blacks out) by this vague track
Of brick and thatch and birdsong any June
Galactic pollen will have overstrewn.

It might be said that without the larger fiction of the entire poem this moment would be lost, and quite impossible to place. And it is true that a phrase like "galactic pollen" withholds its proper meaning unless we have kept up with JM's eccentric discoveries about Akhnaton, nuclear energy, the Bermuda Triangle, and the acquaintance of an immortal patron with his *First Poems*, any of which on its own merits we would gladly tie to a stone and sink deep in the Euphrates. Our regret, however, has nothing to do with the argument of the poem, by which only camp-followers or pedants would pretend to judge it, but everything to do with its gradually narrowing sympathies, and the consequent tendency to allow fewer and more modest occasions of human eloquence, while the prattle of patrons increases in both volume and ambition. Merrill is by nature suggestible to the point of simple faith, and in *Mirabell* he takes his full swing. Part of this is of course the buoyancy of Wilde, but we could wish it had been tempered, as for Wilde it generally was, with a little more of the heritage of Wordsworth. As it is, a voice from There burbles "Leave for Cape Wrath tonight!" and the auditor Here does leave, without ruffling a map or consoling his neighbors.

Like its predecessor, *Mirabell* is centrally furnished not only with the ouija board and makeshift indicators, but also with a mirror. The board and mirror by themselves, we remember, generated two impressive poems in an earlier volume, *The Country of a Thousand Years of Peace*; and both poems now make curious reading, for what they tell of the inward evolution and specialization of Merrill's interest in the esoteric. The mirror once refused to *teach us how to live*, but still felt a tug of vulnerability in the voices of the world's children, which could be heard wondering aloud, *If not you, who will*? Refusing a mirror's responsibilities in their full Elizabethan sense, it knew what help could come of arrangement alone and kept up appearances with a partly moral purpose of instruction. But the mirror has now become merely an adjunct to the board; and the board, loved at first (in "Voices from the Other World")

Because, once looked at lit
By the cold reflections of the dead

> Risen extinct but irresistible,
> Our lives have never seemed more full, more real,
> Nor the full moon more quick to chill

—this capricious medium is now to be loved in itself, and perhaps all the more because it makes our world *less* real. Throughout *Ephraim* the voices were overheard as splendid possibles, which drew from Merrill a luminous attentiveness to the particulars of "Our life, our life, our life." The pathos of skepticism having departed, we are left with the dark religions of the wandering teacup, a long way from "the very world, which is the world / Of all of us."

> —This outside world, our fictive darkness more
> And more belittles to a safety door
> Left open onto light. Too small, too far
> To help. The blind bright spot of where we are.

Even more grimly chastened, later in the poem, Merrill confesses: "Dear Mirabell, words fail us. But for you / How small our lives would be, how tedious." It is the photographic negative of the poem written twenty years earlier. In between, the autobiographical quest which looked as if it would yield the story of a supreme fiction, several times as long as Stevens' poem and miraculously no less personal, has, with its *longueurs*, its trial-and-error cosmogony and important messages from important friends, come more and more plainly to resemble the typical long poems of our time, *Paterson* and *The Cantos*.

Where, in *Ephraim*, the wish for systematic salvation was the gentlest rustling of an angel, candid and calm, never bent on giddy transcriptions, in *Mirabell* there is a panic rush and waste, an earnestness that is really the reverse of *Nil admirari*. Everything must be set down immediately. This urgency is akin to that of the tabloids, with the same profusion of uppercase lettering. Once, Merrill had a store of negative capability; now, his spirits do not!—and they are running the show. It would be less troubling if the mirror did something other than duplicate. It cannot. Merrill looks up there and finds—exactly what he has down here: a very cosy, comfy place for a seventy year lay-over, filled with the gossip of friends, the vigilance of easy and uneasy relations; a little by-chamber of infinity, built by Time and Matter and the God Biology, but upholstered in the finest taste. Johnson thought the good and evil of eternity too ponderous for the wings of wit. Merrill's wit is a little flattering, a little light, and airy, to be employed on the good and evil of eternity. He is in fact everything he calls Auden, and derides him for (less gently than he evidently supposes). He reveals *sub specie aeternitatis* that Auden's besetting flaw was "THE MIS-MARRIAGE / OF LYRIC TO BALD FARCE." No patron was required to tell us this—yet before passing it on, Merrill should have heeded the admonitions of an *un*familiar ghost, named Tu Quoque. The boldest upper-case sections of *Mirabell* are farce too far advanced to admit the lyric impulse. The most moving, on the other hand, like Number 8.9 beginning with "WE MET ON THIS FAIR FIELD & SEEM BY ITS EASE TO BE / IN CONVERSE"—are pure Auden.

All objections to the symbolism of *Mirabell* Merrill has nicely met by anticipation. Robert Morse, "Closest of summer friends in Stonington," reminds the by then thoroughly indoctrinated and cauldron-stirring players that "Everything in Dante knew its place. / In this guidebook of yours, how do you tell / Up from down? Is Heaven's interface / What your new friends tactfully don't call Hell? / Splendid as metaphor. The real no-no / Is jargon, falling back on terms that smell / Just a touch fishy when the tide is low." An equally telling criticism was floated in *Ephraim*, where an analyst hearing the adventure of DJ and JM unshockably classified it as *folie à deux*, and asked the poet himself to supply the motive. To which JM replied: "Somewhere a Father Figure shakes his rod / At sons who have not sired a child? / Through our own spirit we can both proclaim / And shuffle off the blame / For how we live." Merrill can be, when he chooses to be, not less exquisite in sobriety than in extravagance. But this turns out to be one of the ruses by which from time to time he recites an unflattering sentence against himself, in order to be freed for further indulgences; and in *Mirabell* we are invited to share, with who knows what mingled emotions, an especially awkward siege of aesthetic bigotry: DJ wonders, "Are we more usable than Yeats or Hugo, / Doters on women, who then went ahead / To doctor everything their voices said?" And JM replies, in a great many punning words, Yes: reproductive man has squandered his mind on sex, so that only "the docile takers-in of seed" remain as undissolved intellect. We leave it to the Archangel Michael, in Part Three, to say why the metaphor is corrupt.

The ouija board ought to be regarded as an object of experience rather than belief. We would then criticize its products not on scientific grounds but because, in *Mirabell*, they represent an arbitrarily selective range of experience. These table-rappings have become what schoolchildren call a *closed game*—something they get when all the players are there and nobody else can join. Almost any irregularity can still be introduced without bringing the game to an end; on the contrary, this is when the playmakers really take control; it ceases to be a game and becomes a ritual of identification. *Mirabell* exhibits the obscure but powerful system of hierarchies proper to any such ritual. Because the rules are secret, Merrill's patrons are always divulging more than they realize, and getting into trouble.

> Peacock, what's wrong?
>> I AM HERE   I AM MORE CAREFUL
> Poor darling, were you punished?
>> WE MUST GO ON

The poem grows more exacting of its ceremony in proportion as it grows more distraught in the pursuit of mystery. But the resolve that William James found a condition of genuine belief—"It favors gravity, not pertness; it says 'hush' to all vain chatter and smart wit"—is as far from the scene as Ephraim's poignant irony: "Must *everything* be witty? AH MY DEARS / I AM NOT LAUGHING I WILL SIMPLY NOT SHED TEARS." Memories from actual life, like the dog hit by a car at Number 9.5, are put into the poem as honest encumbrances, but they are not understood. We have stayed too long in the theatre.

In much of his enterprise Merrill resembles Cocteau's Orpheus, who writes down the numerical sequences broadcast by the "unknown station" of the car radio, and keeps Eurydice in check with the words, "How does one know what's poetry and what isn't?" (But it is Cegeste, the inferior poet, too clumsy to be entrusted with walking through mirrors, who has been inventing the messages all along and transmitting them from Eurydice's bedroom.) This review may nevertheless be the work of a peevish empiric: it certainly omits the charm of *Mirabell*, especially in the first half, on which others have preferred to dwell. On one point the poem as we have it is consistent throughout. It is radiant with self-confidence. Merrill may have a surprise for us at the bottom of his cup, and anything is possible to the author of a dozen small masterpieces and an unclassifiable but perfect something, *The (Diblos) Notebook*. His example, in spite of the jungle of complications, is invigorating; and there are other signs that we are entering a period congenial to the long poem: Daryl Hine's *In and Out* and John Hollander's *Reflections on Espionage* both come to mind. These poets have nothing in common except genius and an editor—together with the ability to make irritables melt away, and perhaps the conviction that the language of the cultural entrepreneur may no longer be adequate to the demands of a poem. Merrill's enchantress incidentally brought him the gift of apt quotation, and, confronted with the familiar line of Francis Bacon at the end of the last paragraph, he might respond with a less familiar one: "For if a man can be partaker of God's theatre, he shall likewise be partaker of God's rest."

# Late Settings

◆

## Fears and Farewells

### Helen Vendler

At the heart of James Merrill's new collection of lyrics lies his farewell to Greece, where he used to spend part of each year. Merrill urges a grace in losing "Greece itself," a Greece no longer what it was:

> Corrupted whites and blues,
> Taverns torn down for banks, the personnel
> Grown fat and mulish, marbles clogged with soot . . .
> Things just aren't what they were—no more am I.

The leave-taking, commemorated in a poem called "Santorini: Stopping the Leak," is done under the aegis of various lurking horrors. Merrill has just undergone five sessions of radiation to destroy a plantar wart, and the radiologist's waiting room offers vistas of future cancer; a servant in Greece recalls her brother's drowning; the island of Santorini brings up the legend of the destruction of Atlantis by an earthquake. A wave of self-doubt enters Merrill's praise of poise in endings:

> We must be light, light-footed, light of soul,
> Quick to let go, to tighten by a notch

Reprinted from *The New Republic* 193 (5 August 1985), 34–39. Reprinted by permission of *The New Republic*, © 1985, The New Republic, Inc.

> The broad, star-studded belt Earth wears to feel
> Hungers less mortal for a vanished whole.
> Light-headed at the last? Our lives unreal
> Except as jeweled self-windings, a death-watch
> Of heartless rhetoric I punctuate,
> Spitting the damson pit onto the plate?

The recommendation of lightness is made more serious by its own final self-interrogation. Joy's grape is burst, as in Keats, upon the fine palate. But in Merrill the metaphor has soured until it fastens no longer on the flesh of the fruit, but rather on the pit. Keats's deathwatch beetle has become the deathbed vigil and also the ticking time-piece of meter, its motive force the jeweled self-winding of the writer. Merrill's stanza in this poem is a version of Yeats's (and Byron's) ottava rima. Merrill adds a fourth rhyme for English ease, but keeps the terminal couplet, its finality clamping each stanza shut.

Throughout the poem "the vanished whole"— youth, love, and a country lost—is treated with comedy, irony, and pathos. In the nightmarish middle of the poem, Merrill has a vision of himself being drained of all existence through the "leak" in his irradiated foot. Other existences, borne in images, begin to invade his consciousness, thousands of other potential beings eager to take his place in the universe, as his own vitality seeps away. The press of images toward embodied being is like the press of a crowd to be admitted to a restaurant:

> Vignettes as through a jeweler's loupe descried,
> Swifter now, churning down the optic sluice,
> Faces young, old, to rend the maître d's
> Red cord, all random, ravenous images
>
> Avid for inwardness, and none but driven
> To gain, like the triumphant sperm, a table
> Set for one—wineglass, napkin, and rose-bud.

A passage like this one tests the reader's affinity for Merrill. Those of us who find in him something that nobody else now writing affords us would have to point to the combination, visible here and frequent in Merrill, of savagery and civilization. The demands of biology, blood, and nerves (the optic sluice, the ravenous bodily appetites, the triumphant sperm) intermix in him with their utmost ritualizing in formality (the stylizations by which a restaurant surrounds appetite, the scrutiny, at once magnifying and miniaturizing, of the jeweler's eyeglass). Both are here imitated by the verse, beginning in observation, accelerating in momentum, and then brought up short by the absurd and yet touching tableau of the formal table set for one—a metaphor for existence conceivable only in Merrill.

But this is all written, as I have said, in the service of fear—the fear of existence leaking away. Throughout this volume Merrill faces his own extinction, and suggests fantasies of survival:

> Could a soul that clung
> To its own fueling senses crawl at last
> Away unshriveled from the holocaust?

In fact, in the poem on Santorini, Merrill does survive. A small moth— Psyche—appears, reassuring him that his soul still lives, and a familiar pain in his foot tells him that the plantar wart has begun to grow back, "stopping the leak":

> In gloom the peevish buzz
> Of a wee wingèd one-watt presence short-
> Circuiting compulsively the panes
> Gone white. My drained self doesn't yet . . . yet does!
> From some remotest galaxy in the veins
> A faint, familiar pulse begins. The wart,
> Alive and ticking, that I'd thought destroyed.
> No lasting cure? No foothold on the void?

"The last kiss," Yeats wrote, "is given to the void," but Merrill has not quite reached that point. Life and the wart start up anew.

Other poems exhibit a less comic resolution of the shadow of death. All sorts of death take place here, notably in three short lyrics grouped under the title "Topics." In the first, a poem about terrorism, a woman tourist is shot dead. In the second, the governments of Russia and the United States survive in their bunkers after an atomic war. In the third, a poem on knowledge, man has traded earthly happiness for the knowledge of nuclear fission. For this last lyric, Merrill borrows Shelley's and Yeats's prophetic four-beat closed quatrains, and retells, with a Frostian force, the origin and ultimate glory of the universe before the earth blew itself up. (The poem is called "Caesarion," after the son of Caesar and Cleopatra, who was put to death by Octavian.)

> A glow of cells in the warm Sea,
> Some vaguest green or violet soup
> Took a few billion days to loop
> The loops we called Eternity.
>
> Before the splendor bit its tail
> Blake rendered it in aquatint
> And Eddington pursued a glint—
> Recoil, explosion—scale on scale.

> What stellar hopefuls, plumed like Mars,
> Sank to provincial rant and strut,
> Lines blown, within the occiput?
> Considering the fate of stars,
>
> I think that man died happiest
> Who never saw his Mother clasp
> Fusion, the tiny naked asp,
> By force of habit to her breast.

Merrill's pen turns to such subjects with a degree of anger, an anger turned even against writing itself (that the sign of vivacity should become the sign of extinction). This anger turns even against his own poetic masters, who were too quick to praise the word as moral and life-giving. In a poem about the bombing of Beirut, death appears again:

> By noon, fire from the same blue heavens
> Had half erased Beirut.
> *Allah be praised*, it said on crude handbills,
> *For guns and Nazarenes to shoot.*
> "How gladly with proper words," said Wallace Stevens,
> "The soldier dies." Or kills.

Merrill's quarrel with Stevens's aphorism marks a change in our 20th-century perceptions of government. Stevens's words were written in the idealism of World War II, an idealism about war impossible for Merrill, who quarrels too with Yeats's admiration for Renaissance Italian dukes:

> Above
> Lie field and vineyard, castle built
> To nurture intellect, art, love
> Together with, let's face it, guilt,
> Deception, strife.

The same consciousness of disintegration, catabolism, entropy ("Coils of shot film, run-down DNA") quarrels with Rilke's idealization of art in the archaic torso of Apollo, which spoke to him in shining potency, saying, "You must change your life." Merrill's exhumed Greek gods have a different, more impatient message:

> *Expect no*
> *Epiphany such as the torso*
> *In Paris provided for Rilke. Quit*
> *Dreaming of change. It is happening*

> *Whether you like it or not,*
> *So get on with your lives. We have done.*

Merrill's art, so apt for sensuality, travel, and domesticity, recently passed through the purgatorial trial of *The Changing Light at Sandover*, a long three-part poem that consisted of conversations with the dead. That poem now seems to be a threshold over which Merrill had to pass in order to translate himself from one of the living to one of the (potentially) dead. The punning title of the present volume, *Late Settings*, looks toward a jeweler's art, a last music, and a setting sun. The sober coloring of the sunset diffuses itself through the book, sometimes glimmering in afterglow, sometimes flashing in fission.

Merrill's Herbertian variety of technique appears here in experiments variously successful, but always interesting to watch. Merrill can imagine, for instance, a stanza like a house of cards for a poem ("An Upset") about the collapse of a table that had belonged to his grandfather. Everything falls on the floor, "ashtray, lamp, magnifying glass," books:

> Whew. A disaster zone
> Facing therapy: sandpaper, clamps and glue,
> Jetsam and overflow's diversion to shelves
> Unbuilt, if not to plain
> Oblivion. . .
> Another "flood" behind us,
> Now to relearn
> Uprightness, lightness, poise:
> First things—the lamp supposes, prone
> Yet burning wildly on.

The interleaving of five-, four-, three-, and two-stress lines (marked by differing marginal indentations) is as "upsetting" as the disorder on the floor; and yet the very order of the indenting reflects the lamp of intellectual light, inquisitive even in disaster, "prone" and almost rhymeless, but "burning wildly on."

Throughout this book, things burn and are burned, scorched, irradiated. The divine Greek sun even burns a hole in Merrill's film. The smallest sparks of burning in the collection shine in the poem that is placed first. They come from the cigarettes lit in the dark "between Earth and Venus"—two other spots of light in the night sky—as Merrill and his companion stand on the courthouse lawn at dusk. The poem, a small prospective self-elegy in dimeter, is called, innocently enough, "Grass":

> The river irises
> Draw themselves in.

> Enough to have seen
> Their day. The arras
>
> Also of evening drawn,
> We light up between
> Earth and Venus
> On the courthouse lawn,
>
> Kept by this cheerful
> Inch of green
> And ten more years—fifteen?—
> From disappearing.

Here, and elsewhere in this volume, Merrill returns to some of his earliest experiments in rhyme: rhyming two words of which one has an extra syllable ("irises" with "arras," "between" with "Venus"); rhyming two words by their penultimate syllables alone ("ch*eer*ful" with "disapp*ear*ing"); rhyming aslant ("seen" with "in"); keeping a single rhyme going throughout a whole poem ("in," "seen," "between," "Venus," "green," "fifteen"). There are graceful non-signifying "rhymes," like the internal orthographic resemblance between "*river*" and "*irises*," and the phonic resemblance between "*even*ing" and "*Ven*us" (the evening star). Merrill is still fond of zeugma, the figure that links two unlikely words in syntactic twinship (here "inch" and "years": "We are kept from disappearing into the earth by this cheerful inch of lawn and by ten—or fifteen?—more years"). Zeugma is the figure most emblematic of the comic union of body and soul; the body stands on the grass, the soul extends itself into certain and uncertain future time. As in this case, Merrill's formal figures almost always carry meaning; his metaphors brim with signification. His allusions are not inert, but transformative. He remembers, for instance, the Rubáiyát:

> The Moving Finger writes; and having writ,
> Moves on: nor all your Piety nor Wit
> Shall lure it back to cancel half a Line,
> Nor all your Tears wash out a Word of it.

Merrill's grim and witty reversal of Fitzgerald, in which the Writing Finger becomes the Erasing Snail, is spoken by one of the fish in the sonnet called "Think Tank":

> . . . at our best we were of one mind,
> Did our own sick or vital things
>
> Within a medium secured by trick
>
> Reflections over which, day, night, the braille

Eraser glided of the Snail
Our servant, huge and blind.

In the past few years Merrill has substituted Florida for Greece during
the winter, and many of these poems take a wild new energy from the
contradictions of the Florida scenery. The most remarkable among this group
is a poem about Palm Beach, to which I will come in a moment. But first
I want to mention, as an example of Merrill's "Florida writing," a poem
about innocence being caught by experience. Tropical fish are being caught
from a pier by fishermen using other fish as bait; young prostitutes are being
hauled into court. These two narratives are combined, at the end of the
poem, with a reminiscence of Merrill himself, at eight, entering into experience. Here are the central stanzas, full of brilliant concision:

These floozy fish—

Ceramic-lipped in filmy
Peekaboo blouses,
Fluorescent body
Stockings, hot stripes, . . .

Jailbait consumers of subliminal
Hints dropped from on high
In gobbets none
Eschews as minced kin;

Who, hooked themselves—bamboo diviner
Bent their way
Vigorously nodding
Encouragement—

Are one by one hauled kisswise, oh
Into some blinding hell
Policed by leathery ex-
Justices each

Minding his catch, if catch is what he can,
If mind is what one means—
The torn mouth
Stifled by newsprint, working still. If . . . if . . .

The little scales
Grow stiff. . . .

This lyric imagining of "The bite. The tug of fate" is what poets can do to
bring the various foci of perception (nature, others, self) into one point of

attention. Caught fish, street crime, growing up are not three subjects in
the poem, but one, and the distress in the disintegration of meaning ("Minding his catch, if catch is what he can, / If mind is what one means—. . . /
If . . . if . . .") finds its visual embodiment in the torn mouth of the fish,
and the callous reporting in newsprint of police-blotter scandal.

Merrill's fusion of levels of perception at high emotional temperature
is brought off most brilliantly in "Palm Beach with Portuguese Man-of-
War," an elegy of sorts for Merrill's wealthy thrice-married father (who is
buried, as a note tells us, in West Palm Beach). The poem uses no punctuation, letting its images rise surrealistically untethered. The title suggests a
tropical painting like those of Martin Johnson Heade, in which an exotic
object like a hummingbird or an orchid is set against a carefully rendered
landscape: Merrill's object is the "baby gorgon," a man-of-war jellyfish blown
ashore on the long spine of sandy beach, waiting to be reclaimed by the
Whitmanian sea. The poem owes a good deal to Hart Crane's and Elizabeth
Bishop's tropical poems, but is nonetheless wholly Merrill's own in its
anatomy of tycoons, their female hangers-on, their sexual and social forays,
their eventual tombs. The poem offers no editorial explanations for its processional images. It begins with the virgin beach itself:

> A mile-long vertebrate picked clean
> To lofty-plumed seableached incurving ribs
>
> Poor white the soil like talcum mixed with grit

The beach is then colonized, irrigated, built up:

> But up came polymorphous green
>
> No sooner fertilized than clipped
> Where glimmerings from buried nozzles rose
>
> And honey gravel driveways led
> To the perpetual readiness of tombs

Tombs and rooms are indistinguishable in Merrill's Florida:

> Shellwhite outside or white-on-white
> A dropping bird motif still wet
>
> Pastel and madrepore the shuttered rooms'
> Nacreous jetsam wave on wave

The poem turns satiric on the subject of the newly divorced and lustful
aging tycoon at dinner parties:

Having swept our late excrescences
The wens and wives away to mirrorsmoke

Place settings for the skin
Diver after dark the extra man

Drowning by candlelight whose two minds reel
How to be potent *and* unsexed

Worth a million *and* expendable
How to be everybody's dish

The poem envisages the tycoon's destruction by women as an underwater holocaust by cannibal fish:

And not to have seen through the glass visor
What would be made of him some night

By the anemone's flame chiffon gown
Like those downtown in the boutiques

By razor labia of hangers-on
To territories this or that

Tiny hideous tycoon stakes out

The destruction takes place on a coral reef:

Empire wholly built upon albino

Slaves the fossil globules of a self-
Creating self-absorbing scheme

Giddy in scope pedantic in detail

Over the coral reef float the jellyfish:

Over which random baby gorgons

Float without perception it would seem
Whom their own purple airs inflate

And ganglia agonizingly outlive
Look out! one has been blown ashore

> For tomorrow's old wet nurse to come
> Ease from the dry breast and sheet in foam

Hatred and pity coexist in this impersonal elegy. Merrill has so often written in the first person that this chilling drift of images unanchored to a personal speaker is the more noticeable. The poem makes no concessions; and while this may annoy some readers (those who want personal speech, autobiographical narrative, explicit editorializing, "communication"), I think it is a proof of strength in Merrill to resist the temptation to annotate his images. After all, all intelligible poems become understood in time.

There is no poem in this volume that is not worth reading. Some are slight, grace notes and observations. Some are chapters in Merrill's continuing verse autobiography (notably the genial "Clearing the Title," on acquiring a house in Key West); some continue the exploration of Merrill's favorite images (the soul-moth, the peacock, the Greek world). Merrill has added yet one more poem to his "Days of . . ." series (the title borrowed from Cavafy) with "Days of 1941 and '44," a fierce sonnet sequence in which we see Merrill at 15 ("in those days less than nothing, / A shaky X on panic's bottom line?") experiencing his aesthetic conversion:

> In vain old Mr Raymond's sky-blue stare
> Paled with revulsion when I spoke to him
> About my final paper. "Jim,"
> He quavered, "don't, *don't* write on Baudelaire."

But Merrill does write on Baudelaire ("Faith rose dripping from the false"), and goes on to enter the Army, where he reads Proust ("basic training") and hears of the death of a schoolmate who had, a few years before, tormented him:

> The nightmare shower room. My tormentor leers
> In mock lust—surely?—at my crotch.
> The towel I reach for held just out of reach,
> I gaze back petrified, past speech, past tears.

Now the tormentor is killed in battle, and the 18-year-old Merrill does not know how to absorb that death: "The nothing you'd become took on a weight / No style I knew could lighten." The oblique and beautiful ending of the sequence shows Merrill in battle-training under real fire:

> Beneath unsimulated fire he'd crawl
> With full pack, rifle, helmeted, weak-kneed,

And peeking upward see the tracers scrawl

Their letter of atonement, then the flare
Quote its entire red minefield from midair—
Between whose lines it has been life to read.

As the poet-to-be reads between the lines of the tracer bullets and perceives the entire red minefield of life, baffled by the death of his schoolmate who has been transformed from the tormentor into the tormented, lines of life and art begin to intertwine, as hatred ("you were my first true hate") and atonement converge.

Merrill is not often praised for concision; he is considered an elaborate, and elaborating, writer. Yet his lines, here as in "Palm Beach," tell a great deal in a short space. His drive toward the concise is, interestingly, not a drive toward the aphoristic or the epigrammatic, the two modes toward which concision tends. On the contrary, it is a drive toward the complex and dense image that will be perceptual, personal, social, and philosophical at once ("the floozy fish . . . subliminal jailbait . . . hauled into some blinding hell policed by ex-justices"). Such images become impatient of syntax, of commentary, even of punctuation (as in "Palm Beach"). A "cinéma-mensonge," as Merrill calls it in "Santorini"—a free-floating film of hallucinatory imagery—replaces, as objective correlative, the too-logically articulated process of explanation. The *mensonge incontinent* of poetry has here been brought to a level of high inner articulation, so much so that it explains itself by its consummately accurate choice of substantive and epithet.

I would not trade this rendered essence for the more conversational séances of Merrill's trilogy. But I am glad that traces of Merrill's poignant early style remain, not least in a triumphant poem about Proustian memory (reductively called "The House Fly"). In earlier volumes there were love poems to a Greek named Strato; later there were angry, ironic, and bittersweet adieus to him. Now, in a poem at once factual, comic, touching, and ghostly, Strato is named and remembered, the earlier bliss and the later blight of love both subsumed in the ritual of memory provoked by the annual return of the house fly, a "low-mimetic" version of Merrill's psyche, the winged soul. The first stanza compares past kisses to present psychic malaise:

Come October, if I close my eyes,
A self till then subliminal takes flight
Buzzing round me, settling upon the knuckle,
The lip to be explored not as in June
But with a sense verging on micromania
Of wrong, of tiny, hazy, crying wrongs

> Which quite undo her—look at that zigzag totter,
> Proboscis blindly tapping like a cane.

Merrill says somewhere in the volume that he wants a tone that avoids both levity and leadenness, and this stanza will serve as an example of what he means, in its portrait of the self-as-pensioner—fretful, tottering, blind, obsessive in complaint.

The second stanza shows us a more frightful self—the middle-aged self as compulsive artist, unable to leave off the rhythmic self-grooming motions that have become a habit. The house fly resumes her "grand toilette":

> Unwearying strigils taken to the frayed,
> Still-glinting wings; the dull-red lacquer head
> Lifted from its socket, turned mechanically
> This way and that, like a wristwatch being wound.

These passages, with their irritable and bitter Popian accuracy, are the best in the poem, and may be taken to represent Merrill's sense of having been unwittingly deprived of motive while still in the habit of motion. Stevens called this state "desire without an object of desire," and diagnosed it bleakly. But Merrill, for better or worse, does not end his poem in the desert of the present. Instead, he turns gratefully back to memory and its assuaging images, telling us that the fly-Psyche is still worthy of her cult:

> Downstairs in this same house one summer night,
> Founding the cult, her ancestress alit
> On the bare chest of Strato Mouflouzélis
> Who stirred in the lamp-glow but did not wake.
> To say so brings it back on every autumn
> Feebler wings, and further from that Sun,
> That mist-white wafer she and I partake of
> Alone this afternoon, making a rite
> Distinct from both the blessing and the blight.

This daring passage evokes at once the utter foolishness of love—its symbol a fly on the chest of someone absurdly named Mouflouzélis (who is nonetheless the sleeping Eros of the lamp-glow)—and its utter imprinting of existence, so much so that we are all willing to take that "last communion in the haze" (Dickinson) of the Indian summer sun. Merrill insists on the value and meaning of early love in later life, even if memory brings it back on ever-feebler wings.

Those of us who read Merrill to know what to do with our sentiments, even to know what our sentiments are (since poets are more expert than the rest of us in human diagnosis), are told by this poem—on the level of its last message—that the infection of general disappointment and dismaying mechanical habit of middle age is not particular to us. The poem suggests that the erotic idealizations of the past are not entirely invalidated by the frayed and fretful present. We may agree or disagree, but the question has been put, and an answer of sorts given, in the homage to memory.

The poem puts its question and answer in painfully particular terms— "tiny, hazy, crying wrongs," a "proboscis blindly tapping," "unwearying strigils," "the dull-red lacquer head," "the bare chest of Strato Mouflouzélis," all of them at once exactly descriptive and either grimly or absurdly ironic. Aside from the experience reenacted in the little personal drama of the poem—the annual return of the house fly and the earlier self it calls to mind—the poem belongs to the classical tradition of autumn elegy and of cult celebration, at once revising these forms in an ironized modernism, and paying tribute to their staying power in the lyric tradition. If the forms remain, perhaps eros remains as well; under the mechanical turnings of the tired head, something stirs in the lamplight. It comes as a balm that Merrill should suggest as much. But for me it is a greater balm to see the baffled proboscis and the weary dull-red head put into words, the ultimate relief of poetry being the knowledge that such tenuous states of feeling are finally expressible. And though *Late Settings* is, as I have said, full of holocausts and upsets, apprehensions and irritabilities, it shows undiminished luster in its still-glinting wings of consummate expression.

# A Scattering of Salts

◆

## The End of More Than Just a Book

### W. S. Merwin

There may exist somewhere a cache of juvenilia by James Merrill, early verses, precocious but clumsy, scarcely formed, patently imitative, perhaps even pretentious. But it is hard to believe. First because Merrill, disciple of perfection that he was, might well have destroyed any such crudities unless he had been tempted to save them as relatively simple memorabilia, for we see his (and our) ambivalent attitudes toward childhood and childish things surfacing again and again through his poems: the venerable resolution to "let go / Of the dead dog, the lost toy" conflicts with the continuing seductiveness and lightplay of what is forever lost and still pulsing in the present. But in fact it is difficult to imagine Merrill ever writing anything raw, inept, infelicitous. His poetry seems to have begun always with something already pertinent and realized, because that was the way he was.

The page proofs of this latest collection of his poems, "A Scattering of Salts," suggested such a conclusion repeatedly. It was not only the varied brilliance of the individual pieces. Taken together, the retrospective quality of them—a recurring allusion to a body of work that was part of the past, a note of summation and, in every sense, of setting—gave the volume an implication of finality that I kept refusing to take literally. It led me back to earlier poems of his, decade by decade, to all of his published poetry from the late 1940s on. The new book seemed to be telling me that the extraordinary cumulative wealth of this corpus was arriving at a final form; the image that recurs throughout his work, but flashes with piercing insistence in these late poems, is that of crystallization. While I was reading them and trying to persuade myself that what all this amounted to was merely a timely apprehension of mortality, word came of his sudden death. Heart.

Viewed from afterward, the immediate cause of death seems to have been prefigured in the poems, however skeptical one may be, or may try to be, about such notions. Tropes and asides all through this new book seem to be pointing to something of the sort, nowhere more directly than in the final poem, which opens:

> *O heart green acre    sown with salt*
> *by the departing    occupier*
>
> *lay down your gallant    spears of wheat*
> *Salt of the earth.*

Though he wrote poems after this manuscript was finished, and indeed was writing in bed in the hospital during the last few days of his life, these lines clearly address the end of something more than a book.

And his death, announcing completion in any case, at once puts the sequence of his writings into a new, sharp focus. A light goes out, another goes on, and suddenly we are looking at stills, in series. It is, as we knew, a large and dazzling achievement, and for all its variety and extent a remarkably coherent body of work. From the first poems that Merrill published in Poetry and The Kenyon Review at the end of the 40s, until those he was writing during the last year of his life, the tone, the charge and tension of the language, the formal turns and their manners of disclosure, are distinctively his. But during that period of almost half a century he used those qualities to project and articulate a constantly growing, unpredictable range of character, mood, subject, genre and experience.

To say he wrote with unfailing style would be like pointing out that his poems are in English, but to ponder even for a moment the role of deliberation in that style is to encounter the abiding mysteries of his personality and his art. The extremes, the poles, the contradictions that they fuse are far apart in ordinary life. His writing is verbally dense and formal and at the same time a current of white-water rapids, the utterance of a taut freedom. He spoke of loving to be carried away by language—his own language, of course, as it came to him. His poetry is compounded of immense personal reserve, dramatic transformation and startling autobiographical candor, in proportions and mixes that doubtless will excite scholarly speculation and disagreement for a long time to come. The mind that it represents to us is swift, decisive, in no way naïve, in command of a vast treasury of literary, linguistic, musical, visual, social, geographical and erotic education and experience, a profound respecter of conventions yet endlessly impatient with limitations.

It is almost 25 years since he first invited us to take seriously—whatever that may mean—a private pantheon whose dramatic revelations were set before us, in his account, through the medium of a teacup on a Ouija board under the fingers of Merrill himself and a very few intimates: a work within his work, first coalescing in the luminous, eerie, powerful alphabet of "The Book of Ephraim," the series of poems that then evolved into "The Changing Light at Sandover," whose subject is nothing less than cosmic existence and the play of love within it in this world and, the voices suggest, before and after it. "Nine Lives," one of the poems in "A Scattering of Salts," is a small encore to that enormous light show, and its introductory verses say some definite things about Merrill's own conception, or at least his late view, of the enterprise.

To begin with, he places it in the lineage of "the ancient comic theater." These poems are parts, roles, the words of performances and performers, among whom he himself figures, thrilled, as he says, "to find oneself again on stage, / In character, at this untender age." And here, as in the main cycle this poem alludes to, the characters, his own included, appear or simply speak out of what Prospero calls a deep "backward and abysm" of unmeasured and unspeaking darkness.

The stage itself, and the voices of theatrical personae, had fascinated him for years, perhaps since he fell in love with opera while he was still a child—something that he describes in this book—and he wrote plays, in a translucent masque-like mode, from the 50s on.

The prologue to "Nine Lives" invites the reader to attend it too as a piece of intimate theater—which may help to satisfy those who continue to worry about how they are supposed to take the Ouija-board pronouncements. Though how one is supposed to take them, in fact, is the kind of question that comedy, and theatrical presentation as a whole, raise and leave in the air. "Nine Lives" is another farewell: to a stage, a house in Athens, a history, an appetite, a mode, even to a subconscious. It is the breaking of a wand, ending the revels:

> To all, sweet dreams. The teacup-stirring eddy
> Is spent. We've dropped our masks, renewed our vows
> To letters, to the lives that letters house,
> Houses they shutter, streets they shade. Already
> Empty and dark, this street is. Dusty boughs
> Sleep in a pool of vigilance so bright
> An old tom skirts it. The world's his tonight.

Writing for a cast of voices also, and by no means incidentally, displayed another of Merrill's gifts, his mastery of rhyme. In theatrical speech and in the whole spectrum of his poetry it seems natural, a realization of the empirical sureness of his ear, of the liveliness and apparent ease of his voice and pace, of all their high comedy.

He is the obvious immediate heir of W. H. Auden, who is an orbiting character in the Sandover cycle, an avuncular if somewhat irascible benefactor. Merrill's other immediate forebears are less evident. There was Elizabeth Bishop, whom he revered as friend and poet; in this book, "Overdue Pilgrimage to Nova Scotia" is an elegy not only for her but for what she comes to signify, a world that is departing:

> *Out from such melting backdrops*
> *It is the rare conifer stands whole, one sharp*
> *Uniquely tufted spoke of a dark snow crystal*
> *Not breathed upon, as yet, by our exhaust.*
> *Part of a scene that with its views and warblers,*
> *And at its own grave pace, but in your footsteps*
> *—Never more imminent the brink, more sheer—*
> *Is making up its mind to disappear.*

And before Bishop, perhaps her own mentor, Marianne Moore, whose "No Swan So Fine" may be refracted behind one of Merrill's first published poems, "The Black Swan," in which:

> *The blond child on*
> *The bank, hands full of difficult marvels, stays*
> *Now in bliss, now in doubt.*
> *His lips move: I love the black swan.*

Before them I think of the poems of Byron, and of Pope, whom Merrill loved, as ancestors of his poems. But he was never derivative, never to be mistaken for another. He wrote of change from within it, watching the crystal turn, remembering it as it passed. His opus is work of utter integrity, and he was able to suspend within it wit, frivolity, apparent frivolity, irony, grief, a vast gatherum of the minutiae of existence including drag, the G.N.P. and the paper substitute Tyvek, without loss of style. Like every authentic voice of such substance and distinction, he calls into question all the words he suggests that might designate him, and he resettles them as he goes on taking his own place.

# ESSAYS

♦

# [On "Lost in Translation"]

## STEPHEN YENSER

Being committed to duality, like Yeats, Merrill has been sharply aware of the divergent demands that art and life make; and like Yeats, being dedicated to unity, he has devoted himself to confounding the dichotomy. When he defines the poet as a person "choosing the words he lives by," he chooses his words with care. Eupalinos, Valéry's architect and spokesman, could speak for him as well: "I truly believe that, by dint of building, I have built myself."[1] His work strives to embody a process epitomized in the transformations traced near the end of section S in *The Book of Ephraim*, the first of the *Sandover* volumes, where JM addresses a Russian character named Sergei, whom he figures as a plant and whose lineage he traces to a former neighbor in Stonington:

> When he was cut down I took slips of him
> To set in tidy ballad stanza-boxes
> Made, one winter, about Stonington.
> His pliant manners and sharp-scented death
> Came up Japanese. You came up Russian
> —Next to a showy hybrid "Mrs. Smith."
> Here you are now, old self in a new form.
> Some of those roots look stronger, some have died.
> Tell me, tell me, as I turn to you . . .

The actual old man became Ken, the Japanese houseman in "The Summer People," then turned into Sergei in *Ephraim*, and then—by what means and to what ends I shall detail later—into the poet himself. The process appears at a different level in the *Sandover* trilogy at large, which habitually revisits its earlier incidents and figures and discovers in them its later ones. There, one often has the impression, as in dialectic, whether Hegel's or Dante's, of "a single process growing in subtlety and comprehensiveness, not different senses, but different intensities or wider contexts of a continuous sense,

Reprinted by permission of the publishers from *The Consuming Myth: The Work of James Merrill* by Stephen Yenser, Cambridge, Mass.: Harvard University Press, 10–30. Copyright © 1987 by the President and Fellows of Harvard College.

unfolding like a plant out of a seed" (though I do not mean to invoke a simple emanationist view of poetic creation).[2]

Such a process is one thing Merrill means by "translation" in "Lost in Translation," which seems to me more completely expressive of "the unities of home and world, and world and page" than any of his poems of a comparable length. It is at once a memoir and a poetics with metaphysical and epistemological aspects. Ripe and full at every turn, it is the kind of venture that "Tintern Abbey" is—and "Mont Blanc," "Fra Lippo Lippi," "When Lilacs Last in the Dooryard Bloom'd," "Sunday Morning." A poem with structural integrity—Merrill has always been a writer of poems, not of poetry—it is nonetheless absorbent and reflective and anticipatory of his other work. It all comes to *this*, the poem seems to say. Merrill altered its position in the sequence of poems from *Divine Comedies* included in *From the First Nine: Poems 1946–1976*, his selected poems excluding the *Sandover* trilogy.[3] He decided to make it the last poem from these first nine volumes, and he did so, I think, because it is a consummation—and thus a place to begin.

Written in 1972, probably not long before the first inklings of *The Book of Ephraim*, and published first in *The New Yorker* and then in *Divine Comedies*, "Lost in Translation" reaches back to 1937, shortly before Germany's aggressions would "shake / This world . . . to its foundations." In 1937, James Merrill was about to have his family world shaken to its own foundations. He had been born on March 3, 1926, in New York City, the only child of Hellen Ingram Merrill, whose maiden name is her son's middle name, and Charles Edward Merrill, the founder of the brokerage firm Merrill Lynch, Pierce, Fenner and Smith. Charles Merrill had been married once before, to Eliza Church, with whom he had had two children: Doris, the older, who was to marry Robert Magowan and become a benefactor of the arts, and Charles, writer and founder of the Commonwealth School in Boston, whose experiences as an educator are set down in *The Walled Garden*.[4] The marriage to Hellen Ingram was of about the same length as the first marriage—and as far as that goes of the third marriage, which was already casting its shadow over the summer of 1937. Merrill wryly summarizes his father's adult life in the second poem in the sonnet sequence "The Broken Home":

> My father, who had flown in World War I,
> Might have continued to invest his life
> In cloud banks well above Wall Street and wife.
> But the race was run below, and the point was to win.
>
> Too late now, I make out in his blue gaze
> (Through the smoked glass of being thirty-six)
> The soul eclipsed by twin black pupils, sex
> And business; time was money in those days.

Each thirteenth year he married. When he died
There were already several chilled wives
In sable orbit—rings, cars, permanent waves.
We'd felt him warming up for a green bride.

He could afford it. He was "in his prime"
At three score ten. But money was not time.

The poet, who identifies himself by a circuitous route with another "flyer"
in *Ephraim*, would eventually decide precisely "to invest his life / In cloud
banks well above Wall Street and wife."

Having lived almost exactly that span allotted to us by the Psalmist,
Charles Merrill died in 1956. That was the year after his son's play, *The
Immortal Husband*, opened off-Broadway on Valentine's Day, and the year
before the publication of his first novel, *The Seraglio*, in which (we are told
in *Ephraim*) his nearly quadrigamist father served as a "Model / For 'Benjamin
Tanning,'" the novel's sultan, whose last name has overtones of his hardiness
and his severity alike. In 1937, at fifty-two, Charles was on the verge of his
second divorce, an event that would occur in February 1938 and that was
to be a turning point in his son's life. We might infer something of the
boy's feeling during the summer of "Lost in Translation" from his response
to his parents' inadequately explained absences and his corresponding obses-
sion with an enormous jigsaw puzzle, rented from a New York shop and
late in arriving, which he and his governess, "His French Mademoiselle,"
have planned to assemble during the school vacation: "A summer without
parents is the puzzle, / Or should be. But the boy, day after day, / Writes
in his Line-a-Day *No puzzle*." Isn't there something of the determined or
fearful disregard about that way of putting it? Even though to work at the
one puzzle, when it finally arrives, is to work at the other, the family crisis
is never explicitly acknowledged. (One reason it need not be acknowledged
is that by this point in his career Merrill has written about it so often that
he can take for granted his reader's acquaintance with it. And a more important reason is that he has come to write *as though* he could rely on the
reader's acquaintance. His allusions conjure the familiarity they seem to
presume.)

"Lost in Translation" calls into play three autobiographical situations.
In the most recent one, which the poem outlines last, the setting is Athens,
where Merrill had his second home, on Athinaion Efivon Street at the foot
of Mount Lykabettos, from 1959 until the late 1970s, and the subject is
his rereading of Valéry's magnificent lyric, "Palme," and his subsequent
search through the city's libraries for Rilke's translation of that poem into
German. Merrill half-recalls having seen the translation years earlier, but
when he cannot turn up a copy, he wonders whether he hasn't imagined it.
That the translation does exist, and that he eventually finds it, his epigraph—

an excerpt from Rilke's version—attests. The memory of the French and the German poems, and the memory in particular of the exhortation to "Patience," calls up "His French Mademoiselle," in whose care he spent that summer in the family's home in Southampton and on whom he had a crush, though she must have been a good thirty years older than he, since "In real life" she had been "a widow since Verdun." That summer is the second situation in the poem. It occupies sections one, three, and four of five unmarked sections. The moment at which this memory of 1937 begins to unfold in the poet's mind, one of his variations on the celebrated madeleine passage in *A la Recherche du temps perdu*, comes at the end of his second verse paragraph:

> Noon coffee. Mail. The watch that also waited
> Pinned to her heart, poor gold, throws up its hands—
> No puzzle! Steaming bitterness
> Her sugars draw pops back into his mouth, translated:
> "Patience, chéri. Geduld, mein Schatz."
> (Thus, reading Valéry the other evening
> And seeming to recall a Rilke version of "Palme,"
> That sunlit paradigm whereby the tree
> Taps a sweet wellspring of authority,
> The hour came back. Patience dans l'azur.
> Geduld im . . . Himmelblau? Mademoiselle.)

By setting out first the remembered experience and only then, in the parenthesis, exposing the cause of the memory, the rereading of Valéry's poem, Merrill's narrative sequence reverses Proust's. One result is that we are reminded of the elusiveness of a "source." Is the poem's real source the relationship with Mademoiselle? Or is it indeed Valéry's lyric? Life or literature? To whose soft, imperative "Patience" is it finally traceable? Or is the source better represented by Rilke's translation? Merrill foreshadows the answer formulated at poem's end in this passage's little vortex of metamorphoses, where the sugar cubes translate the coffee's taste, the coffee's bitterness renders the boy's disappointment, that disappointment is sweetened by Mademoiselle's counsel, and her words accidentally predict his knowledge of Valéry's lines—which antedate them. Through it all, the past moment of bittersweet anticipation and the present moment of nostalgia figure each other.

Given such density, it is remarkable that the poem's five parts make up such a clearly structured, nearly symmetrical arrangement. The first part, about the wait for and the arrival of the puzzle, is in a flexible mode that Merrill devised for poems in *Water Street* and has been refining ever since: verse paragraphs of occasionally rhymed iambic pentameter lines. This part concludes when, after the puzzle's pieces have all been spread out face up on a card table in the library, "The plot thickens / As all at once two pieces interlock." Because the "plot" is the poem's in addition to the puzzle's, the page's as well as the home's, the first section interlocks just here with the second, where Merrill gives up the blank verse for a line that is shorter and more and more insistently accentual and alliterative. The situation changes too, to the third situation mentioned earlier, as the poem records an experience that "lay years ahead" of the boy—in London, where the poet witnesses a demonstration by a medium. Ostensibly an afterthought, this second section fits with the first partly because it too takes place in a library and partly because it involves a piece of a puzzle—though there are also fundamental congruences. Merrill shifts back into blank verse for the central section's two paragraphs, where he describes the progress made on the puzzle by the boy and his Mademoiselle even as he reveals the latter's background, which is a good deal more complex than he had realized when he was eleven. Like the second section, the fourth has its own distinctive prosody, in this case *Rubaiyat* quatrains. This section describes the completed puzzle, which takes its picture from a painting allegedly done by a disciple of J.-L. Gérôme that has an "Oriental" subject. It breaks off in the middle of a stanza, after not quite two lines, and the last section, which returns to the verse paragraph, tells of the dismantling of the puzzle and the poet's search for the Rilke translation.

Merrill's five-part organization, with its prosodically similar odd-numbered sections and unique even-numbered sections, might also have been modeled on the musical scheme known as rondo form (or second rondo form), which often follows an ABACA pattern. And if it were not, perhaps he would not object to the comparison, since he has commented more than once over the years on the potential usefulness of musical forms to the poet. He has said, for instance, that "whenever I reach an impasse, working on a poem, I try to imagine an analogy with musical form," and he tells us that he solved a certain problem in "The Thousand and Second Night" by "a stroke I associated quite arbitrarily with that moment at the end of the Rondo of the 'Waldstein' sonata."[5] The ingenious structure of the penultimate section of "The Will," in which an entire "sonnet"—seven couplets—intervenes between the octave and the sestet of another sonnet (and thus establishes an 8–7–6 progression that mends even as the interpolation scissors), derives from the Mozart Concerto in E flat (K. 271), whose presto Finale embraces as its middle section a minuet.[6] Music, in the form of opera, was "the first art that came [his] way." As it happens, he began going to the opera in New York—an experience he recalls fondly in "Matinees"—when he was eleven years old, which would have been the year commemorated in "Lost in Translation."

The opening lines of the poem recall the boy's wait for the puzzle, seemingly lost in translation from the puzzle rental shop—and at the same time they conjure that absence, heavy with imminence, that is the matrix of all poems:

> A card table in the library stands ready
> To receive the puzzle which keeps never coming.
> Daylight shines in or lamplight down
> Upon the tense oasis of green felt.
> Full of unfulfillment, life goes on,
> Mirage arisen from time's trickling sands
> Or fallen piecemeal into place:
> German lesson, picnic, see-saw, walk
> With the collie who "did everything but talk"—
> Sour windfalls of the orchard back of us.

Hardly a line here but that tugs in Merrillian fashion in two directions. If the "library" implies intellectual work—the study of German, under the eye of Mademoiselle, or of "Palme" in Rilke's translation—the card table introduces the element of play, and together they go some way toward defining the experience of assembling a difficult puzzle, or the experience of writing a poem. The more and less insistent oxymorons in the phrases "keeps never coming," "Full of unfulfillment," and "Sour windfalls," and the latent antitheses of "Daylight" and "lamplight" and "arisen" and "fallen" embody Merrill's special knotty grain of thought. While the rhyme near the end of this quotation, "talk" and "walk," is a little flourish that acknowledges this tour de force of coupling, the term that sums it all up is "see-saw"—which perhaps also slyly extends the reference to the daily language lesson (with its conjugated verbs), itself opposed (as though to iterate the opening line's balance) by "picnic," whose own rhyming reduplication is echoed by "see-saw."

If we do hear a punning allusion to a language lesson in that last term, that is partly because these lines are rich with a sense of time's own richness. The negated continuous construction at the end of Merrill's second line vibrates with possibility. The present tense and the implied passage of time continue to correct each other through the second sentence, while in the third the "trickling sands" suggest both the seeming desolation of the boy's life and the hourglass that the dragging days keep inverting. Unobtrusive but most piquant of all is the fragment between quotation marks, which unexpectedly introduces the past tense. It would be said, years later, by someone affectionately remembering the collie. The single word " 'did' " suddenly frames the whole scene, a miniature puzzle of activities, in the past. The following line confirms this point of view on things, for "back of us" has a temporal dimension too, so that the phrase "Sour windfalls" summarizes that entire little world, full of love and absence, good fortune and disaster.

This scene will not *stay* past, however. As "The clock that also waited / Pinned to her heart, poor gold, throws up its hands," Merrill again resorts to the past tense. Waited—throws, see—saw. No wonder the watch, which ought to be able to tell exactly what time it is, throws up its hands. As the hands meet at noon, so past and present keep converging in the poem. Though these early conjunctions, if noticed at all, are likely to seem merely quirky, they indicate the profound relationship between past and present implicit in the poem's wizard initial sentence—as transfixing in its way as "Longtemps, je me suis couché de bonne heure." And make no mistake: Proust is behind this poem as much as Valéry and Rilke are, as he is behind so much of Merrill's work. If Marcel solves his long-standing problem and embarks on his "vocation" in the Guermantes's library at the end of *A la Recherche du temps perdu*, Merrill assembles his puzzle in the family library, and then in the London library, and finally in the unnamed library that presumably yields the Rilke translation. And it is Proust who adopts the relevant stereoscopic view of his youthful experience, and who uses "translation" as a further metaphor for the elucidation of the artwork:

. . . ce livre essentiel, le seul livre vrai, un grand écrivain n'a pas, dans le sens courant, à l'inventer, puisqu'il existe déjà en chacun de nous, mais à le traduire. Le devoir et la tâche d'un écrivain sont ceux d'un traducteur.

. . . the essential, the only true book, though in the ordinary sense of the word it does not have to be "invented" by a great writer—for it exists already in each one of us—has to be translated by him. The function and the task of a writer are those of a translator.[7]

In such a passage as the opening verse paragraph of "Lost in Translation," the smallest pieces fall into place partly because of the poet's tolerance for perfecting. One recalls that Marcel notes how some stitching done on the inside of Madame de Guermantes's cloak is finished as nicely as the ordinarily visible stitching. That detail speaks volumes about Proust's work—as Reuben Brower's student might well have noticed, since Brower himself had such an appreciation for seeming trifles. "The failure of much eighteenth-century poetry," in his eyes, "is not due to over-generality but to the lack of a metaphorical sense which connects and gives meaning to detail."[8] It would be hard to make too much of Merrill's concern with detail, for it has as much as anything to do with the kind of writer he is. Take his evocation of Rilke's translation of "Palme," with its sacrificing of many a Gallic nuance "in order to render [Valéry's] underlying sense":

> . . . that ground plan left
> Sublime and barren, where the warm Romance
> Stone by stone faded, cooled; the fluted nouns
> Made taller, lonelier than life
> By leaf-carved capitals in the afterglow.
> The owlet umlaut peeps and hoots
> Above the open vowel.

Only a poet of the fiercest concentration would find in the stark translation a whole miniature acropolis, discover the pun on "capitals," and not only make us see in the umlaut the eyes of an owl but also let us hear its hoots in his assonance ("owlet," "umlaut," "vowel"). When the boy's puzzle arrives, we learn in the third verse paragraph, it turns out to be "A superior one, containing a thousand hand-sawn, / Sandal-scented pieces." These last words, with their lovely run of sounds ("thousand," "hand-sawn," "sandal"), are the exact analogy to those pieces.

From one angle, then, "Lost in Translation" is itself an intricate puzzle. It is a confirmation of this intricacy that there are several other dimensions to the relationship between puzzle and poem. For example, the puzzle's scene, when it finally takes shape, implicitly stages the situation in the boy's family. Again, the puzzle's composition reflects the poet's material. If much of Merrill's life has been devoted to writing and reading, so that the new poem will avail itself of forms tested before by him and by others, the cutter of the puzzle's pieces has his tradition:

> Many take
> Shapes known already—the craftsman's repertoire
> Nice in its limitation—from other puzzles:
> Witch on broomstick, ostrich, hourglass,
> Even (surely not just in retrospect)
> An inchling, innocently branching palm.
> These can be put aside, made stories of
> While Mademoiselle spreads out the rest face up. . . .

These specific shapes have their own immediate relevance; Merrill invites us to put them aside and make stories of them that will suit "Lost in Translation." Thus we might say that the ostrich figures the boy's state of mind and the poem's manner. Left to his own devices, fearful of what he might see, the young Merrill has hidden his head in the puzzle's diverting desert— repeated here in the hourglass's recovery of the first verse paragraph's "trickling sands" and "tense oasis." Of course the oasis has also given the "inchling, innocently branching palm" a place to take root. It is as though these two were opposing impulses in the same life, responding to different sides of one experience: the cheerful and the awful.

The "Witch on broomstick" has a place in this story too, for she is a crucial element in what the boy has been overlooking. Although the original witch never appears here, she is represented in the puzzle, which pictures a sheik's new consort, who threatens his "old wives." This shadowy figure, who appears in *Ephraim* in the lead role in the unwritten drama of Merrill's youth that he thinks of as *The Other Woman*, will be one reason for the divorce. She also shows up in *Ephraim* in the guise of a character named Joanna, who flies into the poem carrying a Ouija board. Like her, the hourglass has figured in Merrill's other work: he has poems called "Hourglass" and "Hour Glass II," and the hourglass is an important motif in *Scripts for the Pageant*, the last of the *Sandover* books. The palm comes up in a number of his poems and of course in Valéry's lyric. Merrill has absorbed much of "Palme" in "Lost in Translation," and lines especially relevant to this constellation of puzzle pieces occur in Valéry's seventh stanza:

> Ces jours qui te semblent vides
> Et perdus pour l'univers
> Ont des racines avides
> Qui travaillent les déserts.

Merrill quotes Rilke's translation as his epigraph:

> Diese Tage, die leer dir scheinen
> und wertlos für das All,
> haben Wurzeln zwischen den Steinen
> und trinken dort überall.

And here finally is Merrill's own rendering, published several years after "Lost in Translation":

> These days which, like yourself,
> Seem empty and effaced
> Have avid roots that delve
> To work deep in the waste.[9]

So beneath Merrill's "inchling, innocently branching palm" lies an untold, virtually untellable story. In addition to his own pain and regret, and his years of language study, of reading Proust and others, of writing and of waiting (for the puzzle to arrive, for the angel to descend, for the right word, the right moment for this poem or story or translation), there is Valéry's poem, with all the experience stored in it and implied in his superb address to the tree:

> Patience, patience,
> Patience dans l'azur!
> Chaque atome de silence
> Est la chance d'un fruit mûr.
> Viendra l'heureuse surprise:
> Une colombe, la brise,
> L'ébranlement le plus doux,
> Une femme qui s'appuie,
> Feront tomber cette pluie
> Où l'on se jette à genoux!

In Merrill's translation:

> Patience and still patience,
> Patience beneath the blue!
> Each atom of the silence
> Knows what it ripens to.
> The happy shock will come:
> A dove alighting, some
> Gentlest nudge, the breeze,
> A woman's touch—before
> You know it, the downpour
> Has brought you to your knees!

And there is Rilke's experience and his writing, which Merrill knows well and which contains its own eloquent apologies for patience—including the passage in the third of the *Letters to a Young Poet*:

Allow your judgments their own silent, undisturbed development, which, like all progress, must come from deep within and cannot be forced or hastened. *Everything* is gestation and then birthing. To let each impression and each embryo of a feeling come to completion, entirely in itself, in the dark, in the unsayable, the unconscious, beyond the reach of one's own understanding, and with deep humility and patience to wait for the hour when a new clarity is born: this alone is what it means to live as an artist: in understanding as in creating.

   In this there is no measuring with time, a year doesn't matter, and ten years are nothing. Being an artist means: not numbering and counting, but ripening like a tree, which doesn't force its sap, and stands confidently in the storms of spring, not afraid that afterward summer may not come. It does come. But it comes only to those who are patient, who are there as if eternity lay before them, so unconcernedly silent and vast. I learn it every day of my life, learn it with pain I am grateful for: *patience* is everything![10]

Proust too has his version of this faith:

Alors, moins éclatante sans doute que celle qui m'avait fait apercevoir que l'oeuvre d'art était le seul moyen de retrouver le Temps perdu, une nouvelle lumière se fit en moi. Et je compris que tous ces matériaux de l'oeuvre littéraire, c'était ma vie passée; je compris qu'ils étaient venus à moi, dans les plaisirs frivoles, dans la paresse, dans la tendresse, dans la douleur, emmagasinés par moi, sans que je devinasse plus leur destination, leur survivance même, que la graine mettant en réserve tous les aliments qui nourriront la plante. Comme la graine, je pourrais mourir quand la plante se serait développée, et je me trouvais avoir vécu pour elle sans le savoir, sans que ma vie me parût devoir entrer jamais en contact avec ces livres que j'aurais voulu écrire et pour lesquels, quand je me mettais autrefois à ma table, je ne trouvais pas de sujet.

And then a new light, less dazzling, no doubt, than that other illumination which had made me perceive that the work of art was the sole means of rediscovering Lost Time, shone suddenly within me. And I understood that all these materials for a work of literature were simply my past life; I understood that they had come to me, in frivolous pleasures, in indolence, in tenderness, in unhappiness, and that I had stored them up without divining the purpose for which they were destined or even their continued existence any more than a seed does when it forms within itself a reserve of all the nutritious substances from which it will feed a plant. Like the seed, I should be able to die once the plant had developed and I began to perceive that I had lived for the sake of the plant without knowing it, without ever realizing that my life needed to come into contact with those books which I had wanted to write and for which, when in the past I had sat down at my table to begin, I had been unable to find a subject.[11]

Although Proust had "pas de sujet"—in effect, *"No puzzle"*—when he sat down at *his* table, it was all the while ripening within, eventually to be "translated" into a form that would also nourish others, including Merrill.

And then beneath each writer's experience is his mother tongue, with its incalculable depths. This heritage is one subject of the poem's second section, the parenthetical digression in which Merrill recalls the medium's performance. This last consists of solving another kind of puzzle, of identifying without seeing it an object that has been shown to an audience, then "planted in a plain tole / Casket." Merrill's translation of the man's musings aloud "Through shut eyes" moves back in time, as the medium hears in his mind's ear "'a dry saw-shriek, / Some loud machinery—a lumber mill? / Far uphill in the fir forest / Trees tower, tense with shock, / Groaning and cracking as they crash groundward.'" As the medium tunes in that episode earlier in the object's history, the reader begins to hear the poet's own machinery. Rather like Pound in his first Canto's palimpsest, Merrill turns to a quasi Anglo Saxon verse to remind us again how the present translates the past. The transformations in a poem like this one, Merrill implies as the medium identifies the hidden object, are nothing compared to those of the forces that have produced its materials:

> "But hidden here is a freak fragment
> Of a pattern complex in appearance only.
> What it seems to show is superficial
> Next to that long-term lamination
> Of hazard and craft, the karma that has
> Made it matter in the first place.
> Plywood. Piece of a puzzle." Applause
> Acknowledged by an opening of lids

> Upon the thing itself. A sudden dread—
> But to go back. All this lay years ahead.

The real marvel is the ogygian linguistic and historical process, which, like the poem, and indeed like the life, involves plan and accident. Such are the unities of world and page.

While that thought has its reassuring side, it also holds a certain "dread." To have one's eyes opened to this karmic process is not only to see how one's present uses one's past days, however "vides / Et perdus" they might have seemed, but also to see that one is but an ephemeral form of this always economizing flux. The "opening of lids" on "the thing itself" causes a *frisson* because in addition to the medium's eyelids, the "lids" include the one on the "tole / Casket." When the poet tells us that "All this lay years ahead," we hear not only a reason for breaking off this divagation on the medium but also relief at the thought that he can avoid for some time yet Henry James's "distinguished thing." In other words, "this" lies in the future from the point of view of the boy and in either the past or the future, depending on the referent, from the point of view of the man writing the poem. He has characteristically gone ahead and back at once. Somewhere the poor gold watch will be throwing up its hands again—while Proust will be clapping his.

"But to go back. All this lay years ahead": Merrill's use of the past tense in connection with the future event has much to do with the line's allure. We return to it because it rises above time so, and as we return, it takes still other forms. While "All this" is the evening in the London library, as well as the truncated vision of death, the phrase refers us also to this poem's account of that evening and of everything else. "All *this*." Furthermore, since this account that is the poem lies years ahead of the boy, there is a strong sense in which his youth itself lies years ahead of him, to be found in "translation." The poem is a heuristic instrument, a way of discovering the self and knowing it.

But then who is to distinguish between discovery and creation in this area? It is only in view of what he has since become that Merrill can appear *then*—in the form of a figure in the puzzle, which in the third section begins to take shape—as "a small backward-looking slave or page-boy." He finds this figure in the puzzle exactly because in the middle of his own puzzle of a life he is looking backward. In looking backward, that is—and by "backward" I mean "over the shoulder" and "to the past," but not "shy," though Merrill means the latter too—the figure in the puzzle looks forward to the poet who will create him. His "backward-looking" figure prefigures and calls into being the artist, whose work (in Proust's words again) "exprime pour les autres et nous fait voir à nous-même[s] notre propre vie, cette vie qui ne peut pas s' 'observer', dont les apparences qu'on observe ont besoin d'être traduites et souvent lues à rebours et péniblement déchiffrées" ("expresses for others and renders visible to ourselves that life of ours which cannot effectually observe itself and of which the observable manifestations need to be translated and, often, to be read backwards and laboriously deciphered").[12] This is one reason that to speculate as to whether Merrill has imagined this figure (or the whole puzzle) or has remembered him would only be to cloud the issue. One cannot say which is the case in the same way that one cannot say whether the poem began forty years ago, or in the "present" deciphering, or in the medium's performance. It "begins" in several places at once—as this account does, and as a puzzle does: "Mademoiselle does borders. Straight-edge pieces / Align themselves with earth or sky / In twos and threes, naive cosmogonists / Whose views clash."

The "small backward-looking slave or page-boy," "whose feet have not been found" yet, appears beside "Most of a dark-eyed woman veiled in mauve" whom he helps down from her kneeling camel. Mademoiselle perhaps thinks the boy is the veiled woman's son, and if so she might be swayed by her own maternal feelings or by her keen awareness of her employers' domestic plight. We know that she knows a divorce is in the offing, because the boy sneaks a look at her letter to a curé in Alsace, where he reads " 'cette innocente mère, / Ce pauvre enfant, que deviendront-ils?' " The boy assumes that these are the figures in the puzzle, but Merrill lets us understand, as we fit together our own pieces, that she is worried about him and his mother. This is pure Merrill, this casting of the poem's one direct reference to its emotional and dramatic center in French and the misinterpreting of it. The principle of restraint is honored even as the imminent trauma is specified and authenticating detail is provided. These lines tell us that Mademoiselle, contrary to the boy's superior observation about what she "thinks mistakenly," would not be all that wrong to believe that the "slave or page-boy" is the veiled woman's son. Although he is not literally her son, this pair mirror the young Merrill and his mother—as we know partly because the veiled woman looks "across the green abyss" at another figure: "a Sheik with beard / And flashing sword hilt (he is all but finished) / Steps forward on a tiger skin. A piece / Snaps shut, and fangs gnash out at us!" And we associate the Sheik with the father—what a delicate house of cards this is!—not only because of the pun on "finished" but also because, as we learn in the poem's last section, the boy's home has its own "mangy tiger safe on his bared hearth." These last words might stand for much of this poem's paradoxical quality, for Merrill's "hearth" hides his "heart" and the heart of the family's crisis, even as the adjective "bared" discloses their presence.

"One should be as clear as one's natural reticence allows one to be": Marianne Moore's dictum might have been the guiding light in this as in many another poem by Merrill.[13]

Mademoiselle has her own family matters to conceal. Years later, speaking French to a French friend, the poet discovers that he has a German accent. Thus he finds out that Mademoiselle's first language was German. French by marriage, she finds it practical, in the prewar atmosphere, to pass. The poem's ubiquitous dichotomizing takes the form in her of "French hopes" set against "German fears." But her heritage is jigsaw-complicated itself, since she is the "Child of an English mother . . . And Prussian father" and was evidently raised in Alsace. No wonder she likes to do the borders of puzzles. No wonder either that her nephew turns out to be a "UN / Interpreter." That last detail is one of several that indicate the relationship between her and the poet, who, in his capacity as translator of Valéry and Rilke and the others, has an analogous occupation. He after all learned French and German from her—not to mention much else that would help make him the kind of poet he is. (Might not that be why Merrill tells us that she is a "remote / Descendant of the great explorer Speke"? Though in fact she seems to have descended from the American explorer Edmund Fanning, John Hanning Speke fits into the puzzle better.[14] Just as Speke discovered the source of the Victoria Nile, so we might find in him, with his convenient name, an emblem of Merrill's own fluent explorations.)

A partner in the boy's creative enterprises, Mademoiselle is muse as well as substitute mother. When we hear that the UN interpreter's account of her background has "Touched old strings," those strings are not only those that sound a metaphorical chord. Besides helping him with puzzles, she "Sews costumes for his marionettes, / Helps him to keep behind the scene / Whose sidelit goosegirl, speaking with his voice, / Plays Guinevere as well as Gunmoll Jean." Indeed there exists a program, dated August 11, 1937, which advertises "*The Magic Fishbone*, by Charles Dickens, as interpreted by the Jimmy Merrill Marionettes. Given for the Southampton Fresh Air Home for Crippled Children." According to the program, "The action takes place in 'The Land of Make Believe,' and Jimmy Merrill himself will play King Watkins, I, the Queen, and Jerry, the Announcer."[15] Just as Jerry, the Announcer, looks forward to that other Master of Ceremonies, Ephraim, so the goosegirl will one day emerge as Psyche in "From the Cupola" and Jean in "Days of 1935." (As for the King and Queen: one cannot but think of God Biology and Mother Nature in *Sandover*.)

Perhaps he would recognize, years later, something of Mademoiselle's manner and their mutual interests in the operas of Bernard de Zogheb— "not operas so much as librettos set to popular tunes of variable vintage and familiarity," as Merrill defines them in his "Foreword" to the text of Zogheb's *Phaedra*.[16] These mischievous, enchanting productions—"designed for that small red theatre in the soul where alone the games of childhood are relived and applauded," acted out by puppets, the music sung by men and women "in the wings"—are sui generis, though as Merrill hints, their melding of heroic emotions and frivolous tunes has precedents in Verdi and elsewhere. (Phaedra drinks poison and she and Thésée part forever to the strains of "I'll Be Seeing You" and "It Had To Be You.") The language of the librettos, "so richly macaronic, so poorly construed and spelt," derives in part from Zogheb's growing up in Alexandria and his acquaintance there with "the bad Italian cultivated by the *gratin*, and a kind of lingua franca used by their domestics." Merrill's fondness for Zogheb's puppet theater, especially its salad of the hilarious and the "exalted and terrible," attests to his belief that "the world needs to be seen [as] cheerful *and* awful, transparent *and* opaque." The light at Sandover is a changing one.

The boy and Mademoiselle are so close as to shade off into each other. If she is "Herself excited as a child" when they get the puzzle, her "world where 'each was the enemy, each the friend'" has its equivalent too in his family life. By the beginning of the fourth section, everything seems to fit:

> This World that shifts like sand, its unforeseen
> Consolidations and elate routine,
> Whose Potentate had lacked a retinue?
> Lo! it assembles on the shrinking Green.

"This World" is at once the political world of the 1930s and the puzzle's world, the Sheik's, with its unanchored sections that combine in surprising ways. It is also the world of the poem as poem, its languages and forms and diverse resources—the poem which exemplifies *its* "elate routine" in the interlacing of "routine" and "retinue" and the internal rhyme of "Potentate" and "elate" and its "consolidations" in the shift at just this point into *Rubaiyat* quatrains, so that the puzzle's exotic form conforms to its matter. The puzzle's subject, the arrival of the new favorite in the Sheik's harem, is said to be "Hardly a proper subject for the Home," but it is the inevitable subject for *this* home. Even the progressive clarification of the puzzle's scene, which also suggests the boy's increasing understanding of his circumstances, parallels the development of the actual domestic situation. As we are first allowed to interpret the Sheik and the veiled woman, they stand in for the boy's father and mother. At this juncture, however, as though to trace the change in the father's affections, the veiled woman has become the mother's rival. Not for nothing is the woman veiled.

After some further shifting of its pieces, the puzzle represents more clearly than ever the boy's world:

> While, thick as Thebes whose presently complete
> Gates close behind them, Houri and Afreet
> Both claim the Page. He wonders whom to serve,
> And what his duties are, and where his feet,
>
> And if we'll find, as some before us did,
> That piece of Distance deep in which lies hid

> Your tiny apex sugary with sun,
> Eternal Triangle, Great Pyramid!

The Page transparently corresponds to the boy, on the verge of having loyalties divided between mother and father and of losing his footing—as the precarious shift in mid-sentence across the stanza break from third person to first person brilliantly confirms. Even as the identification is made, however, the poet retains a significant detachment, since the puzzle so wittily translates his story. Even to be able to see the family in terms of such archetypal patterns as the Oedipal triangle is partly to answer the boy's silent question as to whether he will find a "piece of Distance," for that is also a peace that comes with distance on an emotionally trying situation.

As Merrill moves his units about, they take on the polysemy of allegorical elements; as one's mental focus changes, now the subject is the puzzle proper, now the domestic microcosm, now the political alliances of 1938–1939, now the composition of the poem. The poem even makes a gesture or two in the direction of *Sandover*'s macrocosmic and metaphysical concerns. The "shrinking Green" of the card table reminds us of the world's expanding deserts and the possible death of the planet, while the remark that it is "Quite a task / Putting together Heaven, yet we do" touches on the theme of the creation of God. It begins to seem that there is no subject "Lost in Translation" cannot handle as it shifts among home and world, world and page, often by virtue of the manifold richness of its particulars. At the end of the fourth section, in a bit of bravura, Merrill slips the last piece of the puzzle into place, as he recalls finding the Page's missing feet where they had fallen:

> It's done. Here under the table all along
> Were those missing feet. It's done.

But then whose should those feet be, "under the table," if not the boy's? And if the boy's, then the poet's, "*Here* under the table" on which the poem is being written. The poet is the boy is the Page. Or he is the page on which the poem's words reconstitute him, "a backward-looking slave" to his own needs. Thanks to such "under the table" transactions, it all comes right, it seems. "The correction of prose, because it has no fixed laws, is endless," Yeats wrote to Dorothy Wellesley, whereas "a poem comes right with a click like a closing box." The solution of the last outstanding mystery and the reiteration of "It's done" make just such a "click."

Or is this case closed so easily? We need to notice that this fourth section does not come out even. These two lines on the feet, which seem to conclude it, are a kind of remainder. It is not even clear that they are part of a quatrain; they stand alone and fit neither with the preceding stanzas nor with the following verse paragraphs. In another moment, Merrill would have had to commit himself, for had the second line been carried to its end, it would have had to rhyme with "along," in which event these lines would have been a fragment of a *Rubaiyat* stanza, or not, in which event they would have been a short paragraph. It is a matter of "missing feet"—and of a missing metrical foot or two. A closure that is an opening, this passage is irrevocably in transition.

As the one form comes apart, so does the puzzle—as though *this* UN interpreter were an *un*interpreter:

> The dog's tail thumping. Mademoiselle sketching
> Costumes for a coming harem drama
> To star the goosegirl. All too soon the swift
> Dismantling. Lifted by two corners,
> The puzzle hung together—and did not.
> Irresistibly a populace
> Unstitched of its attachments, rattled down.
> Power went to pieces as the witch
> Slithered easily from Virtue's gown.
> The blue held out for time, but crumbled, too.
> The city had long fallen, and the tent,
> A separating sauce mousseline,
> Been swept away. Remained the green
> On which the grown-ups gambled. A green dusk.
> First lightning bugs. Last glow of west
> Green in the false eyes of (coincidence)
> *Our* mangy tiger safe on his bared hearth.

Because Rilke looms so large in this poem, one is likely to recall his adumbration of the poetic process in the eighth *Duino Elegy*: "Uns überfüllts. Wir ordnens. Es zerfällt. / Wir ordnens wieder und zerfallen selbst" ("It fills us. We arrange it. It breaks down. / We rearrange it, then break down ourselves").[18] But in Merrill's lines, along with the sense of an ineluctable cycle, there is the sense of synchronic events. Even as there are certain threads "que la vie brise," life is ceaselessly making new connections. The very same words that describe the breaking up of the puzzle create in themselves a subtle pattern. They begin to weave one of the new "costumes"—a mantle or a mantilla, say—with "Dismantling" itself. The "lace" in "populace," the more evident for "Unstitched" and "gown," takes the form of the attachments among "Unstitched" and "witch," "down" and "gown," "blue" and "too," "mousseline" and "green." The disintegration of the one narrative is part of another—to be specific, a little apocalypse. For if we are responsible for "Putting together Heaven," we are also responsible for destroying it along with our cities. These lines trace out in lyric form the story of much of *Sandover*. The underset of retrogression in this passage, the drift (reminiscent of the medium's reverse construction of the puzzle piece's history) from its "populace" and "city" back through "tent" to a virtually Edenic "Green" ("gambled" is also "gamboled"): this is a movement found also at a pivotal moment in *Scripts for the Pageant*. Before that, and before "Lost in Translation," Merrill ran his poetic film backward at the end of "18 West 11th Street," another poem about a childhood home that was destroyed, which concludes with an "Original vacancy" and a "deepening spring." As he puts the adage at the beginning of yet another poem about the partial destruction and rebuilding of a house, "Everything changes; nothing does."

Nothing does: nothing changes. And nothing will *do*: no thing or poem or theory will finally suffice. Nothing will do, partly because something is always missing:

> Something tells me that one piece contrived
> To stay in the boy's pocket. How do I know?
> I know because so many later puzzles
> Had missing pieces—Maggie Teyte's high notes
> Gone at the war's end, end of the vogue for collies,
> A house torn down; and hadn't Mademoiselle
> Kept back her pitiful bit of truth as well?
> I've spent the last days, furthermore,
> Ransacking Athens for that translation of "Palme."

Not finding that translation is comparable to Rilke's not finding equivalences for Valéry's phrases. Having translated Valéry's poem—as well as a variety of other works ranging from maxims by Chamfort through poems by Montale to stories by Cavafy and Vassilikós—James Merrill knows all too well "How much of the sun-ripe original / Felicity Rilke made himself forego / (Who loved French words—verger, mûr, parfumer) / In order to render its underlying sense."[19] But the plight is not just that of the literary translator. The lines just quoted pertain also to the unrealizable vision that motivates any poem, not to mention other projects. As Helen Vendler has seen, Rilke's rendering of Valéry "mimics the translation—by Merrill himself, among others—of life into art."[20] Not that "life" here need mean sensuous or concrete experience alone, whatever that might be. Rilke's passion for Valéry's poems, for the French language, for language—these were part of his "life."

To fail to translate exactly, or rather to have to translate and thus to be inexact, to create a difference between the putatively original and the necessarily substitutive: this might be thought of as our very condition. It is no coincidence that Merrill's felicitous "Felicity"—meaning "bliss" and "good fortune" as well as the very "stylistic aptness" that the line break highlights—and the echo, by way of "sun-ripe" and the French words, of the "orchard back of us" call into play again the concept of Eden. The parenthesis itself, with its untranslated and by implication untranslatable words ("orchard," "ripe," and "to sweeten" or "to scent," respectively), is almost a tiny, tantalizing paradise, an enclosed orchard or *hortus conclusus* (as "paradise" means in its remote Old Persian origins). The orchard and the windfalls are always "back of us." Nothing will ever quite do.

Then one begins to see that for Merrill nothing will not do either. The Rilke translation is found. Mademoiselle, although she "kept back" her bit of truth, was not able to bury it. From one point of view, the piece of puzzle that the boy pocketed was lost, but from another it has been found, by the medium—"This grown man" who is also a translator of sorts, an agent of communication with an extrasensory world, a variation on the JM of the *Sandover* books. The "house torn down" rises again in the form of Sandover. Everything changes. To lose is to create an emptiness that must be operated in, a vacancy that will be filled. "Verger," "mûr," "parfumer": these words are rendered inexactly in German and English, but the approximation is a matrix of possibility. Underlying the phrase "underlying sense," because it comes on the heels of the French words, for example, are the "scents" connoted by them. In that marvelous ruin that Rilke's translation is, "that ground plan left / Sublime and barren, where the warm Romance / Stone by stone faded, cooled," after a rain, "A deep reverberation fills with stars"— and what is such a "reverberation" if not at once an emptiness and a plenishing? "Reverberation": the word means a redounding of sound or repeated reflecting of light (or heat), a re-echoing, as of Merrill's echoing of Rilke's echoing of Valéry (echoing his own sources). "Reverberation" might almost be a translation of "translation," and even though *verberare* is unrelated to *verbum*, Merrill wants us to catch a Cratylean glimpse of "rewording" behind the term, much as Stevens, for instance, means us to see "luminous" shining through his phrase "Voluminous master folded in his fire."[21]

To translate, then, is as much to discover in transference as to lose. Here is Merrill's concluding verse paragraph:

> But nothing's lost. Or else: all is translation
> And every bit of us is lost in it
> (Or found—I wander through the ruin of S
> Now and then, wondering at the peacefulness)
> And in that loss a self-effacing tree,
> Color of context, imperceptibly
> Rustling with its angel, turns the waste
> To shade and fiber, milk and memory.

Two orders of proposition appear here. In the first place, as in "A Fever," Merrill is aspiring, like Henry James, to be one on whom nothing is lost. But when nothing is lost at this level, that is largely because of an original openness to experience and a later strenuousness of memory. Nothing is lost, not because it cannot be lost, for indeed it might be that everything is lost in some sense, but because the possibility always exists that one might recall it in some form—as Proust is said in *Ephraim* "Through superhuman counterpoint to work / The body's resurrection, sense by sense." Nothing is lost in Proust because Proust lost himself in his life's work, or in his work's life, in his own "translation"—his "consuming myth," to adapt a phrase from Merrill's "From the Cupola." In the concluding lines in "Lost in Translation," the Proustian presence is the "self-effacing tree," the palm that appears and disappears as a blue puzzle piece in the blue sky and that conceals the poet's effort; or that gracefully translates his wrestling with his angel into a "Rustling" of fronds and wings, just as the patient palm invisibly "turns the waste" (Rilke's "Steinen," Valéry's "déserts") into the sheltering fronds and the nourishing coconut. As Merrill's poem resurrects his child-hood, so its last line recovers, by way of "Palme," its opening lines. As though to prove that nothing is lost, his "milk" translates Valéry's "lait plat," which appears at the beginning of "Palme," along with "le pain tendre" that "Un ange met sur ma table." The table is there in the first line of Merrill's poem, where it has become the card table, while the milk and angel have been kept back until the end. But not lost.

In the second place, this passage concerns the nature of things. All is metamorphosis, it suggests; the world is all "context," its elements are all a fugacity whose interactive events may be either continuations of earlier phases of themselves or ever-new processes. Merrill will make a harder and deeper sense of the idea in *Ephraim*. This poem does not have to decide whether it intends a neo-Hegelian faith in evolution or a neo-Heraclitean hypothesis of flux. It is content to approve, in addition to memory, metamor-phosis—rather in the vein of Merrill's recent sonnet "Processional," which sets forth the adventures of a "demotic raindrop" that is first "Translated by a polar wand to keen / Six-pointed Mandarin" and dreams of being further promoted into "a hitherto untold / Flakiness, gemlike, nevermore to melt":

> But melt it would, and—look—become
> Now birdglance, now the gingko leaf's fanlight,
> To that same tune whereby immensely old
> Slabs of dogma and opprobrium,
> Exchanging ions under pressure, bred
> A spar of burnt-black anchorite,
>
> Or in three tidy strokes of word golf LEAD
> Once again turns (LOAD, GOAD) to GOLD.[22]

If that "tune" had a title, it could be "Plus ça change." As early as Merrill's first play, *The Bait* (1953), he had set similar words to it: "our cold virtues, once thought durable, / But now abstract and frail as snowflakes / Alter to lazy water in the sun. / Fluidity is proof against major disasters. / The marbles melt and wink at me." (And Merrill winks at us, since his prose has crystallized to verse within this one speech.)

One remarkable thing about "Processional," really less hymn than scherzando, is its blithe overriding of categories, as in the conversion to "anchorite" of "anthracite." In the translation envisioned here, alchemical, rhetorical, and natural metamorphic processes themselves change into one another. How could we not be somewhat lost in it?

## NOTES

1. Merrill's remark is in "The Poet: Private," 45. The original version of Valéry's *mot*, quoted as an epigraph to this chapter, is in "Eupalinos, ou l'Architecte," *Oeuvres de Paul Valéry* (Paris: Bibliothèque de la Pléiade [Gallimard], 1957), II, 142.

2. Northrop Frye discusses dialectic in these terms in *The Great Code: The Bible and Literature* (New York: Harcourt Brace, 1982), 221.

3. In *From the First Nine*, in addition to omitting poems published in the original volumes, Merrill has juggled the order of a few others. But these changes are rarely dramatic, and indeed the only other one of much import is the shifting of "For Proust" from an undistinguished seventh position to the penultimate position in the selections from *Water Street*. In no case except that of "Lost in Translation" does he change a volume's concluding poem.

4. Charles Merrill, *The Walled Garden: The Story of a School* (Boston: Rowan Tree Press, 1982).

5. "An Interview with James Merrill" (by Donald Sheehan), *Contemporary Literature*, 9 (Winter 1968), 7. Cf. "An Interview with James Merrill" (by Ashley Brown), *Shenandoah*, 19 (Summer 1968), 12. The "Waldstein" rondo form is different from the second rondo form outlined here.

6. This structure is pointed out by David Lehman, "Elemental Bravery: The Unity of James Merrill's Poetry," in *James Merrill: Essays in Criticism*, ed. David Lehman and Charles Berger (Ithaca: Cornell University Press, 1982), 60.

7. *A la Recherche*, VII, 209. *Remembrance*, III, 926.

8. *The Fields of Light*, 37. Cf. also p. 29: "Our whole aim in analysis of tone is to delineate the exact speaking voice . . . but we can succeed only by attending to the special, often minute language signs by which the poet fixes the tone for us." In "An Interview" (by Donald Sheehan), 7, Merrill says of Brower's course at Amherst that "it was chiefly a course in tone, in putting meaning and the sound of meaning back into words."

9. Valéry's original, accompanied by a translation by David Paul, can be found in Paul Valéry, *The Collected Works*, ed. Jackson Matthews, I: *Poems*, Bollingen Series XLV (Princeton: Princeton University Press, 1971), 228–235. Rilke's translation of the poem into German is included in Rainer Maria Rilke, *Übertragungen* (Frankfurt am Main: Insel Verlag, 1975), 281–283. Merrill's translation originally appeared in *New York Review of Books*, 18 March 1982, 10, before it was included in *Late Settings*.

10. Rainer Maria Rilke, *Letters to a Young Poet*, trans. Stephen Mitchell (New York: Random House, 1984), 23–25. In "An Interview" (by Ashley Brown), 9, Merrill touches on the influence of Rilke: "What I got from Rilke was more than literary; that emphasis on the *acceptance* of pain and loneliness. Rilke helps you with suffering, especially in your adolescence." One thinks of those capitals in Rilke's translation, "lonelier than life." Merrill had written about Rilke as early as "The Transformation of Rilke," *Yale Poetry Review*, 1 (Spring 1946), 22–27.

11. *A la Recherche*, VII, 217–218. *Remembrance*, III, 935–936.

12. *A la Recherche*, VII, 214–215. *Remembrance*, III, 932.

13. "Idiosyncrasy and Technique," in *A Marianne Moore Reader* (New York: Viking, 1961), 171.

14. On Mademoiselle and her background, see "Condemned to Write about Real Things."

15. The puppet show flyer is in Merrill's possession.

16. "Foreword" to Bernard de Zogheb, *Phaedra: An Opera in Two Acts* (New York: n.p., n.d.), 3–4. The sensibility behind these librettos is close enough to Merrill's that it has been thought that Zogheb is a pseudonym for the poet. For the report of Merrill's correction of this rumor, see Jack W. C. Hagstrom and George Bixby, "James Merrill: A Bibliographical Checklist," *American Book Collector*, 4, NS (November / December 1983), 44, under *Le Sorelle Bronte, Opera in Quattri Atti*, a work by Zogheb to which Merrill contributed a similar foreword.

17. *Letters on Poetry from W.B. Yeats to Dorothy Wellesley*, introduction by Kathleen Raine (London: Oxford University Press, 1964), 22.

18. *The Selected Poetry of Rainer Maria Rilke*, ed. and trans. Stephen Mitchell (New York: Random House, 1982), 194–195.

19. Indeed, Rilke wrote poems in French, and the title of one of his collections of French poems is *Vergers*. In "The Transformation of Rilke," in discussing Rilke's poetic evolution, the young Merrill speculates that the "German idiom, rich as almond paste," would not let him wholly renounce "'things,'" and that he could do so only in French, whose "airiness" was conducive to the spiritual essences he sought. Merrill's own translations from three languages include "Selections from Chamfort," *Semicolon*, I, no. 1 (n.d.; 1955?), unpaginated; "The Three T's," by Vassili Vasilikos, *Shenandoah*, 27 (Fall 1975), 44–48; "In Broad Daylight," by C. P. Cavafy, *Grand Street*, 2 (Spring 1983), 99–107; and four poems (one with Irma Brandeis) in *Eugenio Montale: Selected Poems*, introduction by Glauco Cambon (New York: New Directions, 1965).

20. Helen Vendler, "Chronicles of Love and Loss," *New Yorker*, 21 May 1984, 127.

21. John Hollander points out that Stevens's line itself might echo Valéry's "Le Cimetière marin," where "Midi le juste y compose de feux / La mer, la mer, toujours recommencée." (He goes on to note wisely that in "all phenomena of this sort, we must always wonder what our contribution was—how much we are always being writers as well as readers of what we are seeing." The poem also is "toujours recommencée.") See *The Figure of Echo* (Berkeley: University of California Press, 1981), 99.

22. Published in *Atlantic Monthly*, 250 (November 1982), 68. "Word golf," the game that John Shade and Charles Kinbote play in *Pale Fire*, was invented by Lewis Carroll, who called it "Doublets." It involves changing one word into another, usually its opposite, by way of intervening words, each of which differs from its predecessor in only one letter, as in Merrill's example. For more information, see Tony Augarde, *The Oxford Guide to Word Games* (Oxford: Oxford University Press, 1984), 184–189.

# Rethinking Models of Literary Change: The Case of James Merrill

### MUTLU KONUK BLASING

No one has accused James Merrill of being postmodern. If anything, his accomplished formalism and his reliance on traditional verse forms and conventions have made his poetry seem slightly anachronistic. If we are not to dismiss Merrill as a reactionary but to try to define his place in postmodern American poetry, we need to rethink the models of literary history and change with which we have read American poetry since World War II, for his work challenges the ways we have configured the aftermath of modernism.

In poetry, the slippery term "postmodern" is used to refer primarily to poets working in various experimental traditions, in free verse or even prose. For example, Donald Allen's retitling his influential 1960 anthology, *The New American Poetry*, as *The Postmoderns* in 1982 claims this designation for poets whose preference for "formal freedom or openness as opposed to academic, formalistic, strictly rhymed and metered verse" places them "among the most truly authentic, indigenous American writers" (9). Similarly, while declining to use the term "postmodern," James E. B. Breslin envisions the history of poetry after modernism as an opposition between formalist verse, which represents the orthodoxy of a rigidified modernism, and an "antiformalist revolt," with which American poetry in the 1960s "once again became modern, 'of the present' " (xiv, xv). For him, Merrill is part of the "New Rear Guard," one of the "New Formalists" (xiv, 25) who are countered by open-form poets out to "capture temporal immediacy" (xv) and revive the early spirit of modernism. Marjorie Perloff, who follows open forms to the 1980s, uses "postmodern" to designate the LANGUAGE poets, in whose postlyric work "the Romantic and Modernist cult of personality has given way to what the new poets call 'the dispersal of the speaking subject,' the denial of the unitary, authoritative ego" (x); for her, "the pivotal figure in the transformation of the Romantic (and Modernistic) lyric into what we now think of as postmodern poetry is surely Ezra Pound" (181). These representative readings of poetic change since the late 1950s all tend

Mutlu Konuk Blasing, "Rethinking Models of Literary Change: The Case of James Merrill," from *American Literary History* 2 (2) (1990): 299–317. Reprinted by permission of Oxford University Press.

to value open forms. In David Antin's terms, the tradition is a "metrical-moral tradition" (120), and open forms, with their emphasis on presence, immediacy, and temporal flux, also bespeak progress toward liberation on the political, moral, and metaphysical fronts.

The species of postmodern poets who oppose the "metrical-moral tradition" is associated with William Carlos Williams and Charles Olson, along with Pound, and they read their historical relationship to their predecessors progressively, in an ongoing commitment to the imperative "Make it new." For example, the work of the most recent practitioners of open forms is said to supersede the Williams-Pound-Olson model of a speech-centered, projective verse, because making it new *now* entails dissociating voice from text, disrupting organicist models of "traditional" free verse, and rejecting physiological models of composition. Thus the LANGUAGE poets' break with their predecessors in open forms also affirms an underlying continuity of a shared faith in technical progress and the avant-garde value of a "break" or "rupture" as "necessary," in Michael Palmer's terms, "as a counter to certain notions of continuity, consistency, oeuvre" (2, 3).

This aggressively autotelic and nonreferential strain of contemporary poetry, which implicitly subscribes to a progressive model of artistic history, is beset with the internal contradiction that has traditionally plagued the avant-garde. While the avant-garde denounces liberal bourgeois culture, it shares the dominant culture's view of history in rejecting the past and upholding the values of novelty, immediacy, and change. For instance, the LANGUAGE poets are explicitly political and critical of bourgeois subjectivity in their deconstructing the speaking subject into a network of social, political, and economic discourses that prescribes its subjectivity. But this political figuration of the poet's self enables them to evade the literary past, which becomes largely irrelevant in its blindness to the culturally constructed nature of the subject. Although they would dissociate themselves from the avant-garde rhetoric and "myth of innovation" (Palmer 10), they in effect claim novelty, originality, and so on, by failing to engage the past much beyond the work of, say, Gertrude Stein.

I do not mean to suggest that there is anything naive about the LANGUAGE poets; as Palmer admits, "a new poetry comes along and thinks it's going to be right and true this time; that's a myth too. Each time one replaces a given model with another model, a theoretical model, whatever, you are inscribing yourself in the larger myth of innovation (and / or myths of recovery, renascence, et al.). . . . I think that avant-gardism is so clearly commodified now, so clearly simply a matter of what perfume or what soap you're selling, that no one I know believes in it, as they might have, say, in 1919, or for twenty or thirty years after that" (10). Yet in the same interview he acknowledges that while Williams, Pound, and Stein were important in his development, they are finally "problematic in many respects": "I find myself on the point of rather desperate re-evaluation of what they stand for in relation to any of the work that needs to be done now" (8). This stance amounts to inscribing oneself in an authorizing "myth of innovation," going beyond one's experimental models to do properly "the work that needs to be done now." Palmer's comments on the relationship between Black Mountain and LANGUAGE poetics again suggest that the new poets have replaced the earlier theoretical model with another, "truer" model: what certain LANGUAGE writers "have done is to undermine the univocal, the presumptions about speaker and subject still carried out in a breath-projected model, with the bodily origins of that metaphor" (9). It turns out, then, that one metaphor or model does have a greater claim to truth than another.

Merrill's work stands at quite the opposite end of the spectrum of contemporary poetry. He inhabits conventional metrical and stanzaic forms quite comfortably, at least without any anxiety that ruffles his surfaces. Yet his verse also registers its historical position of coming after modernism, and his work matters because it begins by questioning novelty, progress, and modernity—the possibility of new beginnings. Merrill's postmodernism, then, is not merely a late phase of modernism but represents a dismissal of the very ideology of modernity. His anachronistic gestures, which invoke traditional forms and subjects while rendering them problematic, are timely because they question progressive history at the same time that they resist nostalgia and remain only gestures of tradition and form, rather than aiming for substantive recuperations of the past. Such formalism not only precludes an easy equation of a set of techniques with ideologies but escapes any simple model of progressive history, which can only view the use of traditional forms as reactionary. This model, in fact, underlies any avant-garde stance. For instance, Palmer envisions his "opposition"—in 1986 yet—as a mainstream of conservative writing, which is "unquestionably something that rejects the major discoveries and the impetus of modernism in favor of a return to a kind of centered, commodified mode of working that was called for by the generation of Randall Jarrell and others; they felt that things had gone far enough and that it was time to close the windows and lock the doors and get the house in order" (2).

When an interviewer suggests this very scenario to Merrill, proposing that a period of consolidation set in after World War II in the wake of modernism, he responds: "As for consolidation, I'm not so sure. Anybody starting to write today has at least ten kinds of poem, each different from the other, on which to pattern his own" (*Recitative* 25). Merrill's implicit equating of the "at least ten" different models acknowledges that each formal model, each technical option, represents a rhetorical choice, and this reading of post–World War II poetic history seems accurate. As Peter Bürger has argued, while the avant-garde movements of the early decades of the century failed to destroy the institution of art, they did destroy the possibility that any given school of art, any given style, could claim greater validity than another. The avant-garde has transformed "the historical succession of techniques and styles" into a "simultaneity" of "radically disparate" styles, none more "valid" or "historically more advanced" than another (63). Thus "today" (1980) a "realistic" and an "avant-gardiste" art can exist side by side, both equally valid (87), for the choice of any given style signals only a rhetorical stance and cannot make any claim to historical authority.

Merrill's formalism should be seen in this context as a rhetoric of formalism. His forms, posed as rhetorical gestures in their exaggerated artificiality, decorum, and anachronism, register his awareness of their marginality to what are in fact the prevalent modes of post–World War II American poetry. Such formalism questions the historical and metaphysical authority of conventions as much as it challenges free forms that appeal to "experience"—whether personal or sociopolitical—for their legitimation and authority.

Locating Merrill's work historically, then, involves the larger question of what exactly changes in literary change. In order to accommodate contemporary uses of conventional forms, literary change must be understood as more complex than a linear progress. For example, Antony Easthope's history of the iambic pentameter line in English poetry concludes: "in the aggressive early days of the struggle for bourgeois hegemony [and bourgeois figurations of subjectivity], especially around 1600, the pentameter had a novelty and glamour that was long gone in 1900. Now the pentameter is a dead form and its continued use (e.g. by Philip Larkin) is in the strict sense reactionary" (76). This judgment follows from a progressive model of literary change: forms are at first novel, then grow old and die. That a "dead" form can still be used necessitates a historical modification of the organic paradigm: such use is reactionary. With Eliot and Pound came new forms, which "foreground signifier over signified," insist on the poem as production, and assert the construction of the subject as "an effect of discourse" (134–35). Actually, this describes a rhetorical stance, which would characterize Merrill's work as much as the early modernists'. For Easthope, however, the issue is strictly technical, for the position he outlines as modern is an advance linked to the death of the iambic pentameter, which is obvious to all but a few reactionaries. Easthope's model of progressive (evolutionary and revolutionary) literary history places his critical values themselves within the framework of modernism: formal verse in iambic pentameter can only be reactionary, because history marches on.

Formulating an alternative to such simple models of progress requires dissociating form from function, for forms are not what change. Iambic pentameter, for example, has not disappeared; nor is its use limited to the reactionary—to a habitual use that upholds the authority of custom and convention. For a more adequate model of change, we might consider the Russian formalist Tynianov's proposal. According to Tzvetan Todorov, he distinguishes forms from functions, "which are understood as relationships between forms." Literary change involves a "redistribution of forms and functions": now *"the form changes function, the function changes form.* The most urgent task of literary history is to study 'the variability of the function of a given formal element, the appearance of a given function in a formal element, the association of the formal element with this function.' For example, a certain meter (form) serves sometimes to introduce 'higher' epic poetry, sometimes to introduce the vulgar epic (these are among its possible functions)" (146). Here literary change is not represented as an evolutionary or revolutionary process; it is not like technological history, in which forms may become permanently obsolete. Poetry, which emphasizes the signifier over referentiality, depends on a history of coding phonic and temporal relations, and is at once more formal and more historically determined than more novel genres. In poetic change, chronology—the order of events— may break down into a network of anachronisms: retrievals and reappropria- tions—of given forms for different functions, of given functions for different forms—and recombinations of various forms and functions. To be resilient enough to accommodate the variousness of twentieth-century American po- etry and account for its discontinuities as well as its continuities, our model of literary change must be attentive to functional and rhetorical discontinuities within formal continuities and to formal discontinuities within functional continuities. Finally, we must also attend to the rhetorical varieties—to different tropological models or figurations—of temporality, precedence, continuity, and change that inform the work of different poets. With such a flexible approach, we can account for the fact that, in the postmodern period, closure (metaphysical, moral, or political) can occur within open forms, which have become only one more "tradition," and openness is possi- ble within conventional, closed forms.

In their introduction to *The Line in Postmodern Poetry*, Robert Frank and Henry Sayre acknowledge that free verse, once conceived as a challenge to "repressive, academic traditions," has become, "especially in the eruption of the culture industry since the late 1950s, as writing programs and art schools have proliferated, part and parcel of the academy itself" (xvi). "The point is," they remark, "both free verse and expressionist painting attempt to register the immediacy of experience, but both have been transformed into images. It is as if the prosody of free verse, the gestural brushwork of expressionism, are now used only as codes. We no longer see subjective expression, we see a signifier—i.e., the form of the poem itself—which stands for 'subjectivity.' " As free verse has come to *represent* authentic self- expression and sincerity, "the specter that its gestures might be masks, effects, the very signs of an inauthentic production, is raised" (xvii). The editors' dissociation of current free verse from organicist and experiential defenses of it is valuable, as is their acknowledgement that free verse can be *"conceptually* closed" (x). They question the contemporary viability of the Whitmanic identification of poetic, personal, and political liberty and admit the "ideological foundations" of free verse in bourgeois culture: it is "safe to suppose" that "as anti-aristocratic, bohemian, and avant-garde as free verse supposed itself to be, it was equally . . . thoroughly implicated in the rise of bourgeois culture as a whole and, particularly, in the democratization of leisure, and the attendant individual freedoms enjoyed by bourgeois culture, in the late nineteenth century" (xx). Yet Frank and Sayre have little doubt that the "postmodern condition" of the "loss of poetic authority and control" (xi)—however we evaluate this development—is addressed and observable in poetry in free verse; they do not consider the possibility of "conceptual" openness within a poetry "strait-jacketed by the 'closed' forms of rhyme and meter" (x). Similarly, Perloff restricts the postmodern questioning of a unified and authoritative subject to poetry in fragmented forms, experiments that follow from Pound's fracturing the lyric speaker into "multiple voices or voice fragments" arranged and juxtaposed in the mode of collage (183). She reduces the rhetorical deconstruction of the subject's authority to a specific set of techniques, and a project like Merrill's eludes her framework.

Merrill's work calls for a model of literary change that is not based on contests between such binary oppositions as past and present, convention and originality, tradition and experiment. If the possible uses of the past are confined to the reductive models of iconoclasm, nostalgia, and reactionary recuperation, we cannot account for Merrill's project, which is rhetorically and functionally discontinuous with the canonical tradition his forms invoke. "An Urban Convalescence," which opens *Water Street* (1962), has been singled out by Merrill's readers as marking the beginning of his mature work. I propose, however, to cast this poem on a larger, historical stage as an exemplary postmodern "beginning" at the end of the modern idea of history as progress. To highlight Merrill's "lateness" to modernity and progress, we can approach "An Urban Convalescence" by way of a detour and consider Paul de Man's remarks on the figure of convalescence. "The human figures that epitomize modernity," he writes, "are defined by experiences such as childhood or convalescence, a freshness of perception that results from a slate wiped clear, from the absence of a past that has not yet had time to tarnish the immediacy of perception . . . of a past that, in the case of convalescence, is so threatening that it has to be forgotten" (157). If this use of convalescence is "modern," Merrill's use of the figure is clearly different. He diagnoses "the sickness of our time" not as a Nietzschean "historical sickness," but precisely as forgetfulness, a series of slates wiped clean in response to a threat posed by the mere presence of the past. Of course the "freshness," this modern erasure of history, is the postmodern poet's very sickness, his particular past, and Merrill's poem traces his "convalescence" from just such "modernity."

The poem begins with an emblematic modern scene:

> Out for a walk, after a week in bed,
> I find them tearing up part of my block

> And, chilled through, dazed and lonely, join the dozen
> In meek attitudes, watching a huge crane
> Fumble luxuriously in the filth of years.
> Her jaws dribble rubble. An old man
> Laughs and curses in her brain,
> Bringing to mind the close of *The White Goddess*.
>
> *(Poems* 81)

Luxuriating in the "filth of years," jaws dribbling "rubble," the crane is doing the work of demolition. While the scene suggests an unseemly overindulgence in the detritus of the past, the crane is also the agent of urban renewal. Making things "new" by tearing them up, it represents a militant commitment to change, which regards the "simple fact of having lasted" as a threat that calls for the swift retribution of a BLAST. And the mystification and even religious awe that attend the scene ironically hint at the spiritual mission of this breaking of the vessels.

With the allusion to Robert Graves, this devastation that leaves "not one stone upon another" reverberates with more specific historical and literary connotations. The "huge crane" brings to mind Graves's *White Goddess*, presumably because cranes were sacred to the goddess—a mother-muse figure who authorizes an Orphic model of a poetic language grounded in nature. Graves also links cranes to the invention of writing and cites a legend that Mercury invented the letters after watching a flight of cranes, "which make letters as they fly" (224). In Egypt, Mercury was Thoth, the god who invented writing and whose symbol was the crane-like white ibis (227). Graves further suggests that the association of cranes with writing and literary secrets makes sense because "cranes fly in V-formation and the characters of all early alphabets, nicked with a knife on the rind of boughs . . . or on clay tablets, were naturally angular" (227). At the "close" of his book, he offers a poem imagining the wrathful second coming of the goddess at her "cannibalistic worst," in the form of "a gaunt, red-wattled crane," to punish "man's irreligious improvidence" that has led to the exhaustion of the "natural resources of the soil and sea" (486).

Merrill's bringing in Graves effects an odd pun. If the reference to Graves suggests that the crane as goddess is punishing "man's" improvidence, its incarnation as a mechanical crane—an agent or, at least, an accomplice of "man's" sins against nature—is problematic. Furthermore, the destruction wrought by the mechanical crane the "old man" operates is purely mechanistic, demystified, and urban, and takes place in the linear time of *Time*; this crane is indeed an agent of forgetfulness. The crane as a goddess incarnate, however, is an elemental force, whose destructions belong to the cyclical time of nature and myth, and she threatens to avenge herself on those who forget. Merrill's conflation of historical and mythic forces and conceptions of change in a pun enables him to equate these mastering "ideologies" and thus lightly to sidestep both. His pun exposes the nostalgia underwriting a modernity that seeks to return to and recover a foundation through technical progress. By positioning himself at the margins as a "meek" bystander, he resists both progressive history and a regressive appeal to myths of return.

In this maneuver, the pun on "crane" becomes a textual "ground" that stages the conflict and continuity between progressive historical time and cyclical myth. Unlike a metaphor, a pun highlights a nonhierarchical, synchronic duplicity, doubleness, or difference internal to the signifier. The distance between the mythic crane, a symbol or reincarnation of the goddess, and the technological crane committed to an urban destruction and renewal is the distance between mythic-pastoral and technological-urban conceptions of death and rebirth. Merrill's pun compresses the conceptual and historical distance between two different systems in a synchronic doubleness and figures it as internal to language. Grounding himself in a purely literal and accidental resource, Merrill questions the claims of both the technological and the mythic "crane"—the Janusfaced deus ex machina of the modernist aesthetic. Thus "the close of *The White Goddess*," with which Merrill opens, is not merely the conclusion of Graves's book but the end of a poetic era.

Discussing Elizabeth Bishop's "Visits to St. Elizabeths," Merrill remarks her distance from Pound's poetics and praises her for not being "prey to . . . those (male?) drives, the one that produced the *Cantos'* huge unruly text, the other that made its bid to change the map of Europe" (*Recitative* 127). Elsewhere, Merrill associates the "monumental" impulse of the major modernist poets with a "male" drive. Speaking of T. S. Eliot, Wallace Stevens, Williams, and Pound as well as Robert Lowell, he observes that "these men began by writing small, controllable, we might say from our present vantage 'unisex' poems. As time went on, though, through their ambitious reading, their thinking, their critical pronouncements, a kind of vacuum charged with expectation, if not with dread, took shape around them, asking to be filled with grander stuff" (*Recitative* 161). The binary opposition of the gender metaphor is simplistic; the monumental impulse seems to afflict "men," Merrill goes on to remind us, "but that's too neat. Look at poor Anne Sexton who, submitting a poem to an editor, wrote: 'I realize it's very long, but I believe it is major' " (161). Merrill admits to having felt and succumbed to a "similar pressure" in his *Changing Light at Sandover*. While it takes Pound almost 800 pages to admit to "many errors" from a "newer" perspective, Merrill begins his own monumental undertaking with a demurral—"Admittedly I err"—which, tonally and rhetorically, scales his "grander stuff" to human size. Unlike Pound, he does not try to "write like a god" (*Recitative* 28).

If Merrill's poetry is marginal to a male will to power, it is equally marginal to an Orphic poetic that enthrones the master myth of the Mother Goddess whose cult revolves around a heterosexual and reproductive center. According to Graves, "man's" offenses against the goddess follow from "enthroning the restless and arbitrary male will" and suppressing the female principle (486). Yet as Pound's grounding his male drive to power in fertility myths and cycles in his *Cantos* suggests, the two powers are not unrelated. The modernist project of the *Cantos* is to rewrite history as rooted in the natural laws the Goddess represents. This "rooted plan" authorizes formal discontinuities like the "breaking" of the pentameter, the "first heave," from which follow other breaks of other syntagmatic continuities like grammatical and narrative orders. Thus Pound's formal discontinuities are grounded in a substantive continuity with Romantic organicism. He can "make it new, day by day" because *it* does not "wobble"; *it* is a pivot history turns on. And he deploys technical novelty to recuperate that foundation.

"Father Time and Mother Earth" in "The Broken Home" (*Poems* 140–43) are Merrill's personae of these master myths. As he explains, "That bit in 'The Broken Home'—'Father Time and Mother Earth, / A marriage on the rocks'—isn't meant as a joke. History in our time *has* cut loose, *has* broken faith with Nature. But poems, even those of the most savage incandescence, can't deal frontally with such huge, urgent subjects without sounding grumpy or dated when they should still be in their prime. So my parents' divorce dramatized on a human scale a subject that couldn't have been handled otherwise" (*Recitative* 72). Their familial placement in the poet's autobiography, as well as their historical place in the "race . . . run below," domesticates these master figures and acknowledges that the poet-child must obey them. But Merrill, unlike Pound, best obeys "inversely." The verse remains verse, that is, metrical: "The pentameter has been a good friend to me," he says; "you'd think I'd have noticed a little thing like a broken back" (*Recitative* 25). And by remaining verse, his poems "invert" these power figures who would claim authority over his text. If the Father rules time and history, the poet resists him by not subscribing to "newspaper" time, which is uncomfortably close to making it "new" daily. If the Mother watches over birth and death, the poet inverts her by growing and letting die his "gilt leaves." To be sure, his marginality to the master myths registers some guilt (see, for example, "Childlessness" and "A Tenancy"). Yet such psychological dramas, like Merrill's ideological and mythic contests, transpire within a framed aesthetic space: "the parents and the child / At their window, gleaming like fruit / With evening's mild gold leaf." The gilt suffuses all guilt, for the stage of these dramas is always already a figure, a text, not a primal ground.

Similarly, while Merrill's mock-sublime "crane" makes light at once of an Orphic poetic and of a now senile faith in technical renewals, he also "obeys" both principles, if "inversely," for a pun is a curious hybrid. Its truth is, after all, technical, residing in its letters; at the same time, it gives of an uncanny double of super- or sub-literal vision. For Merrill's relation to these master myths is not a progressive antagonism: he is not out to destroy them in order to install other, more valid myths in their place. From his postmetaphysical perspective, all truths are rhetorical, and all ideologies, mastering and marginal, are textual options. And he presents this rhetorical position not as a timeless truth but as indicative of the historical state of affairs at "the close of *The White Goddess*."

Merrill's narrative of convalescence unfolds the options that the crane levels. The speaker remembers the figure of a garland decorated the lintel of the building being torn down. The iconoclastic destruction of received structures—specifically structures of closure like buildings—is "inscribed" with a garland, "stone fruit, stone leaves, / Which years of grit had etched until it thrust / Roots down, even into the poor soil of my seeing." Again, the garland "sways" into "focus" as an emblem of the cyclical-mythic time that underwrites the modern project of catastrophic progress, of radical breaks with history. Next, Merrill moves to the memory of another representation of natural force—"a particular cheap engraving of garlands." The engraving evokes an equally fuzzy and belated avatar of the White Goddess, whose link to reproductive forces and "deadly" power still manages to register, just as the forlorn pastoral emblem of "garlands" still manages to be remembered—if at the expense of the history of the buildings and the people themselves, whose features "lie toppled underneath that year's fashions." The engraving was

> Bought for a few francs long ago,
> All calligraphic tendril and cross-hatched rondure,
> Ten years ago, and crumpled up to stanch
> Boughs dripping, whose white gestures filled a cab,
>
> . . . . . . . . . . . . . . . . . . . . . . . .
>
> Also, to clasp them, the small, red-nailed hand
> Of no one I can place.

And this forgetfulness locates Merrill in his "urban" setting; in Graves's words, "The Goddess is no townswoman: she is the Lady of the Wild Things" (481). By forgetting the goddess, Merrill both implicates himself in the modern "sickness" and turns away from a pastoral recuperation. Following this episode, stanzas of drastic "exposure" underscore the poet's new clarity about his place on the margins of progressive history and natural force, which are themselves only figurations of centers of power—emblems and chapters in the "massive volume of the world." Such knowledge of pervasive textuality, which is also "self-knowledge," delivers him "indoors at last" to an explicitly and historically textual "house."

The speaker's move indoors coincides with a formal switch to quatrains. Merrill himself calls this poem "a turning point" for him and associates this turn with a return, with his staged formal switch: "I remember writing half of it and thinking it was going to be impossible to finish. Then I had the idea of letting it go back to a more formal pattern at the end" (*Recitative*

45). Elsewhere, he tells us that " 'Stanza' is . . . the Italian word for 'room,' " and relates his fondness for regular stanzas to his attachment to "interior spaces, the shape and correlation of rooms in a house," rather than the vistas it commands or the "human comedies" it stages (*Recitative* 3). Here, the enveloping *abba* rhyme reinforces the enclosure of the quatrains. And the poem's resolution suggests that convalescence will involve remembering closures and interior spaces, answering a "dull need to make some kind of house / Out of the life lived, out of the love spent." Given the in-and-out movement that constitutes the poem's adventure, from "out for a walk" to "indoors at last," the repeated "out of" in the final line has an added resonance. "Out of" may mean not only "constituted of" but "outside" the lived life, the spent love. If we register both senses, the house-poem made out of the lived life moves out of the life lived. Merrill here dedicates himself to his special brand of transpersonal autobiographical writing. For his move "inside," to the at least temporarily protected space of his own life, is modified by the fact that he also moves into quatrains. Subscribing to such marked conventions without any effort to naturalize his forms effects an impersonal, intertextual erosion of the personal, and Merrill's formalism, always sharply aware of this, does not offer protection but leaves him open to a different kind of history and loss.

Merrill often makes the textual dangers and "losses"—of signature and singularity, of authorship and authority—that are internal to writing his explicit subjects, but his conventional forms also work implicitly to efface the speaking subject, dispersing it in the drift of impersonal time and history. Poetic conventions such as meter, rhyme schemes, and stanza forms, are timing devices that are also always more than mere schemes, because they remember a past and carry with them the burden of a public history. Thus Merrill's urban convalescence inside quatrains represents more than an urbanity of manners that remediates the natural or the oracular. A convalescence that identifies the "indoors" with formal stanzas dissociates the "inside" from the subjective or the intuitive. As the architectural metaphor of house also signals, Merrill is interested in public building, in transmitting a public history. His conventions make for this historical dimension, while his artificial staging of his forms registers their anachronism and thus divests them of historical authority. Urban as well as urbane, Merrill can maintain a critical distance from progress *and* historical authority, from Orphic, oracular, or intuitive speech *and* conventions.

For Merrill, change and continuity are not polar opposites: continuity is infected with change and change with continuity. For example, situating himself inside quatrains in "An Urban Convalescence" allows him to revise himself and question what are presumably his authorizing values. He begins with a diagnosis of planned obsolescence as "the sickness of our time" that requires things be "blasted in their prime." Yet he immediately overturns this judgment:

> There are certain phrases which to use in a poem
> Is like rubbing silver with quicksilver. Bright
> But facile, the glamour deadens overnight.
> For instance, how "the sickness of our time"
>
> Enhances, then debases, what I feel.
> *(Poems* 83)

This "revision" implies that his "conservative" rejection of novelty has itself joined the "great coarsening drift of things" (*Recitative* 60) or "progress." His second thoughts occur, however, in a conventional form that would conserve the past. In this disjunction, his conventional forms divest themselves of authority: they are dissociated from a conservative ideology that would judge the present by taking refuge in the canonical authority of the past. If originality and novelty are outmoded concepts for Merrill, so is the expectation of a correlation between convention and authority. He employs conventions not because they carry a prescriptive authority but as if they did, at once remembering and transmitting a past and denying it any absolute vitality or validity beyond its being there, a shared, public past. For the anachronism of his forms in the time of *Time* and in one's own "life lived" and "love spent" are evident enough. Moreover, to claim any inherent validity or recuperative efficacy for his forms would reinscribe him in the logic of modernity. Indeed, when he stages his more elaborate forms within larger pieces—as when he breaks into quatrains in the middle of a poem containing blank verse or even prose—he presents such forms as quotations cut off from their original contexts, functions, and "grounds." In his hybridizing use, the "quoted" forms both carry historical associations and assume new functions in their new contexts. Such functional discontinuity again subverts any claim to canonical authority, and traditional forms are at the same time technically closed and rhetorically open.

Merrill's distinction is his ability to register at once the textuality and the historical nature of writing. His polyvalent literalism and his fondness for "accidents" and puns in general foreground the play of the signifier and approach an internalization of history within poetic language. His conventional formalism, however, holds this tendency in check by placing poetic language within a public literary history. Thus he can be grounded in textuality, doing without historical or metaphysical foundations, yet stop this side of an ahistorical, self-reflexive subjectivity, for the textual inside is governed by publicly recognizable, historically coded rules, which transmit a past even if they do not carry any inherent validity.

Since Merrill's chosen subject is his personal past, his conventional forms, which recall an impersonal and intertextual past, serve to unsettle his entire project. Since the "I" may be heard only through the chorus or *con*vention of other poems and poets, the subject dissolves or is resolved into the textual medium. Merrill's writing is never naively personal: the writer's repertoire, poetic conventions, and the accidental resources of language always consume the personal source, leaving the poet to conclude "out of the life lived." The poet who would be saved from "more living"—the poet who would "fly" from Byzantium or Istanbul—has his wish granted only too easily and finds himself in another "Byzantium": "Far off a young scribe turned a fresh / Page, hesitated, dipped his pen" (*Poems* 194). There is no need to yearn, like Yeats, to be "out of nature"; the poet *is* a scribe, his source and destination strictly prescribed in a synchronic pun of Byzantiums and his very medium always already spelling out "what is past, or passing, or to come."

Nor is he naively conventional. Conventions, Lawrence Manley proposes, are animated by a tension and interplay between the formal and the social dimensions they encompass, since they derive their "quasi-objective and sometimes normative status from an underlying social dimension" (32). The history of conventions reveals another set of tensions, between the social and historicist phenomenon of convention and what is perceived, by contrast, to be objectively "universal," such as a "timeless" nature, or to be "unique," such as the concrete particularity of the "individual" (33). Merrill's use of convention stands outside this framework. To begin with, he refuses to place socially sanctioned conventions in opposition to individual or natural language. Speaking of "manners," he observes: "One could paraphrase Marianne Moore: using them with a perfect contempt for them, one discovers in them after all a place for the genuine. . . ." Not only are manners "more hospitable to irony, self-expression, self-contradiction, than many a philosophical or sociological system," but "manners for me are the touch of nature, an artifice in the very bloodstream" (*Recitative* 33). "From my own point of view," he tells J. D. McClatchy, "voice in its fullest tonal range—not just bel canto or passionate speech"—would be "utterly unattainable without meter and rhyme and those forms we are talking about." These "obsolete resources" assume a new function in Merrill's work: they make possible a more "natural" tone of voice at the same time that they "breed echoes" and lend an "air of pastiche" to dispel the illusion of an "individual" voice (*Recitative* 80). Yet Merrill's use of convention does not appeal to social sanction, either. Rhymed quatrains, for example, tend to be typical of the kind of convention Merrill relies on, and they cannot be said to carry any social or historical sanction in American poetry, least of all after 1960. That is, the necessity for their use cannot be inferred from "the habitual practice of other writers or . . . the prevailing opinion as to what ought to be done" (R. S. Crane qtd. in Manley 51), any more than from the claims of "natural truth" or individual talent.

The very anachronism of Merrill's particular conventions at a time when it is "too late" to "rely" on them—at a time when a reader can "hardly be trusted to hear the iambics when he opens *The Rape of the Lock*" (*Recitative*

79–80)—situates his work in extraliterary history as well. In fact, his choice of traditional forms implies a social-class position, as suggested by a remark like:

> Must I grow broad- and dirty-minded
> Serving a community, a nation
> By now past anybody's power to shock?
>
> (*Poems* 315)

Robert von Hallberg notes this aspect of Merrill's style:

> During the 1960s, while some of his contemporaries, under the influence of Merwin, were pursuing styles that apparently disowned social relations, and others, like Lowell, were attempting to democratize, with free verse, low colloquialisms and brand names, the densely metaphorical styles they learned in the 1950s, Merrill held on to his meters and chose his phrases with a sense of class.
>
> So distinct a sense of class is implied by his style that he, at least as much as any of his contemporaries, has altered the politics of style in American poetry . . . Merrill's distinction is his skeptical view of that American *idée fixe*, the democratic or classless style. (112)

Yet von Hallberg does not consider Merrill a "culture poet" (116). "Culture" poetry "obviously involve[s] recent cultural history" (2) and engages "the feelings, experiences, and difficulties that are considered the irreducible center of public life" (4). The dominant tone and diction of Merrill's poems define a "camp" sensibility, which is limited and marks "minor" poetry: "By making a virtue of exaggeration, it cannot achieve justness, and a sane assessment of our most difficult experiences is part of what is asked of the greatest poetry" (112). I would argue that our most difficult experience at this time is precisely the problem of a "cultural center," and Merrill's ability to use—while questioning from within—the style and tone of a literature once associated with cultural centering makes his work very much "engaged." His exaggerations and parodic "edge" implicitly criticize the power politics of any "central" discourse, and his anachronistic conventions, which point to the constructed nature of all styles and thus expose fictions of "classless" or "democratic" styles, also hint at the anachronism of the expectation that poetry engage centers, once the politics of centers has come into question. Whose center is *the* center? Whose history is History? By "centering" his work in an admittedly marginal formalism, by highlighting a degree of artifice that flaunts its disengagement from politics, by refusing to naturalize his forms—which might make for a pastoral convalescence but not an urban one—and by aestheticizing the political, his "camp" stance is perfectly clear about its historical position.

Merrill has no illusions about "central" speaking. Just as an aggressive disarticulation of articulate discourse partakes of the same economy of subjugation it would overthrow, any "central" speech is implicated in the very politics of power that establish the center. In "Roger Clay's Proposal," Merrill exposes the complicity of any opposition with the powers that be:

> I may be oversusceptible to news
> But what I see in the papers leaves me numb.
> The bomb. The ultimatum. Wires hum—
> Adult impersonators giving interviews,
>
> As if that helped. What would? I've thought of it.
> With all due ceremony—flags unfurled,
> Choirs, priests—the leaders of a sobered world
> Should meet, kneel down, and, joining hands, submit
>
> To execution: say in Rome or Nice—
> Towns whose economy depends on crowds.
> Ah, but those boys, their heads aren't in the clouds.
> They would find reasons not to die for peace.
>
> Damn them. I'd give *my* life. Each day I meet
> Men like me, young, indignant. We're not cranks.
> Will some of them step up? That's plenty. Thanks.
> Now let's move before we get cold feet.
>
> Music we'll need, and short, clear speeches given
> Days of maximum coverage in the press.
> We'll emphasize disinterestedness,
> Drive the point home that someone could be driven
>
> To do this.
>
> (*Poems* 104)

This point is made explicit in an interview: "every leader—president or terrorist—is responsible for keeping his ranks thinned out. Good politics would therefore encourage death in one form or another—if not actual, organized bloodshed, then the legalization of abortion or, heaven forbid, the various chemical or technological atrocities . . ." (*Recitative* 72).

As Merrill's equating president and terrorist and his blurring the distinction between different options—for *or* against the "boys"—suggest, the only way not to be implicated in the power politics of making history is to keep well grounded in rhetoric. Thus: "In poetry I look for English in its billiard-table sense—words that have been set spinning against their own gravity. Once in competition with today's headlines or editorial page you just can't sustain that crucial, liberating lightness without sounding like a sick comedian" (*Recitative* 38). The "crucial, liberating lightness" that resists gravity sustains itself by doing without the gravity of a foundation exterior to its own forms and rhetoric. This is "English in its billiard-table sense."

Such "groundless" formalism signals Merrill's postmodern challenge to progressive history and metaphysical foundations alike. He questions experimental *and* conservative values, both of which orient themselves in relation to a grounded, linear history, and thus forces us to question a literary history figured on this model. At the same time that he dismisses experimental techniques, "natural" or organic forms, and Orphic models of poetry, he demystifies his inherited, traditional forms and calls into doubt the assumptions of closure, containment, protection, and control that accompany them. Similarly, he dissociates the lyric from notions of a coherent lyric self with absolute power over words, and inscribes his "voice" and personal past as a *con*vention of a variety of intertextual discourses—both literary and extraliterary. And he conveys his postmodern understanding of the poetic self as textual, and all authority as rhetorical, in autobiographical writing in canonical forms. That his traditional, "old-fashioned kind of poem" (*Recitative* 39) is neither innocent nor ahistorical makes for work whose timeliness lies precisely in its reluctance to lay claim to being timely.

*Works Cited*

Allen, Donald, and George F. Butterick, eds. *The Postmoderns*. New York: Grove, 1982.

Antin, David. "Modernism and Postmodernism: Approaching the Present in American Poetry." *boundary 2* 1(1972): 98–133.

Breslin, James E. B. *From Modern to Contemporary: American Poetry, 1945–1965*. Chicago: U of Chicago P, 1984.

Bürger, Peter. *Theory of the Avant-Garde*. Trans. Michael Shaw. Minneapolis: U of Minnesota P, 1984.

de Man, Paul. "Literary History and Literary Modernity." *Blindness and Insight*. Minneapolis: U of Minnesota P, 1983. 142–65.

Easthope, Antony. *Poetry as Discourse*. London: Methuen, 1983.

Frank, Robert, and Henry Sayre. *The Line in Postmodern Poetry*. Urbana: U of Illinois P, 1988.

Graves, Robert. *The White Goddess: A Historical Grammar of Poetic Myth*. New York: Farrar, 1980.

Manley, Lawrence. "Concepts of Convention and Models of Critical Discourse." *New Literary History* 13 (1981): 31–52.

Merrill, James. *From the First Nine: Poems 1946–1976*. New York: Atheneum, 1984.

———. *Recitative*. Ed. J. D. McClatchy. San Francisco: North Point, 1986.

Palmer, Michael. "An Interview with Michael Palmer." *Contemporary Literature* 30.1 (1989): 1–12.

Perloff, Marjorie. *The Dance of the Intellect: Studies in the Poetry of the Pound Tradition*. Cambridge: Cambridge UP, 1985.

Todorov, Tzvetan, and Oswald Ducrot. *Encyclopedic Dictionary of the Sciences of Language*. Trans. Catherine Porter. Baltimore: Johns Hopkins UP, 1979.

von Hallberg, Robert. *American Poetry and Culture, 1945–1980*. Cambridge: Harvard UP, 1985.

# 'I knew // That life was fiction in disguise': Merrill's Divergence from Auden and Modernism

## Lynn Keller

Unlike most modernists, Auden did not strive to reduce the distance between art and life by recreating in his poems the processes of ordinary perception and consciousness. He stressed instead the danger of mistaking the arbitrary rules of poetry, taken up as a game, for the necessary rules of life, which we cannot escape. Once he had rejected the notion that poetry could be politically efficacious, he emphasized the gratuitousness, the frivolity of writing. Even so, Auden's oeuvre—like Eliot's, Pound's, Stevens', Williams'—tells of a continuous effort to make human experience cohere. His was an organizing intellect, fond of ennumerated categories and tidy aphorisms. According to Auden, the best description of the artistic process is Virginia Woolf's:[1]

> There is a square; there is an oblong. The players take the square and place it upon the oblong. They place it very accurately; they make it a perfect dwelling-place. Very little is left outside. The structure is now visible; what is inchoate is here stated; we are not so various or so mean, we have made oblongs and stood them upon squares. This is our triumph; this is our consolation.

This passage leaves little doubt that art is an ordering, and in his later work Auden regards the rules of that order as paralleling the laws of the universe.

Auden's poetic explorations of order reveal a preoccupation with doubleness, and the same is true for Merrill. The younger poet's formalism reveals his own pleasure in the design and symmetry of "squares and oblongs," while his poems are filled not only with double meanings, but with explorations of all sorts of doublings, bifurcations, and polarities. In order to define the significant ways in which Merrill diverges from his "father of forms," this

Reprinted from *Re-making It New: Contemporary American Poetry and the Modernist Tradition* by Lynn Keller, New York: Cambridge University Press, 1987, 226–53. Reprinted with the permission of Lynn Keller and Cambridge University Press.

chapter will focus on the differences between the two poets' conceptions of and attitudes toward duality, first in a brief overview, then in a more detailed look at Merrill's recent poems.

I

According to Auden, "The cogitations of Descartes / Are where all sound semantics start" (CP 169), so it is hardly surprising that one split recurring in his poetry is the Cartesian one between mind and body. Often in his poems one half of his being will address or discuss the other, as in "No, Plato, No," where the speaking mind objects to a disembodied existence, while admitting that the body may well long to be freed from the spirit that animates it. The division between flesh and spirit parallels others that preoccupy Auden either implicitly or explicitly: reason/feeling, public/private, aesthete/moralist, and so forth. The most fundamental of these contrasting pairs in Auden's mature work is the Christian dichotomy of the worldly and the otherworldly, human and divine.

Although the devil is "the great schismatic who / First split creation into two," the consequences of his fall are not entirely devastating: the positive response of creation has been the "wish to be / Diversity in unity" (CP 171). Auden can therefore glorify the "gift of double focus," believing that simultaneous perception of difference or division on the one hand and wholeness or unity on the other creates a precious balance that prevents complete schism. This double focus is embodied in the Carnival perspective Auden celebrates in his late work: Tension-releasing laughter in which "we laugh simultaneously *with* and *at*" (FA 471)—a gesture Auden defines as "the spirit of Carnival"—accommodates the ambiguity of perceiving "that each great I / Is but a process in a process / Within a field that never closes" (CP 167). True laughter can both accept and protest against the double vision of oneself as a unique individual and as an undifferentiated part of a continuous species. Auden's goal is synthetic vision, not the "either/or" perspective the devil advocates in "New Year Letter." He believes that "human folk" are distinguished from the less conscious creatures in the natural world precisely in "hav[ing] their unity to win" (CP 505) by holding the two sides of their nature (manifest in so many contrasted pairings) in symmetrical balance.

Art, in Auden's view, can assist us in attaining this order, so long as we do not mistake art's order for life's, and instead regard artistic order and balance as models of the harmony we should strive for in our lives. In art's reconciliation of contradictory feelings we see an analogue to the paradisal state (an analogue, Auden emphasizes, not an imitation), which enables us to perceive the possibility of regaining paradise. Order, however, is achieved more easily and more surely in art than in living—that is one source of aesthetic pleasure—for only in art are events *caused by* our will to form felicitous patterns (CP 330).

Art's pleasing patterns, then, have a moral purpose, which Auden spells out at the close of "Caliban to the Audience." (How much and how lastingly Caliban speaks for Auden is suggested by his remark in a 1972 interview identifying this "poem written in prose, a pastiche of the late Henry James" as the single work of which he was proudest.)[2] Having shown us our "estrangement from the truth," the "gap between what you so questionably are and what you are commanded without any question to become" (CP 339), the work of art is to inspire us to bridge that gap. Yet paradoxically, as Caliban argues, the more effectively art portrays either our condition or the truth from which it is estranged, the more easily the audience complacently mistakes awareness of the gap for the bridge over it. So the artist must wish for some unforeseen mishap that will direct the audience to the original "real-life" drama inspiring the artist. The image Auden develops for that "first performance" helps explain his allegiance to the theatrical aesthetic outlined in the preceding chapter. The image is that of "the greatest grandest opera rendered by a very provincial touring company indeed" (CP 340). As the limitations of the company would lead us to expect, their (that is, our) performance is a fiasco, and its conclusion leaves the desolate, exposed performers in a position to see themselves as they are: trapped, hanging over the abyss. At that moment, art's moral purpose may be fulfilled: "for the first time in our lives we hear, not the sounds which, as born actors, we have hitherto condescended to use as an excellent vehicle for displaying our personalities and looks, but the real Word which is our only *raison d'être*." Only then are we "blessed by that Wholly Other Life from which we are separated by an essential emphatic gulf of which our contrived fissures of mirror and proscenium arch—we understand them at last—are feebly figurative signs" (CP 340). Art, and most obviously the theater, should remind us of that all-important split between our flawed mortal existence and the perfect immortal life that should be our goal.

This elaborate theory seems worth quoting and paraphrasing at length because it presents so emphatically Auden's belief in a single "raison d'être," in a single correct understanding one can attain "at last," in one grand stage to which all our theatrics point and an absolute reality in relation to which our performances assume their true meaning. James Merrill's sense of human doubleness does not resolve itself in such a final monism, and his sense of performance has no comparably true referent.

The doubleness that preoccupies Merrill is rooted in language, in its dual powers of literal and figurative reference. He is nervously conscious of his inability to resist the pull of metaphor and symbol. In *Water Street*'s "To a Butterfly," he interrupts a heavy-handed allegory that presents the insect's metamorphoses as stages of human biblical history (the fall, the flood, etc.) to lament:

> Goodness, how tired one grows
> Just looking through a prism:
> Allegory, symbolism.
> I've tried, Lord knows,
>
> To keep from seeing double,
> Blushed for whenever I did,
> Prayed like a boy my cheek be hid
> By manly stubble. (WS 43)

Yet he cannot even get through this protestation without slipping in the doubleness of a pun (his cheek), preparing us for subsequent stanzas' acquiescence to the inevitability of such "rigamarole."

Of course Auden shares—even provides models for—Merrill's figurative doublings in allegory and symbolism, as well as his linguistic doublings in puns or etymological wordplay. The important difference between them is that Merrill locates no primal gap that all gulfs between tenor and vehicle signify, no Wholly Other reality where metaphor's buck stops. True, he seems to suggest in *Sandover* that all existent myths are figurative distortions of some ur-truth, but his belief, in that as in all else, proves partial.

The two poets, then, stand in very different relations to the ordering systems they invoke in their poems. Auden's entire career can be seen as a search for the properly fitting ideological system, like a search for the right hat. He was comfortable donning a series of established styles—the Marxist's cap, the existentialist's beret, and so forth; Merrill, by contrast, has refused to try on anything more firmly molded than the wispy veil of manners. Consequently, while the American Auden confidently affirms his belief in God and the Devil,[3] Merrill, when asked whether he believes in the elaborate system spelled out through his Ouija board, can only answer "yes and no." When Helen Vendler asked how real the trilogy's mythology seemed to him, Merrill replied, "Literally, not very—except in recurrent euphoric hours when it's altogether too beautiful not to be true. Imaginatively real? I would hope so. . . . But the point remained, to be always of two minds."[4] When asked a similar question by Ross Labrie, he responded with similar ambivalence: "when you are caught up in it you believe it wholeheartedly; when you cool off you see it as a stylization of various things in your experience or in the world's experience." And when asked whether he believed specifically in reincarnation, a basic tenet in the Ouija board revelations, he answered, "Yes and no. I simply couldn't say. I think it's a very fruitful belief to have. I think it does wonders in a way for the way you live."[5] Beauty and usefulness—and for Merrill the two are almost synonymous, since only the beautiful seems of much use in improving the quality of life—comprise his criteria for acquiescence, not truth in any absolute sense. Happy to entertain orderly systems provisionally, and to be entertained by them, Merrill does not regard the word of his angels as "the real Word."

Thus, when an interviewer remarked upon Merrill's seeming "a bit self-conscious as an 'intellectual' " and inquired about the seemingly "unrelieved meaning" of the trilogy's caps, Merrill cautioned:

> a lot of what we're loosely calling "meaning" turns out, on inspection, to be metaphor, which leads one back towards language, wordplay, etymology, the "wholly human instrument" (as Wystan says [from JM's spirit realm]) I'd used and trusted— like every poet, wouldn't you say?—to ground the lightning of ideas. We could say that the uppercase represented a *range* of metaphor, a depth of meaning, that hadn't been available to me in earlier poems.[6]

In composing the trilogy, Merrill seems to have struggled to balance a coherent narrative—something which tends to take on a comfortably non-metaphorical substance in the reader's mind—against devices (comparable in aim to Ashbery's typical methods) which interrupt that coherence so as to keep us aware of the provisional, purely linguistic nature of its meaning. Periodically, he jars his readers with reminders that the creatures whose voices appear in uppercase are subatomic particles, or faculties of human intelligence, that a crust around the greenhouse earth may also be an outer ring of the atom's structure, an outer orbit of the solar system, a layer of brain matter, and so forth. None of these levels is finally more true than the others; and all, presented as they are through the medium of language, are creations of humankind and of the individual poet (or, in *Sandover*, perhaps of the poet and his double in the form of a same-sex lover).[7]

Although the historical Auden, like his fictive counterpart WHA, would celebrate language as the wholly human instrument, his conceptions of the relation between language and reality nonetheless differ from those Merrill evolved. In discussing language, Auden tends to concentrate on its social validity, on language as a communal possession. The poet, he argues,

> is more protected than [other artists] from another modern peril, that of solipsist subjectivity; however esoteric a poem may be, the fact that all its words have meanings which can be looked up in a dictionary makes it testify to the existence of other people. . . . a purely private verbal world is not possible. (DH 23)

This is not to suggest that he is naively unaware of the conventional and possibly fictive nature of the "external" reality our words denote. As Mendelson has explained, "In his later poems [Auden] treats the gulf between language and world . . . as a condition that must be accepted but that does not prevent language from being shared, or prevent it from illuminating and affecting a physical and ethical world whose order and events are not only verbal ones."[8] "Ode to Terminus" (CP 608–9), for example, acknowledges how easily the solitary thinker can lose confidence in distinctions between inner and outer, literal and figurative. But language for Auden is the thinker's lifeline, not the web from which his confusions are woven; ordered by grammar—and, in poems, by metrics—language supports sanity by attaching the thinker to the world "where all visibles do have a definite / outline they stick to," where the distinction between figurative and literal is firm enough that one can "see a joke or / distinguish a penis from a pencil." Moreover, that world of conventional distinctions is semantically privileged:

> True seeing is believing
> (What sight can never prove)
> There is a world to see:
> Look outward, eyes, and love
> Those eyes you cannot be. (CP 449)

Thus, while he never lost his "sense of theatre" (CP 651), as he grew older Auden modified and restricted his attachment to "conscious theatrical exaggeration" and to the poet's various "ways of not calling a spade a spade" (DH 47–8; 1956). Taking a decreasing interest in the poet's role as Ariel, magical creator of "a verbal earthly paradise, a timeless world of pure play" (DH 338), Auden more frequently wore the robes of truth-telling Prospero, striving to "disenchant and disintoxicate" (DH 27). The extent of the shift in Auden's orientation is apparent in this statement made in 1964:

In so much "serious" poetry—poetry, that is to say, which is neither pure playful song nor comic—I find an element of "theatre," of exaggerated gesture and fuss, of indifference to naked truth, which, as I get older, increasingly revolts me. This element is mercifully absent from what is conventionally called good prose. In reading the latter, one is only conscious of the truth of what is being said, and it is this consciousness which I would like what I write to arouse in a reader *first*. Before he is aware of any other qualities it may have, I want his reaction to be: "That's true.". . . To secure this effect I am prepared to sacrifice a great many poetic pleasures and excitements.[9]

By contrast, Merrill as he grows older seems increasingly willing to acknowledge explicitly that poetic pleasures and excitements are indistinguishable from truth; they *are* truth in its most valuable guise.

In denying absolute truths and accepting fiction as a substitute, Merrill aligns himself with other modernists such as Stevens. Yet his divergence from Auden is in subtler ways also a divergence from modernism. Modernist structures, though reflexively acknowledged as fiction, nonetheless attempt to hold at bay the world's disorder and frame "what is inchoate," while Merrill's often do not. He carries irony and wordplay to such extremes and so highlights the instability of linguistic signs that the world's confusion often seems to have penetrated his poetry as it is embraced and mirrored in his kaleidescopic language.

For Merrill the purpose of art's order must remain purely aesthetic, not moral, since the "truth" upon which systems of morality might be based dissolves for him into shadowy multiplicity. Art's order does not reflect laws governing the universe, but rather those governing language, which is a gorgeously flexible net of humankind's imagining. The artist's primary delight is in self-conscious manipulation of the linguistic material's shifting and blending layers. Examination of Merrill's volumes since the late 1960s will reveal in more detail how these attitudes that distinguish his work from Auden's evolved and were embodied in his mature poetry.

## II

The curious inconsistencies, the experiments and the unevenness, of the two volumes immediately preceding *Divine Comedies* and the trilogy—*The Fire Screen* (1969) and *Braving the Elements* (1972)[10]—document Merrill's development toward an acceptance that truth does not exist apart from fiction, in the face of an opposing desire to establish, as Auden does, a far more straightforward and simple relation between his poetic language and the actual or the "naked truth."

"Friend of the Fourth Decade" (FS 4–9), the opening poem of *The Fire Screen* (excepting the brief invocation with which Merrill customarily opens his collections) announces the more simply referential idea of language that the book will explore, while suggesting, too, its inevitable inadequacy for Merrill. The speaker's alter ego friend finds himself tired of the familiar world governed by manners and by masking—weary of his sophisticated understanding of social nuance, and of all the hypocritical pretense and deception disguised by polite interactions: "knowing / / just what clammy twitchings thrive / Under such cold flat stones / / As We-are-profoundly-honored-to-have-with-us / Or This-street-has-been-torn-up-for-your-convenience." Consequently, he has determined to start a new life in foreign countries where verbal nuance will be totally lost on him, where he intends to learn only enough of the language to "ask for food and love." Before embarking, he erases the ink from his collection of postcards, eradicating the messages that bind him to his past. His aim is to establish a relation to the actual material world in which objects, creatures, sensations will be primary, "Rinsed of the word." The narrator is envious of his friend; inspired to attempt the same liberation, he, however, is less successful in cleansing his postcard's scenes either of words (his mother's) or of memories. His attempt and his failure enact on a smaller scale the course of the larger experiment of the volume's writing—an experiment symbolized also in the love affair between Merrill and Strato that is chronicled in a number of the poems.

"To My Greek" (FS 19–21) finds Merrill's speaker not as far east as his friend's "dung-and-emerald oasis," but as far away as Greece, where he and his Greek lover (Strato) avoid learning words for abstractions like "justice, grief, convention." They limit the terms of their interaction to the material (except for the word "Forbidden") and sensual—"Salt Kiss Wardrobe Foot Cloud Peach"—and to the immediate present. This Edenic "way of little knowledge" is new to Merrill, and he prays to sustain it, using figures of nakedness that contrast with his usual images of masking: He implores, "under my skin stay nude," "[let] The barest word be what I say in you." (The same imagery recurs in "More Enterprise"; living in Greece, the speaker discards his "swank" suit and Roman shoes for the "scant wardrobe of gesture.") For Merrill this sort of interaction, so unmediated by the veils and double meanings of cultivated language, is entirely fresh, lending a "rainbow edge" to experience.

Merrill's speakers have frequently suffered from a sense of unreality or estrangement from reality. The protagonists of his novels provide particularly obvious examples. Francis Tanning in *The Seraglio*, for instance, considers his having always had access to money as having deprived him of a sense of either his own or the world's reality; Sandy in *The (Diblos) Notebook*, for whom life and fiction are interchangeable, is paralyzed by a deadly detachment from reality. Strato suffers no such debilitating skepticism or self-consciousness; his sensibility—crude, direct, raucous, even (in "The Envoys") brutal— seems the opposite of Merrill's. Later, in the O section of "Ephraim," Strato's animal nature is underscored as he is revealed to be in his first human incarnation, having previously been a cat. Merrill explains his attachment: "(This being seldom in my line to feel, / I most love those for whom the world is real)" (DC 95). In "To My Greek" we sense Merrill's hope that the liaison with Strato may permit a shift in his own orientation toward the world.

Yet even in the most glorious days of their romance, he fears for their future and recognizes that "the sibyl I turn to / / When all else fails me, when you do" remains the "mother tongue" in all her elegant subtlety. Aware that his lover lacks "her blessing"—and aware that she is a virago— he dreams of doing away with her, knowing full well that his ties to her will prove more lasting than those binding him to the "Radiant dumbbell" he now adores. Sure enough, "Flying from Byzantium" (FS 29–31), the poem describing the lovers' parting and the searing pain Merrill experiences as he flies alone back across the Atlantic, ends with him praying to his Mother—that is, to the woman who bore him (and to whom he is so

Oedipally attached), to the homeland, and, most of all, to the mother tongue—for help upon his return to her. He prays now to be removed from life, particularly from physical sensation, and retreats from being one who experiences directly to being one who, well distanced, writes about experience: "Far off a young scribe turned a fresh / Page, hesitated, dipped his pen." Again in "Mornings in a New House" (FS 40–1), when the lovers have broken up and the speaker is left "a cold man," he protects himself from further wounds as "Habit arranges the fire screen." Inevitably, he reverts to reliance upon something inherited from his mother—here, an elaborately embroidered design to be placed between him and the flames, preventing direct sensation of passion's heat. He has had to abandon the attempt to remove his masks.

This is not to say that Merrill's love affair with man-as-animal or word-as-thing has simply ended once and for all. He has, however, learned from experience the dangers of oversimplification. In a 1972 review of Francis Ponge's *Things* and *The Voice of Things* Merrill carefully qualified his attraction to experience stripped of the swaddling of ideas, abstractions, and fanciful wordplay.[11] Agreeing with Ponge's expression of disappointment with ideas because they so easily procure consent, "produc[ing] no pleasure in me but rather a kind of queasiness, a nausea," Merrill extends Ponge's logic:

> No thoughts, then, but in things? True enough, so long as the notorious phrase argues not for the suppression of thought but for its oneness with whatever in the world—pine woods, spider, cigarette—gave rise to it. Turn the phrase around, you arrive no less at truth: no things but in thoughts. Was the apricot any more *real* without a mind to consider it, whether this poet's or that starving goat's? We'll never know.

Later, again elaborating a point of Ponge's, Merrill asserts, "For a thought is after all a thing of sorts. Its density, color, weight, etc., vary according to the thinker, to the symbols at his command, or at whose command he thinks. One would hardly care so much for language if this were not the case." The poet, recreating things in words and using objects to reflect thoughts, must love both. Merrill senses, however, that writers of his historical era are likely to forfeit resources of language to retain the admirable honesty of "the barest word." This he laments: "Even today, how many poets choose the holy poverty of some second-hand diction, pure dull content in translation from a never-to-be-known original. 'There is no wing like meaning,' said Stevens. Two are needed to get off the ground." The other wing, balancing that of mere content (or doubling the content with a second meaning generated by wordplay), is feathered with "fantastic gaiety and invention." Merrill turns his attention to that more decorative means of flight in the closing poems of *The Fire Screen*.

Several of these poems deal with the opera, symbol of a very different relation of language to life than that represented by Strato. Taking now less interest in the denotative power of words than either Auden or Strato would, Merrill focuses on music's "sound of sheer feeling—as opposed to that of sense, of verbal sense."[12] The sonnet sequence "Matinees" (FS 47–51) is a formal twin to "Friend of the Fourth Decade"; both are composed of eight sonnets, though appropriately only "Matinees" follows the sonnet's formal rhyme scheme. The structural parallel alerts us that "Matinees" describes another solution to the tedium the friend described, an alternative to stripping away the "swaddlings" of civilization and the refined rites of language: costume rather than nakedness.

"Matinees" depicts Merrill's introduction to opera at age eleven and opera's effect on his life since, thereby exploring the powers and purposes of an elaborately costumed art. Alluding to Yeats's "Sailing to Byzantium" ("Soul clap its hands and sing, and louder sing"), Merrill sketches his own ideal "artifice of eternity" as a fiery operatic extravaganza:

> Soul will cough blood and sing, and softer sing,
> Drink poison, breathe her joyous last, a waltz
> Rubato from his arms who sobs and stays
>
> Behind, death after death, who fairly melts
> Watching her turn from him, restored, to fling
> Kisses into the furnace roaring praise.

The singing masters of his soul are just that, singers, and unlike Yeats's need not be sages. Adopting their operatic perspective in this world lends the vibrance of passion to ordinary routines, "Tongues flickering up from humdrum incident."

Merrill's attitude toward the theatrical diverges from Auden's here. While Auden would delight as much as Merrill in such enlivening embellishment, he would probably be less comfortable with the (a)moral effects Merrill laughingly flaunts:

> The point thereafter was to arrange for one's
> Own chills and fever, passions and betrayals,
> Chiefly in order to make song of them.

For Auden, it is one thing to embellish with song experiences that would otherwise seem drab or painful; it is another to direct significant events so that they may better serve art's purpose, that is, to make "a religion of the aesthetic."[13] Well aware of his own temptation toward aestheticism, Auden has labeled such religion an "error" (and has identified both Merrill's hero Proust and Baudelaire as men who never got beyond that mistake).

Where Auden would caution us against identifying art with life, Merrill encourages their confusion; after all, the passions of opera, however gratuitously evoked, have "fed his solitary heart" in youth and have left him in later years with a large repertoire of grandly romantic scores, "Old beauties" (referring to both the former lovers and the plots he enacted with them) ready to be replayed in memory. Thus, in the second section of "The Opera Company," Merrill savors a union possible only in art, not in life: In a recording ("low fidelity," he puns) the voices of his two favorite sopranos merge in gorgeous harmony, although their relations in life were characterized only by antipathy and discord. No doubt Auden, too, would have savored the recorded performance, but Merrill differs from the older poet in his refusal to proclaim one version of the singers' relation as more true, more real than the other; similarly, he hedges:

> Dependably for either [soprano], every night
> Tenors had sobbed their hearts out, grates
> Fluttering with strips of red and orange paper.
> Such fires were fiction? Then explain
> These ashes if you please.[14]

For Merrill, opera is perhaps the ideal art because it combines verbal sense with the musical sense of feeling, thereby attaining far greater expressive power than words alone. Recalling in an interview why his first grand opera seemed "the most marvelous thing on earth," Merrill explained, "It was the way it could heighten and stylize the emotions—a kind of absurdity dignified by the music, or transformed by the music. There seemed to be nothing that couldn't be expressed in opera."[15] He was particularly excited by "the sense of a feeling that could be expressed without any particular attention to words."[16] Suggesting the symbolist allegiance he shares with Stevens, but not with Auden, he declared, "Words just aren't that meaningful in themselves. *De la musique avant toute chose.*"[17]

Auden's emphasis contrasts:

> through listening to music I have learned much about how to organize a poem, how to obtain variety and contrast through change of tone, tempo, and rhythm, though I could not say just how. Man is an analogy-drawing animal; that is his great good fortune. His danger is of treating analogies as identities, of saying, for instance, "Poetry should be as much like music as possible." I suspect that the people who are most likely to say this are the tone-deaf. (DH 51–2)

He has explained: "One can speak of verbal 'music' [in poetry] so long as one remembers that the sound of words is inseparable from their meaning. The notes in music do not denote anything."[18] One reason Auden valued the experience of translating opera libretti was that the activity "will cure us of the heresy that poetry is a kind of music in which the relations of vowels and consonants have an absolute value, irrespective of the meaning of the words." (DH 499) Merrill would not claim an *absolute* value, but he does believe that poetic music can carry the sound of meaning with little attention to verbal sense.

It is not surprising, then, that Merrill should have taken some different approaches than Auden's to the play of sound in verse; again the difference between the two is that between a poet who wishes to enchant and one who strives to disenchant. While both men are inventive rhymers, exceptionally skillful in controlling rhythm and in weaving elaborate patterns with their vowels, Merrill's sound play is far more obviously lavish and more pronouncedly sensual than Auden's. Even his relatively unlyrical passages ravish us with their music. The opening lines of "In Monument Valley," for instance, serve the prosaic function of locating the poem's action:

> One spring twilight, during a lull in the war,
> At Shoup's farm south of Troy, I last rode horseback.
> Stillnesses were swarming inward from the evening star
> Or outward from the buoyant sorrel mare. (BE 10)

Yet the lulling balance of motion in and out, of the beginning that is spring and the end that is twilight, is sounded for us in Merrill's balancing reversal of vowels near the quatrain's middle—"swarming inward"—and by the echoing sounds preceding and following—war, were, outward, sorrel, mare. Where Merrill's music is more ostentatious than this, his model often seems to be Stevens' exotic vocabulary and chiming consonants, e.g., "Tones / Jangling whose tuner slept, moon's camphor mist / / On the parterre compounding / Chromatic muddles which the limpid trot / Flew to construe" (BE 25). Lines like those make more musical than verbal sense; they communicate with the opera singer's resources rather than the orator's.

They also demonstrate Merrill's appreciation for "clotted poetry" like Mallarmé's. Discussing such poetry Merrill admitted, "I occasionally still work in trying to produce a poem that resists the intelligence almost successfully, as Stevens said."[19] The purpose of this effort is to make the poem more open to the feelings and the subconscious of both writer and reader. Stevens' intoxicating language provides one resource for such resistance of the intellect; near-surrealist privacy of reference provides another:

> Cricket earphones fail us not
> Here in the season of receptions
>
> One prism drips ammonia still
> Penknife-pearl-and-steel ripples
>
> Paring nobody's orchard to the bone. (BE 40)

A clipped telegraphic mode provides yet another:

> To let:
> Cream paint, brown ivy, brickflush. Eye
> Of the old journalist unwavering
>
> Through gauze. Forty-odd years gone by.
> Toy blocks. Church bells. Original vacancy.
> O deepening spring. (BE 28)

Of Merrill's volumes, none offers a heavier dose of this hermeticism than *Braving the Elements*, from which all these passages are taken; in that collection more than any other, Merrill seems intent on finding, perhaps extending, the limits of verbal music's expressive power. Reducing the referential meaning carried by words opens up other ways of, in *Sandover*'s phrase, "making sense of it": If the denotative sense of our language seems feeble because of the uncertainty of our grasp on "reality," a strong sensory experience of the sounds of words can provide some very real compensation. One can at least "[Come] to [one's] senses through a work of art" (BE 68).

The patterns of his poems' lush sounds are stylistic evidence of Merrill's sense that what one experiences as most real may be most fabricated. That notion becomes the central theme of one of the finest poems in *Braving the Elements*, "Days of 1935" (BE 11–21). Even the poem's method depends on regarding fable as fact, for this is one of two ballads in which Merrill presents his personal history in fantastic form.[20] (The other is "The Summer People," with which *The Fire Screen* concludes. In that poem the half-mythical character Jack Frost is half-Merrill—a doodling artist in a Greek revival New England town who looks younger than his years, who loves cats, four-hand piano, and bridge, and who enjoys spending money on food and drink and flowers.) "Days of 1935" narrates the fantasies of Merrill's lonely wealthy boyhood, when he would compensate for the absence of parents and playmates by imagining the companionship he longed for. His dreams took the "plausible" form of kidnapping, imitating the capture of the Lindbergh baby; yet he is abducted not merely by the man he imagines, that "masked and crouching form," but by imagination itself:

> Then sheer imagination ride[s]
> Off with us in its old jalopy,
> Trailing bedclothes like a bride
> Timorous but happy.

The world imagined by the boy is less mystifying than the one he actually inhabits; his mind boggles wondering about his parents: "was it true he loved / Others beside her?" "Eerie, speaking likenesses," he says, referring to his parents' imaginary photos in the newspaper, but suggesting too the almost ghostly unreality his parents possess for him. In such an inexplicable, disconcerting world, what becomes most real is precisely what is imagined: "Tingling I hugged my pillow. *Pluck* / Some deep nerve went. I knew / / That life was fiction in disguise." By similar logic, the boy's highest moment in the imagined drama occurs when Jean, that "lady out of *Silver Screen*," asks him to tell her stories: "Real stories—but not real, I mean. / Not just dumb things people did." Even his captor recognizes that stories are more real than ordinary life. The little boy who fantasizes for his emotional survival is, like Scheherazade, one who lives by storytelling. As he recounts tale after tale—"Wunspontime, I said and said . . ."—he thinks, "Who knows but that our very lives / Depend on such an hour."

Nor is his dependency on the disguised life of fiction limited to his childhood. The adult who looks back upon the fantasy (in the section beginning "Grown up, he thinks how") finds himself carried away by love as he once was by "sheer imagination." If the adult's romances seem less like fairy tales or glamorous movies ("Tehuantepec," "Belshazzar's Feast"), that is only because their creator takes more care to ground them in "fact" with his "fine / Realistic touch." As a grown lover, once again he is taken in fortunate captivity ("Captivity . . . will set you free"), driven far enough to be liberated from the controlling powers of the superego—embodied especially in his mother's "Grade / A controls" and his father's wealth—far enough "To stitch with delicate kid stuff / His shoddy middle age." Moreover, there is a clear continuity between the homosexuality of the child's erotic fantasies involving Floyd (whose name brings to mind the legendary "Pretty Boy Floyd") and the adult's behavior: "I / Will relive some things he did / Until I die, until I die."

Details of the poem suggest that neither the child who acts out his dreams while sleepwalking nor the man who wills himself captive to myths of love is idiosyncratic in confusing life with fiction. Our entire culture decorates kitchen walls with "board / Painted like board. Its grain / / Shiny buff on cinnamon / Mimics the real, the finer grain." What exactly is finer here? The "real" grain of the board hidden under the paint and recreated by it, or the "real" grain of some imagined board thought to be imitated in paint? Such sleight-of-hand decor relies as much on "A golden haze / Past belief, past disbelief" as does any child's, or lover's, "true to life" fantasy.

"Past belief, past disbelief"—we have entered the challenging mode of paradox, a central device in Merrill's work, most obviously in his late volumes. Paradox, of course, was often used by the modernists as they sought to display multiple perspectives, to reveal complexity and not reduce it. Merrill, in using paradox not as a way of containing multifaceted truths but as a way of fostering fluid, open-ended transformations, offers a characteristically contemporary slant on this trope. When asked about his fondness for paradox, Merrill explained, "I suppose that early on I began to understand the relativity, even the reversability of truths." After mentioning some situations in his childhood that might have made him see "there was truth on both sides," Merrill suggests a more fundamental source than biography for his delight in phrases like "Au fond each summit is a cul de sac":

> I believe the secret lies primarily in the nature of poetry—and of science, too, for that matter—and that the ability to see both ways at once isn't merely an idiosyncrasy but corresponds to how the world needs to be seen: cheerful *and* awful [he alludes to the close of Bishop's "The Bight," "awful but cheerful"], opaque *and* transparent. The plus and minus signs of a vast evolving formula.[21]

If science and poetry represent two evolving sides of knowledge, both are true, and consideration of either leads us to the paradoxically double nature of reality as something both created and discovered. This idea recurs often in Merrill's recent works; for instance, it provides the serious underpinnings beneath all the lighthearted paradoxes—for example, that Merrill's goddaughter's clothes are "Priced inversely to their tininess," that a mere baby should be a weighty burden for him, that his finally becoming a parent of sorts seems to coincide with the incipience of his own second childhood—presented with half-genial, half-grudging humor in "Verse for Urania" (DC 30–6). Because his godchild is being named for a science—one "whose elements cause vertigo / Even, I fancy, in a specialist"—Merrill can make it clear that mythmaking, like truth-telling, is as much the province of science as of art. Contemplating primitive astronomy's assignment of names and explanatory tales to the constellations, Merrill suggests (with an almost Wordsworthian hint of the child trailing clouds of glory) that a few of those names reflect some essential knowledge instinctively the child's:

> From out there notions reach us yet, but few
> And far between as those first names we knew
> Already without having to look up,
> Children that we were, the Chair, the Cup,
> But each night dimmer, children that we are,
> Each night regressing, dumber by a star.
> Still, fiction helps preserve them, those old truths
> Our sleights have turned to fairy tales.

At the same time, those "old truths" we are somehow given to know are also sheer invention, orders imposed by "our wisest apes" who "Stared the random starlight into shapes." The same paradox characterizes poetry:

> Take, for that matter, my beanstalk couplet, above,
> Where such considerations as rhyme and meter

> Prevail, it might be felt, at the expense
> Of meaning, but as well create, survive it;
> For the first myth was Measure.

Thus, near the poem's close when Merrill pleads, "help me to conceive / That fixed, imaginary, starless pole / Of the ecliptic which this one we steer by / Circles," the term "conceive" has two very different meanings: He is asking for a more encompassing understanding of what already exists, and he is asking to invent a fiction. What he wishes to conceive, designated by our phrase "true north," is real *and* imaginary.


# III


In differentiating Merrill's sense of doubleness from Auden's, I have suggested that while Auden tries to hold side by side two seemingly contradictory aspects of actuality—e.g., that each person has a body and an intellect, that people are unique individuals and undifferentiated members of a species—Merrill's double focus takes in the fictional and the "actual." Moreover, I have argued that while Auden believes that a single overriding Truth and Order govern our universe, Merrill is skeptical about the reality of the actual or of its apparent orders. More like Stevens than Auden, he therefore embraces the imagined and the beautiful as substitutes for possibly nonexistent truth. A third difference is now emerging, one in which Merrill's stance is characteristically contemporary: that while Auden's doubleness (or other modernists' multiplicity) aims for a stabilizing balance of contradictory views, Merrill's involves dazzlingly fluid movement, constant expansion, contraction, inversion of perspective, simultaneous multiplications and mergings of meanings and identities. "Yánnina" (DC 259), from *Divine Comedies*, will demonstrate further.

According to a revealing interview conducted by David Kalstone, Merrill composed the poem having in mind the theme of "a double life"—that is, the kind of life undertaken by the "Friend of the Fourth Decade," and less dramatically by Merrill, who divided his time between Stonington and Athens.[22] The poem's genesis was, one might say, "operatic" in that things were done, passions induced, just for the sake of having something beautiful to sing about. The poet arrived at Yánnina equipped with some knowledge of its lore and history, and with a hope of finding something to write about: "I didn't spend twenty-four hours on the spot. But the piano had been prepared, and only the notation remained. That whole element—do we dare call it reality?—had to be unforeseeable, accidental, something to fill in then and there." The events of those twenty-odd hours were "experience[d] in the light of a projected emotion, like a beam into which what you encounter will seem to have strayed." In this sort of creation—the notion is by now familiar—"the poem and its occasion will have created one another," with neither one more real nor more an imitation than the other. As we have by now come to expect, Merrill in writing about that occasion tried to let the "succession of scenes convey not meaning so much as a sense of it," hoping to create that deliciously operatic sense "that something both is, and isn't, being said."

As is true, though less obviously, of so much of Merrill's work, an atmosphere of unreality, or half-reality, pervades the scene. The geographically actual city of Yánnina is portrayed also as a realm of dreams where all people are somnambulists. The sun, too, sleepwalks, and the speaker himself seems to doze off in midphrase: "But right now she's asleep, as who is not, as who . . ." Drowsiness spreads even to the reader, who doubles for the speaker's companion, so that the speaker must ask, "Awake?" In this situation the condition of the dead becomes indistinguishable from that of the living: The old Turk by the water, presumably a statue, sleeps too, as does Frossíni, centuries drowned.

Paradoxically, the most active figures are those fixed in works of art. The postcard of "Kyra Frossíni's Drown" seems as immediate as Bishop's depiction of the moment when a boathook catches her traveling companion's skirt. In Merrill's description of the card, "A devil (turban and moustache and sword) / Chucks the pious matron overboard— / Wait—heaven help us—SPLASH!" Art takes on the immediacy of life, and conversely the living are distanced through comparison with artworks; for example, men are selling crayfish scarlet "as the sins in any fin-de-siècle villanelle." In another paradox, historical figures, whether or not depicted in sculpture or painting, seem present (as they do most obviously in *Sandover*)—"It's him, Ali. The end is near," or "Byron has visited. He likes / The luxe." Yet at the same time the poem emphasizes transcience—particularly of its two versions of the feminine, one "brief as a bubble," the other "gone up no less in smoke." We are being forced into seeing "both ways at once," absorbing the notion of "the reversibility of truths."

Byron's presence in the poem—along with the speaker's preoccupation with the oblivion of sleep, death, or love-death—evokes the Romantic poets' reluctant admission of our inability to have it both ways. They acknowledged the impossibility of enjoying both death's permanence and sensation's intensity. Almost smugly, Merrill contemplates the Romantics' dreamy death wish "in full feather." Jokingly extending the figure with several bird images (ravens, pigeons, doves), his passage culminates with an allusion to the questions that conclude "Ode to a Nightingale": "The brave old world sleeps. Are we what it dreams / And is a rude awakening overdue?" But Merrill's fancy, unlike Keats', deceives as well as she is said to, permitting him the comfort of continued sleep and dream. At the end of the poem, Merrill does not plummet to the earth, like the unfortunate Keats; instead he invites his companion, who seems to have been hurt by love or parting, to take his arm and dare with him "the magician's tent"—that is, the space of art. There, what is torn in two heals again (recalling Bishop's desire for the dissolution of dichotomies). "The magician," Merrill explained in the interview, "performs the essential act. He heals what he has divided. A double-edged action, like his sword. It's what one comes to feel that life keeps doing."[23] The poem's image for this double-edged action is a constant "scissoring and mending" taking place in the water as Ali's barge and its reflection (which is also its rendering in art's mirror) travel "outward and away." Doubleness, though inescapable, is at the same time continually being eradicated, particularly by art's "mending" magic.

To the extent that Merrill is willing to point to *a truth*, it is the same one that preoccupies the other contemporary poets whose work we have examined: process. Perhaps in Merrill's case, the proper term for his sense of continuous transformation would be the literary one, "translation," that figures so importantly in his great poem, "Lost in Translation." In that lyric Merrill is less concerned with translation as product, an achieved version in another language (Rilke's version of Valéry's text), than with translation as action, as the transformational process described in both poets' versions of that poem about a palm. Even when considering the translated poem, Merrill focuses on the action of its translator, who is imagined making himself forgo "much of the sun-ripe original / Felicity . . . / In order to render its underlying sense" (ellipsis added). Merrill's interest is in the changes made in turning the poem from the "warm Romance" language French into the cool starkness of German. And while most of the poem concerns memories of the distant past—primarily of the summer when his parents divorced—these past events are not fixed, beyond translation. To remember the past is to make it active in the present and to find it changing, just as the speaker's recent experience with a medium and a puzzle piece changes his sense of his boyhood's many puzzles. Thus, as is appropriate for a poem about translation, the poem's conclusion takes the insistently ongoing present tense:

> But nothing's lost. Or else: all is translation
> And every bit of us is lost in it
> (Or found—I wander through the ruin of S
> Now and then, wondering at the peacefulness)
> And in that loss a self-effacing tree,
> Color of context, imperceptibly
> Rustling with its angel, turns the waste
> To shade and fiber, milk and memory.

For Merrill, all art acts as the coconut palm does, translating loss, absence, waste into something substantial and nourishing.

One meaning of the verb "to translate" is "to express one thing in terms of another." That is also a standard definition of the action of metaphor. In Merrill's oeuvre the text most obviously concerned with the process of translation, and with the action of metaphor, is his trilogy, *The Changing Light at Sandover.*

## IV

Warning against an approach to the trilogy that is "too doggedly literal," Judith Moffett has invoked a useful distinction: "its Message and its meaning are not the same."[24] I would go further and assert that much of the epic's liveliness derives from the radical difference, and the resulting tension, between the two. The message—even though not entirely consistent and though subject to revision—emphasizes determinism, permanent dualisms, rigid hierarchy, and absolutes. The meaning, as I understand it, evolves largely from the poem's metaphorical method and involves "unrelenting fluency," fluidity, relativism, and free play. The differences between message and meaning are essentially those I have been outlining between Auden and Merrill; consequently, if one reads the trilogy with Merrill's divergence from Auden in mind, one can understand the conflicts enacted in the work's structure and method as reflecting the nature and processes of that divergence.

The doses of message administered in the first installment, "The Book of Ephraim," are light, pleasantly sweetened by the skepticism of Merrill and Jackson and by the wit of their familiar spirit. The medicine becomes less palatable early in *Mirabell* when the poet is informed, "ABSOLUTES ARE NOW NEEDED   YOU MUST MAKE GOD OF SCIENCE" (M 19). The voices of 40070, 40076, and 741 (later Mirabell) then provide instruction about the nature and history of the universe by translating their mathematical formulas into terms more or less appropriate to their audience. Mirabell, who most successfully learns the manners and affection that ease communication with humans, explains:

> THUS MATH ENCAPSULATES COMPLEX TRUTHS WHICH AS WITH
> OUR 1ST MEANINGLESS TO U & THERE 4 FRIGHTENING VOICES MUST
> BE RENDERED INTO YR VOCABULARY OF MANNERS (M 130)

The bats' outline of cosmic history, adapted for JM's and DJ's consumption, evokes many legends of Western tradition, but is proclaimed accurate none-theless, since "ALL LEGENDS ARE ROOTED IN TRUTH" (M 68). Centaurs, for example, preceded and evolved into dinosaurs; the Faust legend derives from the actual history of Pope Innocent VI; the evil released by the fallen angels of Christian mythology was in fact atomic energy. Similarly, it turns out

that "IN THE BEGINNING WAS THE WORD" was one man's response to "THE
UNEARTHLY MUSIC OF THE SINGLENOTED ATOM" (M 149), and Dante's
glimpse of God as a brilliant point of light surrounded by concentric rings
of halos (*Paradiso*, XXVII) was a vision looking "INTO THE ATOM'S EYE"
(M 38).[25] Thus, according to the trilogy's message, the truth does exist and,
though veiled by the metaphors and images human limitations dictate, is
revealed to the extent that humans can benefit from knowing it. Sometimes
the Ouija board's metaphors are even translated by those of higher rank and
greater understanding so that their truth will be more accessible to JM and
DJ. Maria, for instance, interprets:

> THESE MYTHS THAT ANTECEDE ALL MYTH ARE COUCHED
> IN DAUNTING GENERALITIES. FOR MICHAEL/SUN
> READ: GENERATIVE FORCE. FOR GENERATIVE FORCE
> READ: RADIATION TO THE BILLIONTH POWER
> OF EXPLODING ATOMS. FOR EMMANUEL,
> H2O. FOR SEEDS, THAT COSMIC DUST
> LADEN WITH PARTICLES OF INERT MATTER.
> FOR GOD READ: GOD. (S 106)

She suggests that while God is not a metaphor, most of the lessons' terms
are metaphors with identifiable referents.

Knowing that his epic's creatures—unicorns, fallen angels, and so
forth—are metaphors standing for atomic formulas, Merrill several times
has to be reassured that he need not render them in their true numbers and
"MAKE A JOYLESS THING / OF IT THRU SUCH REDUCTIVE REASONING" (S
179–80). Metaphor is the poet's permitted freedom, though his proclaimed
discomfort with it persists. JM often appears troubled by the shifting scale
of the board's accumulating metaphors. Early in *Mirabell* he begs the voices
to "Speak without metaphor. / Help me to drown the double-entry book /
I've kept these fifty years" and complains "It's too much to be batwing
angels *and* / inside the atom, don't you understand?" (M 28). He questions
why, having nearly convinced us that their works "include / Ancient happen-
ings of a magnitude / Such that we still visit their untoppled / Bones in
England, Egypt, and Peru," the bats should then

> Imply that we must also read your story
> As a parable of developments
> Remoter yet, at matter's very heart?
> Are we to be of two minds, each nonplussed
> By the other's vast (or tiny) scale?
> Are we to take as metaphor your "crust
> World"—for, say, the brain's evolving cortex?
> Or for that "froth of electrons" locked within
> Whose depths revolve the nuclear Yang and Yin? (M 31–2)

The answer, an approving "HEAD OF CLASS." JM and DJ are to accept their peacock as "both a subatomic x / *And* a great glaring bugaboo"; no doubt they are better equipped to do so since Merrill had already determined many years and poems earlier "That anything worth having's had both ways" (M 80). To further complicate *Sandover*'s doubling of scale, the grand design spelled out by the bats in *Mirabell* and the angels in *Scripts* involves a great many dualisms, among them white and black, matter and antimatter, positive and negative electric charges, God B and the monitor. All these exist in parallel situations of precarious balance. The resistance the paired entities offer one another (their "pressing back," to use Stevens' formulation that Merrill favors) is a universal impulse, operative on all scales. Consequently, when JM asks near the end of *Scripts*

> When we suppose that history's great worm
> Turns and turns as it does because of twin
> Forces balanced and alert within
> Any least atom, are we getting warm?

he is warmly congratulated for having "MADE SENSE OF IT" (S 196). With all its elaborate dualisms, the cosmos, as presented in the trilogy's message, is clearly and firmly ordered. In fact, the primary purpose of the bats' instruction is to warn humankind against the chaos they themselves once worshipped, i.e., the uncontrolled energy of smashed atoms. They insist that the orders, rules, and hierarchies they depict and obey have been established to prevent chaos from slipping in, to protect the inviolability of the atom. One of the most unpalatable but essential lessons they force down the throats of their human pupils is that all things affecting human history are governed by a NO ACCIDENT clause, with even humanity's resistance to that concept having been programmed.

So goes the tidy take-home message, revealing a securely ordered universe, threatened by humankind's predetermined meddling with its primary ordering unit, the atom. But the Auden-like sense of balance and consistency the message precariously achieves is not easily maintained, even on the level of pronouncement, and it is certainly undercut by the poem's method. Examining both the complicating pronouncements and the translational method, we will see that the work's multiplying levels of metaphor often cancel each other out until all that one can hold onto—as is true in much of Ashbery's work—is the process of transformation from one level to another. When Merrill dutifully recites his lessons:

> Bon. We will try to remember that you are not
> A person, not a peacock, not a bat;
> A devil least of all—an impulse only
> Here at the crossroads of our four affections

he has not fully absorbed the dynamics of the bat's meaning. Mirabell gently corrects him, "OR MAKE OF ME THE PROCESS SOMEWHERE / OPERATING BETWEEN TREE & PULP PAGE & POEM" (M 79).

Of the three installments, "The Book of Ephraim" draws the least attention to, or takes least seriously, the revelations about the systematic makeup of the cosmos. Pronouncements of message here lend themselves to interpretation as metaphorical statements not about any aspects of planetary, atomic, or supernatural reality, but about the process of artistic creation. Ephraim's scheme of reincarnation serves largely as an image for the process by which aspects of the artist's self and experience are reborn, transformed, in his successive works of art.[26] This is the point of the poem's interweaving of events from the poet's past, the lost novel, and the poet's present ongoing experience; all are different versions of the same story. Each character the artist creates is an "old self in a new form" (DC 112)—that is, a way for him to revitalize his existence, escaping once more the dreaded fixity of being "cut and dried," and a way perhaps to attain immortality. Consequently, Wallace Stevens and Carl Jung, who have identified God as the imagination and the unconscious, emerge as the book's authorities on the nature of God. Ephraim himself defines heaven as "the surround of the living" (DC 103), and his admission that heaven will vanish if humankind destroys itself (DC 100) also suggests that the mirror world is purely a human creation. Specifically, this heaven is the creation of two individuals, DJ and JM. Merrill's "Book of a Thousand and One Evenings Spent with David Jackson" celebrates not only the reincarnation of the artist in his imaginative creations, but also the continual rebirth and rejuvenation of the love and "refining passion" (here God is also Eros) between him and his chosen mate.

Keeping in mind these personal and self-reflexive aspects of the drama that sound as muted undertones in the pronounced message, we appreciate the epic's machinery as most essentially a means of self-knowledge—one which eases the erasure of conventional boundaries that limit understanding of oneself and one's mental processes. The Ouija board rituals allow an expanded perception of the self as multiple, ambiguous, fluid. The fundamental mysteries illuminated in the trilogy, then, are human, not superhuman. Thus, Merrill not only admits the possibility that the whole Ouija board rigamarole may be an elaborate "folie à deux" by which the two lovers "sound each other's depths of spirit" (DC 74); he goes further to stress the arbitrariness of the poem's frame:

> Hadn't—from books, from living—
> The profusion dawned on us, of "languages"
> Any one of which, to who could read it,
> Lit up the system it conceived?—bird-flight,
> Hallucinogen, chorale and horoscope:

> Each its own world, hypnotic, many-sided
> Facet of the universal gem.
> Ephraim's revelations—we had them
> For comfort, thrills and chills, "material."
> He didn't cavil. *He* was the revelation
> (Or if we had created him, then we were).
>
> (DC 75–6)

The parenthetic statement is an important one, echoed several times in Merrill's interviews. "If the spirits aren't external, how astonishing the mediums become!" he remarked to Vendler,[27] and to McClatchy:

> don't you think there comes a time when everyone, not just a poet, wants to get beyond the Self? To reach, if you like, the "god" within you? The board, in however clumsy or absurd a way, allows for precisely that. Or if it's still *yourself* that you're drawing upon, then that self is much stranger and freer and more far-seeing than the one you thought you knew.[28]

By giving voice to heavenly beings, old myths, dead friends, and then by allowing their identities to merge and reflect, to multiply and fuse, Merrill grows beyond a narrow sense of self, since his own sight and experience expand with those of the beings he has brought to fictive life. Although the process of expansion and contraction could—presumably does—go on indefinitely, Merrill shapes his trilogy so that the overall tendency is first to expand the cast and then to reduce it. This enables him at the end to return to the scale of his earlier lyrics, having acquired (and given his readers) a changed awareness of his creative freedom. A typical example of the epic's fluid identities is provided by the four archangels representing the four elements, who expand to twelve beings, since each has three natures, which in turn reduce to six twins. As the cast shrinks toward *Sandover's* close, we learn that the angels are also the supreme moments of "the five," one of whom is Maria (Plato), and that she in turn is all nine muses. Ephraim turns out to have been an incarnation of the archangel Michael (his only homosexual life to date). Moreover, for all history there is only one Academy (and, by implication, one audience, a select coterie of the living and the dead).

How this play with identities pertains to Merrill's sense of the self is most apparent when *Sandover's* greatest cosmic powers are unveiled as immense projections of the estranged parental figures who have loomed over Merrill's work for decades. God B and Nature (Queen Mum) are versions of the always puzzling divorcing parents of "Lost in Translation"; as Merrill had written in *Nights and Days*, "Always the same old story—Father Time and Mother Earth, / A marriage on the rocks" (ND 28) (even Eden for him "tells a parable of fission, / Lost world and broken home" [M 98]). The

Sandover Ballroom then becomes a magnified version of the one in his first Broken Home, and humankind's uncertain fate the enlargement of one boy's. We return by the trilogy's close essentially to the dramatis personae of Merrill's lyrics—the triangle of estranged parents and contested child, along with a small group of intimate friends. Yet the dynamics of *Sandover* leave us with an altered perspective so that we can regard as neither silly nor presumptuous Merrill's play upon the name of God—ABBA (Aramaic)— as designating his own favorite poetic form, the envelope quatrain.[29] Whether or not God and Merrill's art are forms of one another, they merge in undertaking the same awesome task originally identified by Stevens: pressing back against reality, holding off the darkness. Similarly, after we have for hundreds of pages experienced metaphoric levels that constantly change and identities that fuse and multiply, we do not perceive as reduction the shift into literary terminology that occurs at the climactic moment of the trilogy's plot. This is the epic's most wrenching scene, when JM and DJ must finally let go of their dead friends, Maria, Wystan, George (and soon, Robert), and send them into their new lives by breaking the mirror through which they have communicated. The double-meaning laden language with which the emotional moment is portrayed makes it a literary event:

> JM WILL TAKE THE MARBLE
> STYLUS & GIVING US THE BENEFIT
> OF A WELL AIMED WORD, SEND OUR IMAGINED SELVES
> FALLING IN SHARDS THRU THE ETERNAL WATERS
> (DJ CUPBEARER) & INTO THE GOLDEN BOUGH
> OF MYTH ON INTO LIFE (S 234)

But because we have been made to feel the power of the stylus and the substantiality of imagined beings (or the insubstantiality and fluidity of all beings, real and imaginary), Merrill's conflating the grief-filled moment on the terrace with his laborious writing of the poem no longer seems the reduction of scale or the evasion of emotion it might otherwise have seemed.

The epic's locus of power is the human intelligence, particularly as manifest in the many levels of language and meaning it can control. Early in *Scripts*, WHA predicts that "WE SHALL DISCOVER / [the angels'] POWERS ARE IN US QUITE AS MUCH AS OVER," but the statement turns out fully to apply only to the living. God B's generative light, also associated with the Archangel Michael, can be revealed only to the live humans in the cast because only the humans are capable of imagining its forms: "S/O/L [the abbreviation suggests source of light, source of life, the Latin for sun, and a phonetic spelling of soul] / IS ROOTED IN THE LIVED LIFE ONLY MAN RECEIVES GOD B'S / MAIN MAGIC: IMAGINATIVE POWER." (Elsewhere intelligence is explicitly identified as the source of light [S 14] and imagination as the element fertilizing it [S 11].)

One of the obvious ways in which humanity's divine power is dramatized in *Sandover's* composition is in Merrill's use of language to bestow appearances on the other world. We are frequently reminded that there are no appearances on the other side of the mirror (a notion JM repeatedly asks to have explained), but Merrill goes to elaborate lengths to smother that world in appearances and sensory stuff so that despite all protestations to the contrary, we retain vivid mental images of a trotting hornless unicorn nibbling green hedges, of Maria and Wystan dressed each day in different specified colors, of bats' eyes glowing with the red of "nuclear fire ache," of bat-winged forms perched around the edge of a lit-up mirror, and so forth. When the incorporeal bat 741 is translated into an equally incorporeal peacock and much is made of his gorgeous plumage, MM (a spirit who has literally neither brain nor heart) explains that he appears only "IN US    OUR MINDS (HEARTS) ARE HIS MIRROR" (M 63). The Tinkerbell sentimentality of it all (he is even temporarily de-moted to bat again with a moment of human doubt) does nothing to qualify the resulting recognition of the mind's power: We can make anything real, can sustain the life of any being, in our mind's eye and in the reflecting field of verbal intelligence.

The pretense behind the italic sections of word-painting in *Scripts* is that they are descriptions provided by MM and WHA after the events and inserted earlier by Merrill, but the pretense is thin, and intentionally so: The passages are presented as a playwright's stage directions, and the pleasure provided by all the details of gesture, light, color is once again that of sheer invention, e.g.:

> *At a light footstep all profoundly bow.*
>
> *Enter—in a smart white summer dress,*
> *Ca. 1900, discreetly bustled,*
> *Trimmed if at all with a fluttering black bow;*
> *Black ribbon round her throat; a cameo;*
> *Gloved but hatless, almost hurrying*
> *—At last! the chatelaine of Sandover—*
> *A woman instantly adorable.* (S 125)

We know it is all a manner of speaking, but such writing makes us feel in "the theatre of the blood" how language overpowers "naked truth," creating fable that *is* fact.

While Merrill's play with heavenly appearances often seems sheer camp indulgence, the trilogy's involvement with death and loss reminds us of more essential applications of God B's main magic, in coping with death. Thus, in "Ephraim" section R, an elegy for Maya, the poet is to transform the hellish heat of a painful September and "remake it all into slant, weightless gold: / Wreath at funeral games for the illusion / That whatever had been, had been right" (DC 107). Auden's faith that "whatever is, is right" is inaccessible to Merrill, but for him the artist's role is to revise the appearances of our world to bring us moments of such consoling belief. It is immaterial whether art's recouping of losses is, as DJ suggests, just lies (S 53)—the point is to provide "A WAY OF TELLING THAT INSPIRES BELIEF" (M 112).

Given the outrageousness of the trilogy's Ouija board format, the reader's belief can be only momentary inspiration, not lasting credence— and Merrill would have it so, for all his show of didacticism. Belief here, as in the postmodern perspective generally, is necessarily provisional and processive, as Bishop says, "flowing, and flown." It would be an error to read the progressive revisions of message in the trilogy as closer and closer approaches to *the* truth, despite hints to that effect (apologetic dismissals of previous "satellite truths," "partial fictions," "pearlgray lies," "small charades" that were supposedly necessary means of breaking the truth gradually to mere humans).[30] The revised messages, as much as the earlier ones, remain metaphors, enlarging perhaps with the poet's increasing confidence and daring; they ask of us not simple credulity, but "yes & no." DJ and JM enact a model renunciation of fixed certainty in "The Higher Keys" when they determine not to rendezvous with Maria (reincarnate as an Indian scientist-to-be) in 1991, as they had previously arranged:

> Worse yet, my dear, what if in fact
> Two old parties tottering through Bombay
> Should be accosted, on the given day,
> By Plato posing as a teenage guide?
> What if The Whole of It were verified?
>
> No, henceforth we'll be more and more alone.
>
> (CLS 539–40)

The work demands tolerance of uncertainty as well as resistance to outmoded absolutes and firm boundaries. Merrill's "characters, this motley alphabet, / Engagingly evade the cul-de-sac / Of the Whole Point" while remaining nevertheless "drawn by it."

By clownishly signalling many of his epic's metaphors with (m), Merrill heightens our awareness of the provisional, self-created, and mercurial nature of our truths. His parenthetic letter, instead of signalling an anxiety, allows us to anticipate delightful surprises. The wonder of language—humanity's home and highest achievement (or, more metaphorically, "MANS TERMITE PALACE BEEHIVE ANTHILL PYRAMID" as well as his "liferaft")—is its "unrelenting fluency." Despite all the epic's lessons in hierarchy, its energizing principles turn out to be continuity, flux, and synthesis—continuity between anima and animal, between dead and living, real and imaginary, self and other. The entire poem celebrates Merrill's having outgrown his youthful desire for secure distinctions, for "remission of their synthesis" (a nostalgic desire retained by many modernists facing uncertainty and disorder). Our bicameral minds and the poems they generate operate as puns do—simultaneously contracting or imploding several meanings into one statement and expanding or exploding one statement into many; the process in Merrill's hands is a liberating one and also evidence of human liberty. Both the mirror and the Ouija board are fields of reflection, which is to say they dramatize the action of the thinking mind. That dramatization is only possible with metaphor and other figures of speech that point two or more ways at once. It is the final paradox of Merrill's paradox-packed epic that its ostensibly deterministic frame should contain a vast anti-scheme so empowering of humankind: "The setting nothing, but the scope revealed / As infinite, for *Light* is everywhere, / Awaits the words that clothe it—which we wield" (S 201).

## Notes

1. Auden frequently quoted the passage (see, for example, DH 61); he made this claim in "An Unpublished Interview" conducted by Walter Kerr in 1953, published in the special Auden issue of *Harvard Advocate*, 108 (Fall 1966): 35. The passage from *The Waves* is reproduced as quoted in that interview.
   The following abbreviations for Auden's works appear as parenthetic citations in this essay:

   DH  *The Dyer's Hand and Other Essays* (1968; reprint, New York: Vintage Books, 1972)
   CP  *Collected Poems*, ed. Edward Mendelson (New York: Random House, 1976).

2. "W. H. Auden," *Writers at Work: The Paris Review Interviews*, fourth series, ed. George Plimpton (New York: Viking Press, 1976), p. 257.
3. He announced his belief in the Devil in "W. H. Auden," *Writers at Work*, p. 268.
4. Helen Vendler, "James Merrill's Myth: An Interview," *New York Review of Books*, 3 May 1979, p. 12.
5. Labrie, "James Merrill at Home," pp. 30, 31.
6. "The Art of Poetry," p. 200.
7. See Merrill's statement on language and reality in "The Art of Poetry," pp. 196–7.
8. *Early Auden*, p. 21.
9. Ostroff, "The Contemporary Poet as Artist and Critic," pp. 185–6.
10. The following abbreviations appear as parenthetic citations in this essay:

    WS  *Water Street* (New York: Atheneum, 1962)
    ND  *Nights and Days* (New York: Atheneum, 1966)
    FS  *The Fire Screen* (New York: Atheneum, 1969)

BE       *Braving the Elements* (New York: Atheneum, 1973)
DC       *Divine Comedies* (New York, Atheneum, 1977)
M        *Mirabell: Books of Number* (New York, Atheneum, 1978)
S        *Scripts for the Pageant* (New York, Atheneum, 1980)
CLS      *The Changing Light at Sandover* (New York, Atheneum, 1982)—cited only
         for quotes from *Coda: The Higher Keys*

11.   Quotations in this paragraph are from that review, "Object Lessons," *New York Review of Books*, November 1972, pp. 31, 32.

12.   Sheehan, "An Interview," p. 146.

13.   Critics of Auden's work commonly remark on the doubleness of his allegiances: John Blair, for instance, discusses "a tension between moral seriousness and the inescapable amorality of poetic artifice" (*The Poetic Art of W. H. Auden*, p. 11), and Mendelson remarks on the poetry's "commitment to fact and its deliberate artifice" (*Early Auden*, p. xiv).

14.   Auden does acknowledge the truth of opera's portrait of human willfulness; see "Notes on Music and Opera" (DH). Blair quotes from an article in *Vogue*, 1948, in which Auden suggests that one respond to opera by thinking, " 'What psychological insight to construct so many plots around one or the other of the two most uniquely human acts, laying down one's life for one's friend and cutting off one's nose to spite one's face. How realistic to show that, whatever it may be in between, life at its best and its worst is a *performance* that defies common sense.' " (pp. 162–3). To say that opera is "realistic" in this sense, however, is not to deny that its fires are purely fictional.

15.   Labrie, "James Merrill at Home," p. 24–5.

16.   Sheehan, "An Interview," pp. 144–5.

17.   Ibid., p. 146.

18.   "W. H. Auden," *Writers at Work*, p. 263.

19.   Labrie, "James Merrill at Home," p. 23.

20.   The literary ballad had been recently revitalized both by Auden in his late thirties diagnoses of psychological cripples like "Miss Gee," "James Honeyman," and "Victor," and by Elizabeth Bishop in "The Burglar of Babylon."

21.   McClatchy, "The Art of Poetry," p. 215.

22.   Kalstone, "The Poet: Private"; quotes in this paragraph derive from that interview, pp. 44, 45.

23.   Kalstone, "The Poet: Private," p. 45.

24.   *James Merrill: An Introduction to the Poetry* (New York: Columbia Univ. Press, 1984), p. 161.

25.   The scientific basis of Dante's vision preoccupies Merrill also in his review essay on *The California Dante*, "Divine Poem," *New Republic*, 29 November 1980. He discusses an article by Mark A. Peterson in the *American Journal of Physics*, December 1979, which suggests that Dante's universe "also emerges as a cosmological solution of Einstein's equations in general relativity theory." Merrill's review suggests extensive parallels between Dante's epic undertaking, as Merrill understands it, and his own; in talking about the former he often seems to be describing the latter.

26.   I was led to this understanding partly by David Kalstone's essay "Persisting Figures: The Poet's Story and How We Read It" in *James Merrill: Essays in Criticism*. With his customary elegance and insight, Kalstone argues that Merrill's trilogy exemplifies a contemporary trend of long poems that attempt to absorb the instability of the self into the form of the work.

27.   "James Merrill's Myth," p. 13.

28.   "The Art of Poetry," p. 194.

29.   For an excellent discussion of the nature of God and his names in the trilogy as well as of the duality or unicity of Merrill's universe, see Stephen Yenser, "The Names of God: *Scripts for the Pageant*," in *James Merrill: Essays in Criticism*. Yenser has anticipated much

of my argument in claiming that "What the trilogy gives us in the end is not a belief but rather a dialectical process of thought and imagination—a process such that it will not tolerate any single belief, or even species of belief, whether monistic or dualistic, materialistic or idealistic" (p. 275).

30.   I take issue here with Charles Berger, who argues in "Merrill and Pynchon: Our Apocalyptic Scribes" that the trilogy's "process of revision is grounded in a growing certainty about the truth" and that "the notion of authority remains intact" (*James Merrill*: *Essays in Criticism*, p. 294).

# James Merrill's Masks of Eros, Masques of Love

## ERIC MURPHY SELINGER

Do all poets write, at some point, about love? The most discreet, the most epically distracted temperament will yield some amorous moment: we find them in Milton, in T. S. Eliot. But one love song—say, of J. Alfred Prufrock—does not a love poet make. A certain return to the subject marks the writers we call by that name, those we turn to for pleasures and insights as time goes by. If every romance runs, as subtitles in the *Penguin Book of Love Poetry* suggest, from intimations and celebrations through desolations and reverberations, the best love poets never settle on a single vision of that rocky progress. They shift perspectives, changing tone or structure, then heed the Muse's command to "look in thy heart and write" once more (Sidney, *Astrophil and Stella*, Sonnet 1). Writers like Donne and Spenser, Lowell and Rich, take romantic occasions as occasions for reflection, not only on love's urges, pleasures, and fears, but also on how best to model them in art. What does writing in narrative, diary jotting, verse letter, or sonnet sequence mean, not just for one's accuracy, but for the life lived, the love still unaddressed?

Such self-consciousness can make an author seem "literary," chilly, self-involved. It tugs out of transparency the scrim of convention that lies between us and moments we long to find immediately moving. But this gesture merely underscores that neither "russet yeas, and honest kersey noes" nor the plainest New Jersey "this is just to say" is a more natural language for the wooing mind than rouged-up conceits (Shakespeare, *Love's Labor's Lost* 5.2.413; Williams, "This Is Just to Say" 372). Love is a fair ventriloquist; yet how dull to see love poets merely mouthing, dandled on affection's plaid-clad knee. "Eternity is passion, girl or boy / Cry at the onset of their sexual joy," writes Yeats, but they "awake / Ignorant what Dramatis Personae spake" ("Whence Had They Come" 287). To avoid the ignorance of the childishly passionate, or to re-experience it from an adult perspective, the poet may turn to myth and allusion, to iconic and ironic distances. And in

Reprinted from *Contemporary Literature* 35, no. 1 (Spring 1994), 30–65. Copyright © 1994 by The University of Wisconsin Press, Madison, Wisconsin. Reprinted by permission.

American poetry there is no love poet more knowing—no more undeceived about the sources, the resources, and the limits of his art—than James Merrill.

Only a few of Merrill's poems are the sort we read ourselves into or slyly recite. He's written no "Drink to me only with thine eyes," no "Having a Coke with You." We take his measure in longer narrative, symbolist, and mythographic efforts, where the way life turns into work, and work to life, may be explored in exemplary detail. Since his 1976 collection *Divine Comedies*, Merrill has found this exchange, this "translation," deeply soothing. In it childhood worries and grown-up despairs, as of a long-cold love affair, may be set right:

> But nothing's lost. Or else: all is translation
> And every bit of us is lost in it
> (Or found—I wander through the ruin of S
> Now and then, wondering at the peacefulness)
> *(Selected Poems* 284)[1]

Both "Lost in Translation" and "The Book of Ephraim," the lyric and narrative triumphs of *Divine Comedies*, offer a vision of life and art enriching and repairing one another: the art of poetry in the first; the art of love, called "DEVOTION," in the second. But we do the poet a disservice by reading only retrospectively. The heartsease of his last decade and a half blossoms out of a struggle encompassing three collections—*Nights and Days* (1966), *The Fire Screen* (1969), and *Braving the Elements* (1972)—in which Merrill quarrels with himself and other poets, embraces and loses at least one beloved, attacks and returns to his Muse. In the process he tests a series of myths and metaphors for the relationships between life and art, contact and composition, love, illusion, and the imagination. Each collection may be read as a sequence; together they plot a zigzag course from unease through reconciliation to a new, deeper despair. Only out of these depths does Merrill discover the consoling, chastened vision of his more recent work.[2] It's a trajectory that takes him through a number of the crises that Roland Barthes and Julia Kristeva describe in postmodern amorous discourse, and it places him, with Adrienne Rich and Mona Van Duyn, in the first rank of contemporary American poets of love.

When Merrill chose five poems from his first, privately published collection, *The Black Swan* (1946), for his 1982 selected poems, *From the First Nine*, he did so both to preserve what he calls "the earliest inklings of certain lifelong motifs" and to revise those inklings into questions that his later work would answer (*From the First Nine* 361; see Yenser 33–35). I want to begin with a brief look at one such early poem, a reflection on lost love and artistic gain called "The Broken Bowl." This poem introduces several motifs that

Merrill explores in much of his later, major work, particularly in its focus on the more or less necessary, more or less vexed *interiority* of love poetry, its creation of what he has recently named "A Room at the Heart of Things" (the title poem, more or less, of his 1988 collection *The Inner Room*), which threatens to wall out the beloved as the poem is composed.

As one might expect from the work of a twenty year old, the early version of "The Broken Bowl" stands a bit overawed by its influences. Its title, for example, calls to mind the shattering of Henry James's golden bowl—a moment that reveals the flaw in the gilded crystal *objet* as it does in the marriage of Maggie Verver and her Prince, yet which allows that marriage to be mended at the last (see McWhirter 175–99). But the younger Merrill does not make much use of James's reconstructive pattern; "our last joy" in the affair, he tells his lost beloved with nervous satisfaction, lies in "knowing it shall not heal" (*Black Swan* 9). Thirty-six years later, schooled in his heart's insistent drive to aesthetic restitution, the poet turns his youthful answers on themselves. "Did also the heart shatter when it slipped?" he now demands (6). Yes: "Shards flash, becoming script"; the heart, the bowl, falls from "lucid, self-containing artifice" to a vision of "fire, ice, / A world in jeopardy," only to be restored as the "we" of the later poem "build another, whole, / Inside us" in a "new space, / Timeless and concentric" that resembles, in the best New Critical fashion, the well-wrought and highly allusive poem itself.[3] What lets the bowl, the heart, survive?

> Love does that. Spectral through the fallen dark,
> > Eye-beam and ingle-spark
> Refract our ruin into this new space,
> Timeless and concentric, a spotlight
> To whose elate arena we allot
> Love's facets reassembling face by face,
> > Love's warbler among leaves,
> Love's monuments, or tombstones, on our lives.

In their vision of the poem as an "elate arena" in which "Love's facets" reassemble, these lines recall the confident compensatory structure of Keats's "Ode to Psyche," a poem which "asserts that by the constructive activity of the mind we can assert a victory, complete and permanent, over loss" (Vendler, *Odes* 49). An appealing faith—yet the older Merrill quickly complicates the scene. For if "Love's facets" looks back to the shattered bowl, to the lovers transformed into diamond, "Love's monuments, or tombstones" suggests that there is something essentially elegiac in this transformation, as though the act of preserving faces in facets, love in art, either were or required the death of love as well.[4] Like the Keats of the "Nightingale" ode (to which "Love's warbler among leaves" seems to allude), Merrill finds that "the fancy cannot cheat so well / As she is fam'd to do, deceiving elf"—which is to say, in this context, that the creation of art's inner room may have more to do with the repair and expansion of one's "sole self" than with the building of a temple with "a casement ope at night, / To let the warm Love in!" (203; 206). Creation intervenes between the lovers, so that while the poet may claim that this "new space" is "inside *us*," the poet's plural seems a little disingenuous.

The link between the genres of love poem and elegy, in which the beloved's absence is required so that song may serve as a substitute and self-delighting satisfaction, is as old as the myths of Pan and Syrinx, Daphne and Apollo. And as long as time enforces the poet's solitude, making the act of writing one with memory, the note of elegy on which "The Broken Bowl" ends is inarguably appropriate. (In such retrospective poems as "A Tenancy," the final poem in his 1962 collection *Water Street*, Merrill makes his inner room seem an inviting open house: "If I am host at last," he writes, "It is of little more than my own past. / May others be at home in it" [88].) But when the composing imagination itself shatters the peace, when the poem enforces the beloved's departure in order for its aesthetic and soul-making compensations to accrue, Merrill's tone shifts uneasily. Torn by the attraction of self-creation through writing and the incumbent solitude of composition, he grows increasingly suspicious of the motives and effects of his art (Fraser vii–viii). The collection that follows *Water Street*, *Nights and Days*, wrestles this ambivalence from its first poem, "Nightgown," where the phrase "dear heart" may invoke another person or, more painfully, the poet's heart alone:

> Whom words appear to warm,
> Dear heart, wear mine. Come forth
> Wound in their flimsy white
> And give it form.             (91)

The paired, unsettling intimations here—that words may only *appear* to warm this heart, and that the heart may therefore turn out to be "wound" in words like a corpse in its shroud, coming forth still cold—are posed against the verse's tender, poised entreaty in a way that prepares readers for the more striking split in the speaker of the poem that follows, "The Thousand and Second Night." His face half-paralyzed as the poem begins, his narrative insistently self-interrupting and ironic, this speaker images his transformations of life into art in brutal metaphors. Writing involves "Stripping the blubber from [his] catch" and burning that oil, so that "Mornings, a black film lay upon the desk" (97; see Fraser 23–26). The "elate arena" is far off, any reconstructive structure out of sight.

Merrill is hardly the first poet to have rebelled against the love poem's claim to be an object of desire, the poet and his words the only true and lasting pair. But instead of the witty, satirical turn that characterizes most such rebellions (Rosalind's lessons in wooing in *As You Like It* come to mind), Merrill's musings on his art have a harsher, less self-possessed tone. In "The Thousand and Second Night" writing the love poem entails a reductive stripping away or boiling down of the beloved, as blubber is boiled down into lamp oil—and since "blubber" can mean to weep noisily or speak while weeping, to strip the blubber from one's catch is colder still. In "Between Us" the poet wakes up in bed to find his hand, a metonym for the act of writing, fallen asleep and looking for a moment like something alien, grotesque—a shrunken parody of the beloved's head:

> A . . . face? There
> It lies on the pillow by
> Your turned head's tangled graying hair:
> Another—like a shrunken head, too small!
> My eyes in dread
> Shut. Open. It is there,
>
> Waxen, inhuman. Small.
> *(From the First Nine* 134)

This living hand does not connect the lovers but mocks them with its reductive ("small") and "inhuman" trophies from love's fray. As "Between Us" ends, Merrill begs the hand to open and "deliver" him, in both redemptive and transportational senses of the word. The poem that follows in *Nights and Days*, "Violent Pastoral," tries with its single sinuous sentence to convey the rush and blurring boundaries of such deliverance—an erotic connection described in terms of a Jove-like eagle who "mounts with the lamb [a Ganymede] in his clutch" (104). Yet the moment is brief, the poet still divided, his syntax straining "to link the rut in dust / . . . / . . . / With the harder spiral of making." And the question I posed of "Nightgown" returns: is this a poem of union between lovers, say those of "Between Us," plucked out of their separate subjectivities by the "One pulse pounding, pounding" of sex, or does its myth describe a moment of union within the poet's split, too-conscious self, as the watchful, composing imagination (the "shepherd" of the scene) briefly inhabits both the "Aching talon" of the hand and the body's hapless "bleating / Weight" (104)?

"The self's a fine and private place," quips F. W. Dupee, "Yet none, I think, do there embrace" (qtd. in McWhirter 1). In *Nights and Days* Merrill's stance is mostly one of solitary self-division, and Merrill seems far less concerned than other love poets of the middle and late 1960s—the Lowell of the sonnets, the Rich of *Leaflets*, the Creeley of *Words*—with forcing the lyric to accommodate a beloved's resistant presence. Yet I find it hard to accuse him of Romantic solipsism, nor readily second him when he takes himself to task. For the most part he seems free of hauntings by

Alastor, the Spirit of Solitude who stalks poets from Shelley to Stevens. In part this is a matter of aesthetics, the poet's sense of what human company, *in a poem*, looks like. Praising Wallace Stevens as a model for how to populate a poem, Merrill turns a common accusation on its head. For Hugh Kenner, among others, "the Stevens world is empty of people," his characters insubstantial figments (75). Not so, Merrill responds. Eliot and Pound offered "figures like poor Fräulein von Kulp, frozen forever in a single, telling gesture," and "John Adams wound like a mummy in a thousand ticker tape statistics." Figures in Stevens, by contrast, were "airily emblematic, yet blessed with idiosyncrasy. . . . They served their poet and departed undetained by him" (*Recitative* 118, 119). Psyche, in "From the Cupola," also from *Nights and Days*, is Merrill's Stevensian masterpiece, at once a part of the poet and a realized character, "sheer / projection" and a true "correspondent," as she says of her own beloved, Eros. Merrill's evident tenderness toward her counters Dupee's wry couplet by enacting an acknowledged embrace within the self—one that neither masks nor undermines the embrace of an external beloved. Near the center of the poem, as she despairs, the poet intervenes. "Psyche, hush," he breaks in:

> This is me, James,
> Writing lest he think
> Of the reasons why he writes—
> Boredom, fear, mixed vanities and shames;
> Also love.
> From my phosphorescent ink
> Trickle faint unworldly lights
>
> Down your face. Come, we'll both rest.
> Weeping? You must not.
> All our pyrotechnic flights
> Miss the sleeper in the pitch-dark breast.
> He is love:
> He is everyone's blind spot.
> We see according to our lights.
>
> (125)

Along with the distinct and lively voices of Psyche and her sisters, such musings by the poet populate his inner room to such an extent that his solitude, by the end of the volume, seems hardly to deserve the name.

But artistry alone does not keep Alastor at bay. As Stephen Yenser observes, the "coexistence within the self of Eros and Psyche is not the same . . . as a union of the self with the Eros without; the integration of sensuality and spirit within the self does not assure—though it might facilitate—a close relationship between self and other. . . . The 'touch' of the actual always cracks the mold of the dream" (148–49). What saves the poet, at least for now, is an evolving stance toward his art—one that cushions him against that shattering touch. If the volume *Nights and Days* opens in self-disgust over the split between the life lived and the poem made, it moves by the end of "From the Cupola" to a poetry of reconciliation. Poetry seemed brutally solitary, a matter of "stripping" the "blubber" from one's amorous "catch" to light the writer's desk. Love and such lamplight make an awkward match. But as he reassures Psyche, Merrill reassures himself that affection is at least *part* of his art's motivation, and that love remains "in the pitch-dark breast," still unburned, unawakened by the "grotesque" lamplit investigations of "The Thousand and Second Night." In the last lines of "From the Cupola," using an adjective from "Between Us" to qualify an externalized version of the inner room's "elate arena," Merrill describes the poet's typewriter as a "shrunken amphitheatre." But now the letters in his typewriter form "Ranked glintings" of "a small articulate crowd"; and although art's motives are still mixed, typing and masturbation collaborate to work love's inspiration into "sense":

> We've seen what comes next. There is no pure deed.
> A black-and-red enchanter, a deep-dyed
> Coil of—No matter. One falls back, soiled, blurred.
>
> And on the page, of course, black only. Damned
> If I don't tire of the dark view of things.
> . . . . . . . . . . . . . . . .
>               My hands move. An intense,
> Slow-paced, erratic dance goes on below.
> I have received from whom I do not know
> These letters. Show me, light, if they make sense.
>                   (130–31)

Lines like these ease Merrill's earlier irony and disappointment, suggesting as they do that his sense of his art as reductive and isolating was partial, "black only," and that the self-love inherent in his poetry will not impede love of someone else. "In love," writes Julia Kristeva, paraphrasing Rimbaud, " 'I' has been an *other*" (*Tales* 4). Merrill's ability to speak as Psyche and the other characters of the poem, receiving and articulating through his "letters" a previously unknown otherness within himself, allows the love for another person that we find in the last poem of this volume, "Days of 1964" (see Fraser 60; 68–71)—a poem which tests the poet's developing assurance against the specifics of an evidently intersubjective romance.

If the end of "From the Cupola" turned the inner room into the external amphitheater of the typewriter, "Days of 1964" continues that push to the exterior. Set almost entirely outdoors, in a Greek world that literalizes the "Greek / Revival" architecture mentioned in the poem before it (119), "Days of 1964" is lit at the start not by the "lamp" of artifice but by sunlight, which has "cured" the poet's neighborhood. Far from banishing Eros, lamplight here illuminates intimacies ("We lay whole nights, open, in the lamplight, / And gazed . . ."), while daylight proves just as revealing. At the midday crux of the poem, the poet encounters his cleaning woman, Kyria Kleo, on her way to a rendezvous. He has already hinted that, despite looking "like a Palmyra matron / Copied in lard and horsehair," she's a type of Aphrodite, just as he figures Aphrodite's son Eros. But the apparition of her face among the pines startles him into another myth of love's lineage, one that bears on the tension between love and art that Merrill has explored throughout the volume:

> Poor old Kleo, her aching legs,
> Trudging into the pines. I called,
> Called three times before she turned.
> Above a tight, skyblue sweater, her face
> Was painted. Yes. Her face was painted
> Clown-white, white of the moon by daylight,
> Lidded with pearl, mouth a poinsettia leaf,
> *Eat me, pay me*—the erotic mask
> Worn the world over by illusion
> To weddings of itself and simple need.
>
> Startled mute, we had stared—was love illusion?—
> And gone our ways.
> (133)

Is love illusion? "Too pathetic, too pitiable, is the region of affection," Emerson laments in "Illusions," "and its atmosphere always liable to *mirage*" (1118). But Emerson wants to contrast the world of illusion to a reality inhabited by the solitary soul and faceless, impersonal "gods" quite different from Merrill's lively pantheon; and his insistence that we see one another through the "colored and distorting lenses" of a subjectivity so radical that it "ruins the kingdom of mortal friendship and love" carries him well past the poet's more forgiving acknowledgement that, in love, "we see according to our lights" ("Experience" 487). Likewise when critic Lynn Keller explains that Merrill here "admits that all human love may be merely illusion, a facade applied to beautify crude physical need," she brings to this poem an ironic, even reductive tone ("*merely* illusion") appropriate to earlier poems in *Nights and Days*, but too caustic for this context. In the process she discards the poet's carefully chosen marital metaphor, thus missing the implicit answer to his demand (211). The "wedding of [illusion] and simple need," for which this poem is an ambivalent epithalamion, gives *birth* to love, just as "Resource and Need" bear Eros in Plato's *Symposium* (555). Part illusion, then, love is part necessity also—the "necessary seeming" Kristeva names as "the imagination" (125; 381). Need in this poem is not crude but "simple"—our affections are too mythic and elaborate to think of them in Keller's architectural terms. Love's entanglement with the imagination does not come between lover and beloved, or merely disguise crude need; rather, as historian and philosopher of love Irving Singer attests, it is only "through the amorous imagination," "that one person becomes sexually attractive to another. Our instincts alone would not enable us to love or even to lust in the way that human beings do" (1: 21). "Love makes one generous," Merrill writes in "Days of 1964," thinking in part of our imaginative bestowal of attractive, powerful qualities on those we love.

The poet's image for bestowal is the mask. Masks sustain love, writes Keller; they "enrich our inner lives by transforming everyday perception"— a transformation intimately linked with the poet's "theatrical aesthetic" (208; 213). "The as ifs of love," like those we indulge at the theater, "are imaginative, not delusional," according to Singer (1:17), so that "the amorous imagination bestows value upon a person as the dramatic imagination bestows theatrical import upon an actor" (1:19).[5] We might well think of Merrill's masks as those of a classical drama, played out in a Greece that writes large the "shrunken amphitheater" of the poet's typewriter. It's not just that, masked, poet and beloved can tell the truth. Rather, masked as they are by fictions, these young lovers may be divinely inspired, so that the internal embrace of "From the Cupola," in which self became other and was healed, can be lived out between lover and beloved. "Where I hid my face, your touch, quick, merciful, / Blindfolded me. A god breathed from my lips," the poet sighs (133). A winged Cupid painted blind, the poet is also Socrates covering his head to speak of love in the *Phaedrus*, where we learn that love's enthusiasm recalls the "possession or madness" that Socrates' jaded contemporaries call "not manic but *mantic*" (492, 491; emphasis added). Merrill now adds, so to speak, an extra syllable, restoring the divinatory value once lost. Romantic, even in recollection, he speaks his piece. In a world of love as possession, the touch of the actual is a brush of angels' wings. Is love illusion? "You were everywhere beside me, masked," comes the poet's answer, "As who was not, in laughter, pain, and love" (134).

In its ease with theatrical and amorous bestowal, "Days of 1964" marks a high point in Merrill's early love poetry. And yet, such love is not without its risks. If at some moment, Roland Barthes explains, I as a lover "see the other in the guise of an inert object, like a kind of stuffed doll" on which I bestow virtues and value, that is enough "to shift my desire from this annulled object to my desire itself," so that "it is my desire I desire, and the loved being is no more than its tool" (*Lover's Discourse* 31). How awful to wake up and find one's fine romance, inspiring and inspired, reduced to an imaginative play that is *mere* play, not a possession by the gods but an overdressed rehearsal of *idées reçus*.[6] Something like this shift takes place between "Days of 1964" and Merrill's next volume, *The Fire Screen*.[7] Where love and poetic imagination seemed intertwined at the close of *Nights and Days*, in this collection beloved and Muse are rivals. "Lacking her blessing"— that is, untransfigured by amorous art—the beloved is no longer attractive, but rather "Stout, serviceable, gray. / A fishwife shawled in fourth-hand idiom" ("To My Greek" 152).[8] If the opposite of bestowal is, in Singer's terms, *appraisal*, no wonder the poet worries:

> Still
> I fear for us. Nights fall
> We toss through blindly, drenched in her appraising
> Glare, the sibyl I turn to
>
> When all else fails me, when you do—
>
> The mother tongue!
>
> (151)

By the time of these poems I suspect Merrill had soured on his own facility with bestowal, and with the familiar plots his affections played him through. Barthes describes the poet's lot: "the body, from head to toe, overwhelmed, *submerged by Nature*, and all this nonetheless: *as if I were borrowing a quotation*" (*Roland Barthes* 91). Suppose my sacred drama turned out to be a "household opera" written by others and learned in childhood? "Long beyond adolescence," Merrill writes of himself in the book's penulti-mate poem, "Matinees," "Tissue of sound and tissue of the brain / Would coalesce, and what the Masters wrote / Itself compose his features sharp and small" (163). And even this paints the danger in too broad, too comforting a stroke. By the time we reach "Matinees" in the sequence of *The Fire Screen* we are *happy* to hear that some earlier artist has arranged our affairs. That at least leaves room for someone's creativity, if not ex nihilo then through variations on a theme. In "To My Greek," near the start of the volume, Merrill faces the still more alarming fear—that is, that the mother tongue herself dictates the course of our affections.[9] When he writes of "Common sense veering into common scenes, / Tears, incoherent artifice" we hear the all *too* coherent artifice of the words "sense" and "scenes," as though their proximity made the outburst inevitable (152). "God and the imagination are one," Stevens's Interior Paramour declared (*Collected Poems* 524). Merrill puts language in divinity's place, but joylessly. "The mother tongue! / . . . / Her automation and my mind are one" (151).[10]

The violence of early poems in *Nights and Days* was directed against the poet himself, taking the forms of ironic or cruel metaphors. For fear of his words' revelations, the speaker of "To My Greek" turns to violence as well, but his focus is apparently outward. He threatens to slit the Muse's well, but his focus is apparently outward. He threatens to slit the Muse's windpipe; he twists against syntax and stanzaic structures, warding off clarity and closure. "Let there be no word / For justice, grief, convention; *you* be convention," he proclaims—or is it pleads (151)? Love, at least the love of these two, must be "the way of little knowledge," for the poet knows the conventions of the amorous sequence, how they end with lovers far apart, their love preserved in verse alone (Fraser 89–90, 93). And as we read *The Fire Screen* we learn other reasons why knowledge is so threatening, flaws in the beloved that the poet cannot bring himself to leave unnamed in verse. In "The Envoys" the beloved torments animals who persist in loving their tormenter. In "Part of the Vigil" the poet enters the "little, doorless, crudely lighted chambers" of the other's heart—how different from the rooms we've seen in the poet himself!—and is unable to find his image there (*Fire Screen* 24). "We must step boldly into man's interior world or not at all," says Stevens (*Opus Posthumous* 195); but Merrill's step leads to nervous hope, no more. "Didn't your image, / Still unharmed, deep in my own saved skin / Blaze on?" he asks. "You might yet see it, see by it. / Nothing else mattered" (*From the First Nine* 189). And yet, the fact that "blazon" means both a dazzling display and a merely showy, ostentatious one suggests the poet's ambivalence, the falsity of his claim. Does this vigil mark the funeral of their love? The last four lines deny it, but their tone gives them the lie.[11]

Love poets have always known how love enacts its bestowals through language. Emerson mocked that ascriptive power: "We unjustly select a particle, and say 'O steel-filing number one! what heart-drawings I feel to thee! what prodigious virtues are these of thine!'" ("Nominalist and Realist" 577). Whitman accepts ascription as he soothes our vanity. "None has done justice to you," he reassures us: "O I could sing such grandeurs and glories about you!" ("To You" 376). But neither comes to grips as Merrill does with the peculiarly authorial fear that language might be not just the slippery medium but the motivating force of his affections. I find this fear plangently addressed in "Flying from Byzantium," where the poet first acknowledges the end of his affair. In the second section of this poem Merrill takes the imperative word play of "common sense veering into common scenes" to a tragicomic extreme. If discovering "the hidden wish of words" is part of any poet's creative act (*Recitative* 111), here "the man in the moon," a male Muse, speaks in nothing *but* trouvailles. Rhymes slant with dizzying rapidity; and the poet responds in kind:

> Up spoke the man in the moon:
> "What does that moan mean?
> The plane was part of the plan.
> Why gnaw the bone of a boon?"
>
> I said with spleen, "Explain
> These nights that tie me in knots,

> All drama and no dream,
> While you lampoon my pain."
> *(From the First Nine* 193)

At this point in his affair Merrill might call on his art to preserve love's memory, or simply to keep himself afloat in seas of erotic travail. Yeats in such distress aspires to "the artifice of eternity" (193). But flying from, not sailing to, a Yeatsian solution, the poet exchanges the coruscating densities of "To My Greek" for bravura word play or for minor, amenable forms like the foot-per-line-longer limerick stanza, borrowed from Yeats, that he deploys in section 1:

> The hour has come. I'm heading home.
> We take a cab to the airdrome
> In time for the last brandy.
> I've kept my Kodak handy
> To snap the last unfocused Kodachrome.
> *(From the First Nine* 192)

Why these half-heartedly comic gestures? Perhaps the poet would rather turn the force of art on himself, as he did in "The Thousand and Second Night," than on his lost beloved. Perhaps he fears he's been more in league with the Muse, the mother tongue, than her victim. "The plane was part of the plan," we read—a line that looks at once back to the way language has forced a pattern on events and forward to "Matinees," where a young poet learns how to "arrange for [his] / Own chills and fever, passions and betrayals, / Chiefly in order to make song of them" (165). (A few years later, in *The Dolphin*, Robert Lowell will likewise record his sense of being "maneuvered on a guiding string" as he "execute[s] his written plot," and mourn his having listened to "too many / words of the collaborating muse," though the determinism he fears shades from the literary to the familial, while Merrill's shades from the literary to the linguistic [49, 78].) The poet declares himself the "animal" of his lost love, but he is also "the young ringmaster," putting himself and his beloved through the hoops of a predestined, predictable romantic finale. The image of the poet as ringmaster invokes a second poem of Yeats's, "The Circus Animals' Desertion." Although their affair may have embodied "heart mysteries," to use the Irish poet's phrase, Merrill too might well confess that "Players and painted stage took all my love / And not those things that they were emblems of" (347).

At the close of "The Circus Animals' Desertion," Yeats prepares to lie down for renewal in "the foul rag and bone shop of the heart" (348). At the close of "Flying from Byzantium," we find Merrill "Kneeling" to declare his allegiance to the Muse: "Mother, I was vain, headstrong, / Help me, I am coming back / . . . / That I may be born again / Lead the black fly to my flesh" (*From the First Nine* 194). But the abjection of the flies and flesh is countered by a gesture of cool removal, one that keeps the Muse's powers half at bay. For the end of "Flying from Byzantium" is set in the third person, a quotation of what "he," the poet, said, and this rhetorical move allows the poet to qualify the plea for death and rebirth as a "vague, compliant song." (For all that he asks to be reborn, rebirth has no true place in Merrill's work—hence his failure to engineer the reincarnation of particular souls in "The Book of Ephraim.") The youth of the ringmaster, which signals his distance from maturing experience, is *preserved* rather than *restored* in the final figure of "Flying from Byzantium." "Far off," untouched by the Dionysian energies the repentant poet invokes, "a young scribe turned a fresh / Page, hesitated, dipped his pen." What the young scribe writes would be a poem like "Last Words," which follows "Flying from Byzantium" as a sort of coda—that is to say, a poem where part of the self suffers identifications and ecstasies while another sighs that "There's nothing I don't know / Or shall not know again, / Over and over again" (156).[12]

Is there something innately repulsive about repetition, for a love poet? "Almost every one loves all repeating in some one," says Gertrude Stein in *The Making of Americans*; the notion that both life and writing might find our loved ones playing out some pattern, acting according to type, bothers her not at all (270). But in *The Fire Screen* Merrill finds such patterns hard to take. Through them he glimpses that bleak, unhappy vista where "individual and type are one" ("Friend of the Fourth Decade" 141). We play out love's dramas there, but they're hardly sacred, or even operatic, and each evening teaches the same lesson in romantic dramaturgy:

> First
> the hour, the setting. Only then
> the human being, his white shirtsleeve
> chalked among treetrunks, round a waist,
> or lifted in an entrance. Look for him.
> Be him.
>
> ("Another August" 159)

The word "entrance" is painfully ironic: though we once again see love as theater, no one now has been entranced, swept up in bestowal as in "Days of 1964." As *The Fire Screen* continues, the poet loses his faith in the once-inspiring theatrical metaphor for love, so that by the time we reach "Remora," Merrill describes his former relationship as one of clever parasite to blundering shark. "One sees," he writes dryly, "in spite / Of being littler, a degree or two / Further than those one is attracted to" (160). The deus ex machina of a skin diver (another lover? a rival?) intercedes, but to no good end:

> Who now descends from a machine
> Plumed with bubbles, death in his right hand?
> Lunge, numbskull! One, two, three worlds boil.
> Thanks for the lift. There are other fish in the sea.
>
> Still on occasion as by oversight
> One lets be taken clinging fast
> In heavenly sunshine to the corpse a slight
> Tormented self, live, dapper, black-and-white.
>
> (160)

The "heavenly sunshine" of those last lines is another version of the "appraising glare" of "To My Greek," by which the poet sees "in spite" indeed. In this unforgiving light the other's charms appear to have undergone a cold sea change, and the poet himself, as that sneering "dapper" suggests, has not been spared.

"One begins by unlearning how to love others," Nietzsche observes, "and ends by no longer finding anything lovable in oneself" (142). Drawn into depths of appraisal that one "lives . . . alone to sound and sound" ("To My Greek" 153), Merrill arrives in "Remora" at a cynicism toward his art at least as deep as the one in which *Nights and Days* began, and if only because of its repetition, the emotional impasse is worse. Like other disillusioned amorous sequences—Mina Loy's *Love Songs for Joannes*, Lowell's *The Dolphin*, Robert Creeley's *Pieces*—*The Fire Screen* shows a poet deeply suspicious of aesthetic finish and achievement, which can seem to betray the particulars of a love relationship and win a morally suspect literary victory from loss. Unlike those sequences, however, Merrill's volume refuses to console us or its author with the thought that aesthetic flaws signal a deeper or more valuable achievement of moral or amatory authenticity.[13] The poet undertakes what is perhaps a trickier, threefold task: to restore the value of love as bestowal (which means, in part, love as illusion); to exorcise his self-image as an ever-untouched "young scribe," a "cold man," or "Jack Frost"; and to reconcile himself with the jealous mistress of the volume, the mother tongue as Muse. His efforts span the close of this volume and the love poems of the next, *Braving the Elements* (1972); they enable the emotionally poised, consoling vision of "The Book of Ephraim" and more recent works.

If at this point we wished to diagnose the poet's plight, we might say that he suffers from melancholy. "The belletrist's disillusioned attitude," Kristeva writes, is "a lesser form of the ailment [melancholia] that demystifies wisdom, beauty, style, and eros itself" (*Tales* 77). A full-blown case includes "a constant *anxiety* on the moral level, a painful *impotence* on the sexual one," the patient poised before an "abyss into which one can read the unsurmountable ascendancy of a stifling mother." In its final stages we find that the lively reversible roles of voyeur and exhibitionist, sadist and masochist, gutter out in an undifferentiated "aggregate . . . of stagnation and despair" (77). I hold no brief for lay analysis, and Merrill displays none of the flat affect and numbed, repetitive speech that the theorist leads us to expect.[14] But Kristeva's outline is helpful in reading the close of this volume; and the struggle with the mother that she hints at—for Merrill at once the Muse, his mother, and the mother tongue—will in fact prove central to his cure.

The poet's recovery begins in "A Fever," where the two Muse figures of "Flying from Byzantium," the man in the moon and the mother tongue, merge to form a single intruder into the poet's inner room. The room has been otherwise occupied, for Merrill has apparently begun sharing it with a new friend he names, at the close of the poem, "my girl." When "she leaves," however, as the beloved always leaves, the Muse sweeps in to tidy up and chastise:

> Enter the moon like a maid in silence unsheeting the waste
> Within, of giant toys, toy furniture.
> Two button eyes transfix me. A voice blurred and impure,
> Speaks through lips my own lips have effaced:
>
> "Back so soon? Am I to wish you joy, as usual,
> Of a new friend? For myself, not quite the nice
> Young thing first given to your gentleness,
> These visits are my life, which is otherwise uneventful."
>                                   (*From the First Nine* 200)

Less jealous than hurt and neglected, no longer the imperious force she appeared to be at the end of "Flying from Byzantium," the Muse wants her poet to acknowledge both that she needs him and that he treats her badly.[15] In her defense, and to defend that part of him that she represents, she undertakes an apology for the imagination. The less-deceived and unforgiving gaze of appraisal, which the poet feared in "To My Greek" (it seemed an "appraising glare") and embraced in "Remora" (where it seemed, however bitterly, a "heavenly sunshine"), seemed attractive and compelling because it promised the truth about the loved one and the self. It was a main line injection of what Henry James called "the real . . . the things we cannot possibly *not* know, sooner or later" (279). When the brisk delights of accuracy fade, however, the chill of self-hatred sets in. And is there in beauty no truth, no knowledge granted only in disguise? "The point was to be one on whom nothing is lost," the Muse reminds him. "But what is gained by one more random image / / Crossed with mine at one more feast of crumbs?" (*From the First Nine* 201). Appraisal may be a necessary *part* of love, but on its own it ends in cross-reference and accretion, meager fare for the poetry of love. What's lacking in appraisal, and in Merrill's harshest appraisals of love and poetry, is a place for what James calls "romance"— that which "can reach us only through the beautiful circuit and subterfuge of our thought and our desire" (279).

I bring up James because the Muse's "point" is quoted from the novelist: not the preface to *The American*, my own source so far, but "The Art of Fiction," where James explains what the advice to "write from experience" might, in practice, mean. "Experience," he notes, "is never limited, and it is never complete." Rather,

> it is the very atmosphere of the mind; and when the mind is imaginative . . . it takes to itself the faintest hints of life, it converts the very pulses of the air into revelations. The young lady living in a village has only to be a damsel upon whom nothing is lost to make it quite unfair . . . to declare to her that she shall have nothing to say about the military. Greater miracles have been seen that, *imagination assisting, she should speak the truth* about some of these gentlemen.
>
> (172; emphasis added)

It is as though the poet had until now recalled only the admonition to write from experience, to "be one of the people on whom nothing is lost!" (as James concludes the passage), without recalling how much of experience is mental, imaginative, an extrapolation from crumbs back to the feast. "The tears, the mendings—they all hurt," the Muse admonishes, perhaps to reassure him of her sympathy; then, echoing a phrase he used for love's art in *Nights and Days*, "the consuming myth," she adds that mending, or artistic reconstruction, "entirely consumes" (*From the First Nine* 201). Like her reference to a feast, her admonishments play on the poet's frustrated drive to devour experience—to "live, love," as the man in the moon admonished in "Flying from Byzantium," not "shake [his] fist at the feast"—as well as on his desire to be consumed by passion once again.

Touched by her words, the poet falls to his knees a second time. He awakes from one spell—call it a spell of disenchantment—into another, yet without satisfaction:

> A long
>
> Spell seems to pass before I am found in a daze,
> Cheek touching floor. From a position so low,
> Colors passionate but insubstantial fill the window.
> Must it begin and end like this always?

The insubstantiality of those colors and the solitude of his position ("so low" as "solo") suggest the incompleteness of this scene. How can the poet, "imagination assisting, speak the truth" from this abashed, unprepossessing stance? "A Fever" ends with an image of dawn, and the next poem begins with one, but we sense no new day at hand.

However much the poet may return to the world of desire and bestowal, after all, he still fears that a part of him will remain aloof and critical, watching the rhythm of subjection to and defiance of the Muse start up again. This "young scribe" self seems to compose "Mornings in a New House," with its detached description of the fires of eros lit once more, "By whom a cold man hardly cares." A great deal depends on our reading of "Mornings," which critics have rightly focused on as, in Caroline Fraser's phrase, "the emotional peak of the volume" (126). Yenser finds the poem essentially optimistic, moving "from stiffness through routine to emotional perception" as the poet discovers once again that "passion and craft are knotted, crossed, *double*-crossed, partly because the exercise of the art discovers or creates the emotion" (164). The poet shields himself from a "tamed uprush / (Which to recall alone can make him flush)" by introducing this poem's version of the mask, the fire screen. The poet's mother's "crewelwork," embroidered by her as a child, this screen is for Yenser a figure of the poem, just as the "tamed uprush" is "the 'fire' of inspiring emotion" (163). But suppose that fire were one more "tamed recall," as David Kalstone proposes, "of the shattered (or spent?) affair"? In that case the fact that the poet is recalling *by himself*, "alone" in that sense, makes him flush. The different senses hint at very different scenes.

"It is hard to disentangle the impulses which contribute to this poem," Kalstone says (109). *Caveat lector*—and yet, at the risk of sounding like a poor man's Paglia, I find the cruel work of poetry giving the poet pleasure because in it he at last admits a certain sadomasochistic enjoyment of his ongoing battle with the Mother-Muse. Kristeva's "aggregate of stagnation and despair" (*Tales* 77) sparks into life as the poet imagines himself as a doll to his mother as a child:

> Still vaguely chilled,
>
> > Guessing how even then her eight
> > Years had foreknown him, nursed him, all,
> > Sewn his first dress, sung to him, let him fall
> > Howled when his face chipped like a plate,
> >
> > He stands there wondering until red
> > Infraradiance, wave on wave,
> > So enters each plume-petal's crazy weave,
> > Each worsted brick of the homestead,
> >
> > That once more, deep indoors, blood's drawn.
> >
> > (161–62)

These lines are pivotal, yet critics have by and large misread their tone. Kalstone speaks of an "identification with the 'tiny needle-woman' mother"—a "discovery of . . . entwined accomplished "without guilt" (110). Yenser describes the mother "comforting a doll that she has dropped—and therewith foreshadowing her lover for her son" (164). Nothing could be further from the case. She lets him fall and howls because *she* has been deprived, something belonging to her has been chipped, neglected, damaged. We never see her pick the doll back up. The "Infraradiance" that warms the "worsted brick" of Merrill's new inner room is pre-eminently his anger at having been let fall, bested by a Muse who glares at and seduces, cradles and drops him, brings him to his knees. Roused by this anger, he strikes back, and if it is his own heart's blood he draws, it's taken in a burst of self-assertion. If he cannot slit her throat, as he threatened in "To My Greek," he can at least rejoice in pricking the Mother-Muse's crewel-working finger. If god and the imagination cannot be joined, the poet seems to say, let my mind and her automation at least be set asunder. Doll and needle-woman stand opposed, sparks fly: or, to be more accurate, one bleeds, while the other shuts its eyes in satisfaction:

> deep indoors, blood's drawn,
> The tiny needlewoman cries,
> And to some faintest creaking shut of eyes
> His pleasure and the doll's are one.
>
> (162)

"Sadomasochism," writes Robert Polhemus in *Erotic Faith*, is "a desperate strategy to break through the wall of numb otherness, a fanatical attempt at intimacy and abnormally intense communication through the sharing of pain—the inflicting and the bearing of it" (88). The pleasure and pain of "Mornings in a New House" enact this strategy, as they attempt to warm the cold man the poet fears he is, to set poet and Muse into some vital, charged relation.

After this burst of pleasure, painfully won, "Mornings in a New House" ends with a retreat. "Days later" the poet adds an apologetic footnote, a preview of the note to "Mrs. Livingston" that the boy-poet of "Matinees" must, on his mother's orders, copy out and send.[16] But *The Fire Screen* does not end on this note of self-abasement. It ends instead with a coda, "The Summer People," which recapitulates the volume's battle between poet and Muse, love and art, at the safe aesthetic distance offered by its ballad form and its setting in the "village white and neat" of "Caustic (Me.)."[17] If the previous poems were exhibits from the Caustic town museum, that designation equally applies to the characters of this one: Andrew and Nora, who "had elsewhere played with fire"; Andrew's wife Jane, a painter of sorts; Margaret, Nora's widowed mother. A new inhabitant arrives, linked by rhyme to the failures of love. "I wish I weren't a widow," says Margaret. "I wish you weren't divorced— / Oh, by the way, I heard today / About a man named Frost" (169). Jack Frost's own affections are hammered into us. He "loved four-hand piano," "Loved also bridge," "Loved to gossip, loved croquet, / His money loved to spend / / On food and drink and flowers, / Loved entertaining most" (170). Or does he have some other first allegiance?

> "Proud Grimes, proud loyal kitty,"
> Jack said, "I love you best."
> Two golden eyes were trimmed to slits,
> Gorgeously unimpressed.
>
> (171)

In his feline indifference, and in his later cruelty, Grimes is the Muse cut down to ballad-stanza size.

As long as Jack stays on alone through the off-season, taking the spareness of winter as an opportunity for imaginative embellishment, all goes well. In his eyes bare boughs become "gnarled crystal"—an image that recalls Stendahl's version of bestowal, called "crystallization," in which the lover alone with his thoughts transforms his beloved the way that Salzburg salt miners toss a leafless winter bough into the mine in order to retrieve it, unrecognizable, "covered with a shining deposit of crystals" (135). If winter is the season of intellectual creativity, as the epigraph of "The Summer People" states, it is perhaps because the season writes large the creative impetus of absence. (Inasmuch as the swan is sacred to Venus, we may find a trace of love's departures in the "Flights of the midnight Swan" that decorate snow-white Caustic all season long [175].)

Like the Muse, though, Grimes is a jealous master. The moment Jack's summer neighbors decide to stay through Christmas, Grimes reacts by clawing his master's thigh (as close to a castration threat as a cat-sized Muse can muster). When Grimes attacks someone *else* the forces of sociability recoil. "Two good whiffs of ether," and—as the doll's and poet's eyes closed in "Mornings"—the cat's "gold eyes shut on Jack" (177). But the cycle of punishment is not quite closed:

> That same night, Grimes in ermine
> And coronet of ice
> Called him by name, cried vengeance,
> Twitching his long tail twice.
>
> Jack woke in pitch dark, burning,
> Freezing. . . .
>
> (178)

We recognize these symptoms from "A Fever" and "Mornings." Unable to balance hot and cold selves, winter's art and summer's social pleasures, Jack flees.

Yenser calls Jack Frost "Merrill's Mauberley," for like the character from Ezra Pound's "Hugh Selwyn Mauberley" he is for the poet a distancing, exorcizing fiction (176). Merrill must move beyond Jack's alternating quarrel with and subjection to the Muse into a mature equanimity. This movement will entail an education in—and grudging acceptance of—what Emerson called *succession*, one of the limiting Lords of Life. When Jack tries to segregate cold and warmth, solitude and society, he forces coherence on time's and inspiration's passage—an effort that finds its equally sterile counterpart in his later wish to unite the two in something like a Spenserian "continuall spring, and harvest there / Continuall, both meeting in one time" (qtd. in "Ephraim," *Divine Comedies* 106). The fruits of this union, in the "November mildness" that follows Jack's departure, are the doomed spring flowers planted by Jack's Japanese "houseboy," Ken. Ken's suicide follows their unseasonable bloom.

"The Summer People" ends on a worn-down, tragic note. In the course of the ballad, though, a new source for the poet's troubles has been identified, one that shifts our focus from the internal struggle with the Muse that has held our attention so far. The "Chemical Plant" whose glow floats over the village harbor at the end of "The Summer People"—"gloats" is Merrill's portmanteau pun—foreshadows the world of impersonal forces that the poet will face in subsequent volumes, and it signals a new vision of the world we cannot in the end *not* know: a world of entropy, of atomic and geologic powers; a "realm of hazard" more external than internal ("In Nine Sleep Valley" 216). Learning this new realism, the "uncounselable heart" with which the poet opened *The Fire Screen* drops its rage against the way love's illusions go up in smoke. Near the center of the ballad, in a first-person digression, he thinks of Job. "Logs burned, / The sparks flew upward," Merrill observes, then strikes the new note, startling in its lack of irony: "Time passes softly, scarcely / Felt by me or you. / And then, at an odd moment, / Tenderness passes, too" (175–76). As we will learn in *Braving the Elements*, love's impermanence and reverberations hardly stand out in a world where "nothing either lasts or ends" ("Mandala," *From the First Nine* 252). As cycles go, the Muse's circuit can seem beautiful, familiar, comforting (see Fraser 152–53).

Like the songs of Robert Frost's ovenbird, the love poems of *Braving the Elements* are notes on "what to make of a diminished thing" (76). We take that hint from the book's first lines: "Then when the flame forked like a sudden path," it begins, "I gasped and stumbled, and was less" ("Log" 189). The sublime extremes of love and bitterness we found in *The Fire Screen* are muted here, as the poet returns to now-familiar scenes. In "After the Fire," for example, we revisit Greece. But Kleo, whose appearance startled the poet into his vision of bestowal, his "love-blinded gaze," has aged into troubles. Kleo's mother, "the yiayia, nearly ninety," screams curses at her children: the son once identified with Eros is "a *Degenerate*! a *Thieving / Faggot*!" just as daughter Kleo is a *"Whore!"* These not-inaccurate appraisals call to mind another mother's work:

> *Kill me, there'll be an autopsy,*
> *Putana, matricide, I've seen to that!*
> I mention my own mother's mother's illness,
> Querulous temper, lucid shame.
> Kleo says weeping that it's not the same,
> There's nothing wrong, according to the doctor,
> Just that she's old and merciless. And warm.
>
> (191)

By adding a generation Merrill frees his mother from the burden of being purely mythological, an inhumanly terrible and demanding figure for the Muse. And the merely humanly terrible and demanding yiayia calls up a warmth of pity quite unlike the slow burn of "infraradiance" whose temperature we took in "Mornings." Embracing her, the poet can restore to some degree the "original old-fashioned colors" of the house, and with them both her and himself:

> the room brightens, the yiayia shrieks my name—
> *It's Tzimi! He's returned!*
> —And with that she returns to human form,
> The snuffed-out candle-ends grow tall and shine,
> Dead flames encircle us, which cannot harm,
> The table's spread, she croons, and I
> Am kneeling pressed to her old burning frame.
>
> (192–93)

Their kneeling embrace revises the gesture of subjection that we saw in "Flying from Byzantium" and "A Fever." It hints for the first time at a love between poet and mother, poet and Muse, outside the realm of sadomasochism, and at their joy in the new relation.

Joy is, perhaps, too strong a word. Certainly the poet has not lost sight of the truths he learned in his long sojourn in appraisal, so that when those "dead flames . . . which cannot harm" reappear in another poem near the end of *Braving the Elements*, they take their place in a disquisition on "Proust's Law." "What least thing our self-love longs for most," he observes, "Others instinctively withhold." Thus the corollary: "Only when time has slain desire / Is his wish granted to a smiling ghost / Neither harmed nor warmed, now, by the fire" ("Days of 1971" 235). By now any mention of a man who

is not warmed should raise a flag; but Jack Frost is nowhere in sight. Merrill
is now warmed by other fires than desire's, and he finds himself able to
subject Strato, the heretofore unnamed beloved of *The Fire Screen*, to gently
ironic, only lightly appraising scrutiny:

> I look hard
> At both the god and him. (He loves attention
> Like gods and children, and he lifts his glass.)
> Those extra kilos, that moustache,
> Lies found out and letters left unanswered
> Just won't do. It makes him burst out laughing,
> Curiously happy, flecked with foam.
>
> ("Strato in Plaster" 224)

That foam signals a memory of sensual release, recalling as it does the shallows
the pair braved in "To My Greek"—and, since the poet has read his love affair
through Yeats before, perhaps also the foam where nymphs and satyrs copulate
at the end of "News for the Delphic Oracle." But the even tone of "Strato in
Plaster" is so different from the earlier passion and divine possession that such
feathery touches of allusion, at which Merrill is past master, scarcely bring the
lovers' bliss to mind. It seems distant, almost unbelievable. "The god in him,"
the poet writes, "is a remembered one" (225).

This even gaze and lack of bitterness, toward the once-beloved and the
once-possessed, value-bestowing self, depends on the poet's having reconciled
at last with the Muse, and thus with fiction, with James's romance. It
evinces a victory, in verse if not in life, over melancholy. But when did this
victory take place? To answer that, it helps to remember that what the
melancholic lacks, at least according to Kristeva, is the basis of love itself:
a sense of belonging to an ideal order, to an imaginary, ideal Other who
loves us and with whom we identify. Following Freud, Kristeva names this
figure an ideal father—the sort that Merrill's mother remarries in a poem
from this volume, a "gentle General." But "he" is essentially a combination
of both parents, a "coagulation" in the child's mind of Mama and that *other*
object of her desire, whatever it may be (*Tales* 41). I see such an ideal
combination in the poem of Merrill's cure, "Days of 1935." In this ballad,
which recuperates in its very form the sad plot of "The Summer People,"
Merrill as a boy dreams of being kidnapped by an affectionate surrogate
family: Jean, who watches the boy "As no one ever had"; and Floyd, who
loves Jean with a passion the child knows only from movies. That Floyd
initiates the boy into sex puts an unexpected spin on the Kristevan imaginary
father's "warm but dazzling, domesticated paternity" (*Tales* 46). But their
encounter seems part of the boy's growing ability to indulge in fantasy—
in this case, to imagine an ever-broader sense of "How much [he's] worth
to [his] old man" (195)—and of the adult poet's reconciliation with the

beautiful circuit of desire. When imaginary mother Jean asks the boy for "Real stories—but not real, I mean" (198), she invites him to exchange the appraising glare for a "golden haze," and she validates the paradoxical pleasures of romantic bestowal and Jamesian romance. The child, as Kalstone observes, discovers his own "vitality" in the moment he exercises "his story-telling powers." The adult poet, recalling the dream, learns that "through fiction his parents become available to him in ways never possible in life" (79)—a lesson that applies to lovers, too.

Although "Days of 1935" reasserts the inspired, truth-telling power of illusion last seen in "Days of 1964," Merrill's sojourn in appraisal taught him a few lessons. The boy-poet's speech on the witness stand recalls poems of cold-eyed rejection from *The Fire Screen* ("You I adored I now accuse," he says); the execution of Floyd and Jean reads like a libretto out of "Matinees." But the poet's attitudes toward both love and poetry have matured. Thinking of his treatment of kidnappers in fantasy, and of his parents in the narrative frame, the poet stakes a new claim for the value of the slip between life and its re-creation. "True to life," he writes, the boy has "played them false." The golden haze of fiction may illuminate a world "Past belief," but it is "past disbelief" as well (203). It's not just that the poet nothing affirmeth, and therefore never lieth, as Sidney says. Rather, in a world of boards "Painted like board" and of loves that act out sonnet sequences, art's false play is true (202).

"Life," therefore, "was fiction in disguise" (197). The paradox is easily observed in Merrill's work—*too* easily, I think. We need to remind ourselves of the alternative visions he has tested: that art is a world restored in the poet's inner room ("The Broken Bowl"); that art is reductive ("The Thousand and Second Night") or a matter of plots and types and repetition ("Flying from Byzantium," "Another August"); that the union of art and sociability, while devoutly to be wished, would prove a disastrous forced bloom ("The Summer People"). Merrill's aestheticism stems as much from hard poetic trial and error as it does from innate inclination. The emotional growth behind it shows in his watchful self-portraits in *Braving the Elements*. Instead of looking on as a timelessly "young scribe" or that cold man, Jack Frost, Merrill appears as a love- and dream-struck little boy and, in "Willowware Cup," as a father. He contemplates a teacup decorated with a Chinese scene, perhaps one of farewell:

> Plum in bloom, pagoda, blue birds, plume of willow—
> Almost the replica of a prewar pattern—
>
> The same boat bearing the gnat-sized lovers away,
> The old bridge now bent double where her father signals
>
> Feebly, as from flypaper.
>
> (209)

The watchful self Merrill discovers in the scene is a "father" who is "minding less and less"—and who must, therefore, have minded more before, as the "young scribe" never could. The poet masks his fear of detachment with insouciance: "He must by now be immensely / Wise," the speaker muses, "and have given up earthly attachments, and all that." But even this briefly donned paternal persona is significant. As boy and adult he is allowed a range of closer relationships with the mother. "She kisses him sweet dreams" in "Days of 1935"; in the second part of "Up and Down," she gives him an emerald ring and he returns it—a symbolic marriage in the vault of a bank called "Mutual Trust" (229). And the new roles mark these as poems of *education*. "One learned. . . . / . . . Learned," the poet sighs ("Under Libra: Weights and Measures" 221).

In the face of what he's learned about succession, Merrill abandons the attempt to capture moments of ecstatic union. He may begin "Up and Down" with a vertiginous climb in a chair lift, but as he notes, "Au fond each summit is a cul-de-sac"; and "The rest was all downhill." The puns have a wistful ring, as Merrill forsakes erotic sublimity, or "boundlessness," for the comforts of a "Cozy Cabin" (228)—an ironic figure for those consolations art and memory provide (Fraser 215). He finds the transformative, distilling power of art alive in quotidian intimacies like giving a haircut, which conjures the beloved, "draped in a sheet whose snowy folds / Darken in patches" into a snow-covered mountain, melting as summer comes ("In Nine Sleep Valley" 215). But the sheet wound round the lover is a winding-sheet as well. "Sheeted with cold, such rot and tangle must / In time be our affair," he writes; and all affairs in this book take place, as the others did not, "in time."

And Merrill's education in love's repetitions seems equally a lesson in forgiveness. He forgives himself for "minding less and less"; forgives himself and his lover for their inevitable separation; forgives them too, for being unable to settle for the "feast / Of flaws, the molten start and glacial sleep, / The parting kiss" that love amounts to in the end. *"Forgiveness is aesthetic,"* Kristeva announces: in it we reconcile ourselves, out of all the failures and indifferences, with the realm of the ideal (*Black Sun* 206–7). In the envoi to "In Nine Sleep Valley," the poet concurs. Thinking of America as a nation of "botched" love, then of an image of Eros, he arrives at last at pity for his own poetry, itself only a "sorry" part of the true "art" which is acceptance:

> Master of the ruined watercolor,
> Citizen no less of the botched country
> Where shots attain the eagle, and the grizzly
> Dies for pressing people to his heart,
>
> Truster, like me, of who (invoked by neither)
> Hovered near the final evening's taper,

Held his breath to read his flickering nature
By our light, then left us in the dark,

Take these verses, call them today's flower,
Cluster a rained-in pupil might have scissored.
They too have suffered in the realm of hazard.
Sorry things all. Accepting them's the art.

(216)

Forgiveness, acceptance. The love such terms describe is closer to the affectionate world of "From the Cupola" from *Nights and Days* than to anything we saw in *The Fire Screen*. But the " 'touch' of the actual" that threatened to shatter the dreamy union of Eros and Psyche within the poet (Yenser 149)—and which, in the form of disillusionment, came between the poet and his Greek in later work—has been at last embraced. If all poets, as W. H. Auden suggests, are loyal to either Ariel or Prospero, to the truth of beauty or to the more-than-beautiful value of truth, then Merrill has put on Prospero's robes with an ease and authority that suggest he was never entirely in Ariel's camp to begin with. For all his commitment to poetry as "a verbal earthly paradise," he has in this volume included those elements of "the problematic, the painful, the disorderly, the ugly" that for Auden mark the Prosperian strain (338). The relationship that includes these, yet is not shattered by them, Merrill calls *friendship*. At first a little nervously: "And we are friends now? Funny friends," says the Black Mesa to its landscape (217); "the fracture's too complex, / Too long unmended, for us to be friends," says the old god Strato: "I, he hazards, have made other friends. / The more reason, then, to part like friends" (225). But the volume as a whole moves from an initial address to the lover as "dear light" to "Syrinx," the final poem, addressed to a "dear friend."

The "story of love changing into affectionate companionship" that David Perkins finds in "The Book of Ephraim" thus retells more than the course of Merrill's affections (652). Though the word "friend" jumps out at us in sections G and H, as JM worries, albeit unconsciously, over the ebbing of erotic fires in his relationship with DJ, we also find that the very existence of Heaven, the Other World with which JM and DJ communicate, depends on the upkeep of human affection. Not of erotic love—for though "Ephraim's name / is Eros" in JM's novel, we can't take that name at face value. He better represents what he calls, in the Ouija board's capital letters, "DEVOTION": a devotion at once "TO EACH OTHER TO WORK TO REPRODUCTION TO AN IDEAL," as though these could not, in fact, be opposed to one another (*Divine Comedies* 103). Later in the *Changing Light* trilogy, devotion is called "V work": the work of five elite souls who correspond to various senses and elements, but also "vie work," the anti-entropic work of life and love and poetry, of writing the trilogy itself. As the poet puts it to DJ in "Clearing the Title," *Sandover* is *"Our* poem now. It's signed JM, but grew / From life together, grain by coral grain." And if "Building on it, we let the life cloud over," then the return from composition to life is equally "for heaven's sake" (291).

The art of love is an *art* at last. An art of revision, of mendings which do not "entirely consume" (as the Muse promised long ago in "A Fever") but rather refine both poet and poem. But the art is also once again theatrical, this time not in its use of masks so much as in Merrill's sense of the equally performative natures of love's bestowals and of poetry. "What is at stake," as Kristeva explains, "is turning the crisis [of postmodern love and narcissism] into a *work in progress*," in which love remains a "builder of spoken spaces" (*Tales* 380, 382). The words of love make something happen, enact a new reality. Rather than build a new world, a new room, within the poet himself, the restorative and performative art of love we find in Merrill's work from "Ephraim" onward creates a room that both poet and "friend" inhabit. We see this faith in "Ephraim," where we learn that "We must improve the line / In every sense, for life" (*Divine Comedies* 135), and in "Clearing the Title" and "The House Fly" from *Late Settings* (1985). But I find it best embodied in "A Room at the Heart of Things," Merrill's tender revision of a poem he has said he finds as inspiring as others find the Twenty-third Psalm: Wallace Stevens's "Final Soliloquy of the Interior Paramour" (qtd. in *Voices and Visions: Wallace Stevens*).

"We say God and the imagination are one . . . ," Stevens writes, and his ellipses suggest the lonely disappointment solaced by the claim. Out of the "light" of that claim, he makes his Paramour a "dwelling in the evening air, / In which being there together is enough" (524). Merrill's poem, too, takes place at "the vanishing point / / Inside [the poet's] head" where "vows endure beyond / Earshot of lovers who dissolved their bond" (*Inner Room* 20). Here, though, there are "Two rooms, rather" (*Inner Room* 18); and there seem to be two characters, an actor and a "lover" who writes lines for the other to read, like "the curtain line (Act II): / 'Light of my life, I've made a play for you!' " (19). Since *The Inner Room* is dedicated to actor Peter Hooten, we might be tempted to say that the poet's inner room has at last received a human visitor, not just the Muse or the figure "Ephraim" names "The ancient, ageless woman of the world" (*Divine Comedies* 136). But Merrill makes sure that we cannot tell whether one room or two, one lover or a couple, are involved. All the poignant distinctions that Stevens gathers his courage and sings to overcome—between interior and outside worlds, companionable swordplay and solitary word play, Paramour and poet—are in Merrill's poem, *sin rubato*, undermined. The poem ends on an elegant theatrical pun, in which the powers of illumination and performance, of love and poetry, are joined at last:

But here, made room for, bare hypothesis
—Through swordplay or soliloquy or kiss

Emitting speed-of-light particulars—
Proves itself in the bright way of stars.

(*Inner Room* 21)

## Notes

1. Unless otherwise noted, all page references to Merrill's work are to the *Selected Poems: 1946–1985*.

2. My sense of the shape of Merrill's career, as well as my reading of several key poems, is indebted to the work of Caroline Fraser in her dissertation, *A Perfect Contempt: The Poetry of James Merrill*. She takes the phrase "a perfect contempt" from Marianne Moore's "Poetry": reading with "a perfect contempt," one finds in poetry "a place for the genuine." A similar space, as we will see, may be found there for love.

3. Merrill "teethed" on Brooks and Warren, he confesses in an interview (*Recitative* 54); surely Brooks's "The Language of Paradox" was part of that early learning, with its praise for a poet who "has actually before our eyes built within the song the 'pretty room' with which he says the lovers can be content" (17).

4. "Nor marble, nor the gilded monuments / Of princes shall outlive this powerful rhyme" Shakespeare swore in sonnet 55; here, though, any promise that anything will "live in this, and dwell in lovers' eyes" rings a little hollow.

5. In his essay "Love as Theater"—a curious apology for something like highbrow, high-art prostitution—Ronald de Sousa suggests that the "theater of love" would be superior to commonplace affairs in being "actually more civilized, at least in respect of two attributes of civilization . . . imagination and irony" (489). These attributes characterize Merrill's poetry as well.

6. "False, false the tale," Socrates announces before uncovering his head to give a second speech on love. *The Fire Screen* might take that recantation as its epigraph.

7. This book is, as David Kalstone has said, Merrill's "book of love," one that "reads like a sonnet sequence following the curve of a love affair to its close," in its progress "challenging some of the balanced views of *Nights and Days*" (105).

8. Richard Howard calls this poem "inextricably dedicated to a language and a personality" (409). It seems to me that the personality comes through rather more strongly.

9. I stress, in this reading, the artistic and linguistic roots that Merrill finds in his affairs—the degree to which he takes himself to be one of those La Rochefoucauld described, who would never fall in love unless they'd read about it. For now I will not pursue the question of familial scripting that Merrill, like so many other American poets, most notably Robert Lowell, explored in the 1950s and 1960s.

10. It may be objected that a poet with Merrill's love for word play would hardly mind the sort of loose pun we find in "common sense" and "common scenes." "A Freudian slip is taken seriously," he complains in "Object Lessons," because "it betrays its maker's hidden wish. The pun (or the rhyme, for that matter) 'merely' betrays the hidden wish of words" (*Recitative* 111). The date of this interview, though, is 1972, coinciding to my mind with the reconciliation with the Muse we find in that year's collection of poems, *Braving the Elements*, and not with the tone of *The Fire Screen*.

11. It is worth noting that references to some unnamed "lie" recur throughout the

dense, difficult poem that follows "Part of the Vigil," "Nike." The poet's self-accusal is displaced onto his harsh, lunar mistress. "The lie shone in her face before she spoke it," "Nike" begins (154).

> I held my breath in pity for the lie
> Which nobody would believe unless I did.
>
> . . . . . . . . . . . . . . . . . .
>
>                           She asked,
> Before the eyes were bandaged, the bubble burst
> And what she uttered with what I held back
> Ran in red spittle down the chin,
> Asked why I could not have lived the lie.

In the harsh glare, lunar or solar, of appraisal, the poet's urge to bestow graces, charms, and qualities on his beloved seems at best an instinctive delusion, and at worst deliberate treachery.

    12.   With its weary trimeter, "Last Words" revises yet a third poem from Yeats, "Mohini Chatterjee"; it turns that poem's reassuring recital of multiplied being ("I have been a king / I have been a slave" and so on [247]) into a poem of reductive repetition.

    13.   I explore the goal of amatory authenticity and its aesthetic implications in more detail in my dissertation, "What Is It Then Between Us? Traditions of Love in American Poetry."

    14.   A more dramatic example or more serious case of such melancholy can be found in Louise Glück's recent volume *Ararat*. I give a close, Kristevan reading of this book-length sequence in "It Meant I Loved."

    15.   How badly? As if in resistance or as an example, he goes so far as to urge the very embodiment of his craft to "Speak freely, without art" (*From the First Nine* 200), an insulting, impossible demand. In a later poem of reconciliation with his lost love, "Strato in Plaster," Merrill will give such behavior the Greek name "malakía," a "word in common use / Which means both *foolishness* and *self-abuse*," with the latter term here applicable in a purely emotional sense. He cannot hurt the Muse without abusing himself.

    16.   "Mornings" and "Matinees" are linked by more than etymology. It's as though the "Flue choking with the shock" of anger in "Mornings" caused the "coughing fit" the boy declares himself "so sorry" for in the later poem (161; 166).

    17.   Merrill ensures the ballad's place in the volume through a series of echoes. The village is built of "Greek revival houses" drawn from the world of "To My Greek"—and thence from "Days of 1964" and "From the Cupola"—while references to a shortage of "good-sized fish" reminds us of the caustic metaphors of "Remora." The later reference to "Time and Tenderness," who "write upon our faces / Until the pen strikes bone," likewise recalls the first poem of *The Fire Screen*, "Lorelei," where "Love with his chisel" deepened "the lines begun upon your face" (176, 137).

## Works Cited

Auden, W. H. *The Dyer's Hand and Other Essays*. New York: Vintage, 1989.

Barthes, Roland. *A Lover's Discourse: Fragments*. Trans. Richard Howard. New York: Hill and Wang, 1978.

———. *Roland Barthes*. Trans. Richard Howard. New York: Hill and Wang, 1977.

Brooks, Cleanth. *The Well-Wrought Urn: Studies in the Structure of Poetry*. New York: Harcourt, 1947.

de Sousa, Ronald. "Love as Theater." *The Philosophy of (Erotic) Love*. Ed. Robert C. Solomon and Kathleen M. Higgins. Lawrence: UP of Kansas, 1991. 447–91.

Emerson, Ralph Waldo. *Essays and Lectures*. New York: Library of America, 1983.

Fraser, Caroline Anne. *A Perfect Contempt: The Poetry of James Merrill*. Diss. Harvard U, 1987. Ann Arbor: UMI, 1988. 8806081.

Frost, Robert. *Selected Poems of Robert Frost*. New York: Holt, 1963.

Howard, Richard. *Alone with America: Essays on the Art of Poetry in the United States since 1950*. New York: Atheneum, 1980.

James, Henry. "The Art of Fiction" and "Preface to *The American*." *The Art of Criticism: Henry James on the Theory and the Practice of Fiction*. Ed. William Veedar and Susan M. Griffin. Chicago: U of Chicago P, 1986. 165–96; 271–85.

Kalstone, David. *Five Temperaments: Elizabeth Bishop, Robert Lowell, James Merrill, Adrienne Rich, John Ashbery*. New York: Oxford UP, 1977.

Keats, John. *The Poems*. Ed. Gerald Bullett. New York: Everyman's-Knopf, 1992.

Keller, Lynn. *Re-making It New: Contemporary American Poetry and the Modernist Tradition*. Cambridge Studies in American Literature and Culture. New York: Cambridge UP, 1987.

Kenner, Hugh. *A Homemade World: The American Modernist Writers*. New York: Morrow, 1975.

Kristeva, Julia. *Black Sun: Depression and Melancholia*. Trans. Leon S. Roudiez. European Perspectives. New York: Columbia UP, 1989.

———. *Tales of Love*. Trans. Leon S. Roudiez. New York: Columbia UP, 1987.

Lowell, Robert. *The Dolphin*. New York: Farrar, 1973.

McWhirter, David. *Desire and Love in Henry James: A Study of the Late Novels*. New York: Cambridge UP, 1989.

Merrill, James. *The Black Swan and Other Poems*. Athens: Icaros, 1946.

———. *Divine Comedies: Poems*. 1976. New York: Atheneum, 1983.

———. *The Fire Screen: Poems*. New York: Atheneum, 1983.

———. *From the First Nine: Poems 1946–1976*. New York: Atheneum, 1982.

———. *The Inner Room: Poems*. New York: Knopf, 1988.

———. *Late Settings: Poems*. New York: Atheneum, 1985.

———. *Recitative: Prose*. Ed. J. D. McClatchy. San Francisco: North Point, 1986.

———. *Selected Poems: 1946–1985*. New York: Knopf, 1992.

Nietzsche, Friedrich. Selections from *Daybreak: Thoughts on the Prejudices of Morality*. *The Philosophy of (Erotic) Love*. Ed. Robert C. Solomon and Kathleen M. Higgins. Lawrence: UP of Kansas, 1991. 140–43.

Perkins, David. *A History of Modern Poetry: Modernism and After*. Cambridge: Belknap-Harvard UP, 1987.

Plato. *Phaedrus and The Symposium*. *The Collected Dialogues of Plato*. Ed. Edith Hamilton and Huntington Cairns. Bolligen ser. 71. Princeton: Princeton UP, 1963.

Polhemus, Robert M. *Erotic Faith: Being in Love from Jane Austen to D. H. Lawrence*. Chicago: U of Chicago P, 1990.

Selinger, Eric. "It Meant I Loved: Louise Glück's *Ararat*." *Postmodern Culture* 3 (3), May 1993. [Electronic journal, unpaginated.]

———. "What Is It Then Between Us? Traditions of Love in American Poetry." Diss. University of California–Los Angeles, 1993.

Shakespeare, William. *Love's Labor's Lost*. *The Riverside Shakespeare*. Gen. Ed. G. Blakemore Evans. Boston: Houghton, 1974: 179–212.

————. *Shakespeare's Sonnets and a Lover's Complaint*. Ed. Stanley Wells. New York: Oxford UP, 1985.

Sidney, Sir Philip. *Selected Writings*. Ed. Richard Dutton. New York: Carcanet, 1987.

Singer, Irving. *The Nature of Love, vol. 1: Plato to Luther*. 2nd ed. Chicago: U of Chicago P, 1984. 3 vols. 1984–87.

————. *The Nature of Love, vol. 3: The Modern World*. 2nd ed. Chicago: U of Chicago P, 1987. 3 vols. 1984–87.

Stein, Gertrude. *Selected Writings of Gertrude Stein*. Ed. Carl Van Vechten. New York: Vintage, 1962.

Stendahl. "From *On Love*." *The Philosophy of (Erotic) Love*. Ed. Robert C. Solomon and Kathleen M. Higgins. Lawrence: UP of Kansas, 1991. 132–39.

Stevens, Wallace. *The Collected Poems*. 1954. New York: Vintage, 1982.

————. *Opus Posthumous*. Ed. Milton J. Bates. Rev. ed. New York: Vintage, 1990.

Vendler, Helen. *The Odes of John Keats*. Cambridge: Belknap-Harvard UP, 1983.

*Voices and Visions: Wallace Stevens: Man Made Out of Words*. Videocassette of PBS broadcast. Dir. Richard P. Rogers. Prod. Jill Janows. Writ. Robert Seidman. Ed. Corey Schaff. New York: New York Center for Visual History, 1988.

Whitman, Walt. *Complete Poetry and Collected Prose*. New York: Library of America, 1982.

Williams, William Carlos. *The Collected Poems of William Carlos Williams, Volume I: 1909–1939*. Ed. A. Walton Litz and Christopher MacGowan. New York: New Directions, 1986.

Yeats, W. B. *The Poems: A New Edition*. Ed. Richard J. Finneran. New York: Macmillan, 1983.

Yenser, Stephen. *The Consuming Myth: The Work of James Merrill*. Cambridge: Harvard UP, 1987.

# Against Apocalypse:
## Politics and James Merrill's
### *The Changing Light at Sandover*

LEE ZIMMERMAN

Admittedly, James Merrill is not a political poet in the manner of, say, Denise Levertov. Although Levertov wants to "attain such osmosis of the personal and the public . . . that no one would be able to divide our poems into categories," she nevertheless bases her answer to the question "What Is Political Poetry?" largely on "political or social content" (128), and, like many contemporary poets, she has been an activist. One recent study of her political poetry distinguishes her "clear moral and ideological position" from much modern poetry which remains "hermetic and socially disengaged" (Smith 232), a description Robert von Hallberg might find suitable for Merrill's work: "Politics, with few exceptions, is a subject Merrill deliberately disdains. . . . From [Merrill's] camp viewpoint politics is stylelessly over-laden with content; it can be ignored because the camp sensibility is prem-ised, as Susan Sontag has noted, on detachment" (110–11). Von Hallberg offers up passages where Merrill no sooner broaches a political issue than he retreats (Merrill refers in *The Book of Ephraim*, section "J," to "nuclear research / Our instinct first is to deplore, and second / To think no more of" [33]) and quotes "The Broken Home": "I rarely buy a newspaper, or vote. / To do so, I have learned, is to invite / The tread of a stone guest within my house" (142).[1] Indeed, Merrill has plainly conceded, "We all have our limits. I draw the line at politics or hippies" (*Recitative* 32). (Spoken in 1967, these must have sounded like fighting words.)

Merrill's poetry makes clear, however, that assertions are reversible. For him (to quote from Wallace Stevens's "Notes toward a Supreme Fiction," a poem Merrill says he "teethed on" [*Recitative* 42]), it is "not a choice / Between excluding things. It was not a choice / Between, but of" (229).

Reprinted from *Contemporary Literature* 30, (1989), 370–85. Copyright © 1989 by The University of Wisconsin Press, Madison, Wisconsin. Reprinted by permission.

Stephen Yenser, our most acute reader of Merrill's doubleness, begins his study with the observation that

> from the beginning . . . Merrill has been a writer uncannily alert to reversals and doublings. The duplicate and the didymous, the obverse and the inverse, the geminate and the specular are part and parcel of his art. Pun, paradox, alter ego, chiasmus, spoonerism, and all kinds of literary double-stopping and counterpointing are his stock in trade, as essential to his writing, to his "poem's world," as perhaps they are to what he thinks of, at least at times, as "the world's poem," where Mother Nature herself "sets meaning spinning like a coin." "Anything worth having's had both ways," he offers in *Sandover*, where he also proposes that we live in "One nature dual to the end." (4)

If the line drawn at politics, then, is a limit, it is also a starting line. (As for hippies, well, who is that lighting up a joint on the courthouse lawn in "Grass," the first poem in *Late Settings*?) Merrill does profess a distaste for political issues—"The lobbies? The candidates' rhetoric—our 'commitments abroad'? The Shah as Helen of Troy launching a thousand missile carriers? One whiff of all that, and I turn purple and start kicking my cradle"—then goes right on to sentences that betray strong political feelings:

> I like the idea of nations, actually, and even more those pockets of genuine strangeness within nations. Yet those are being emptied, turned inside out, made to conform—in the interest of what? The friendly American smile we're told to wear in our passport photos? Oh, it's not just in America. You can go to an outdoor concert in Athens—in that brown, poisonous air the government isn't strong enough to do anything about—and there are the president and the prime minister in their natty suits, surrounded by flashbulbs, hugging and patting each other as if they hadn't met for months. God have mercy on whoever's meant to be impressed by that. (*Recitative* 71)

This passage makes some pretty easy complaints (who is not against dirty air and self-congratulatory politicos?), but it is rife with more complex, and more seriously political, feelings about growing cultural homogeneity and the erosion of local identity. Similarly, the socially disengaged lines from "The Broken Home" that von Hallberg quotes are followed by qualification: "Shooting this rusted bolt, though, against him [the "stone guest" of politics] / I trust I am no less time's child than some / Who on the heath impersonate Poor Tom / Or on the barricades risk life and limb." A few lines later Merrill adds, "I am earth's no less" (142).

"Rarely" buying a newspaper or voting doesn't self-evidently signal a disdain for political concerns. But to declare oneself "time's child" and "earth's" is very much to commit oneself; to feel implicated in history and nature is the very opposite of disengagement. To recognize these parents, though, is to take seriously their divorce. Earlier in "The Broken Home" Merrill writes:

> Always that same old story—
> Father Time and Mother Earth,
> A marriage on the rocks.
>
> (141)

And he has made quite clear how seriously this break is to be taken:

> That bit in "The Broken Home"—"Father Time and Mother Earth, / A marriage on the rocks"—isn't meant as a joke. History in our time *has* cut loose, *has* broken faith with Nature. But poems, even those of the most savage incandescence, can't deal frontally with such huge, urgent subjects without sounding grumpy or dated when they should still be in their prime. So my parents' divorce dramatized on a human scale a subject that couldn't have been handled otherwise. Which is what a "poetic" turn of mind allows for. You don't see eternity *except* in the grain of sand, or history except at the family dinner table. (*Recitative* 72)

Merrill here defines the political urgency in his writing. Before I explore this in the trilogy itself, though, it may be worth briefly pondering one problem his remark raises. You "can't deal frontally with such huge, urgent subjects without sounding grumpy or dated," but is mere grumpiness the only problem? Lurking here is a more troubling one, I think: how can a text—which by its nature unifies, weaves together, makes whole (*text* derives from the Indo-European root *teks*, "to weave")—respond to historical events, especially in the twentieth century, that defy wholeness? Must any attempt to accommodate the nightmare of history to consciousness falsify that horror? Have the Nazis, for example, outstripped our capacity to conceive of what they have done? *Can* we, as *Sandover* puts it, "make sense" of things? Christopher Lasch writes about the Final Solution: "The trouble is . . . that words fail in the face of evil on such a scale. . . . Who can remain silent, having witnessed such events? But a language of extremity, the only language appropriate to extreme situations, soon loses its force through repetition and inflation. It facilitates what it seeks to prevent, the normalization of atrocity" (101).

One sort of answer to this problem may rely on indirection. Although she imagines Truth as dazzling rather than dark, we might still heed Emily Dickinson's directive: "Tell all the Truth but tell it slant—/ Success in Circuit lies" (# 1129). Merrill would likely resist the rather grandiose list of questions I've strung out above, characteristically preferring terms on a more human scale ("grumpy"). But no matter how the question is framed, his answer remains the Dickinsonian one. I'll return in more detail to the relationship between the wholeness of a text and the contingency of the world. The point here is that if you "can't deal frontally with such urgent issues," Merrill also knows you may deal with them slantwise—and that the issues *are* urgent, that "History in our time . . . *has* broken faith with Nature."

The urgent issues are most circuitously broached before the trilogy, while in *Late Settings* the subjects become more explicitly political and there is a pervading sense of imminent nuclear and ecological disaster ("*Nature / Is dead, or soon will be,*" announces one of the statues in "Bronze" [52]; "Radiometer" concludes, "World without end? / Not this one. Look: the setting sun, my friend" [69]). What of *Sandover* itself? Charles Berger argues, "The epigraph to *Mirabell* reinforces the idea that the trilogy's center of anxious concern, its deep origin, however clouded by mythic analogue or autobiographical excursion [tell it slant], is the development of the atomic bomb [but tell all the truth]" (282). (Merrill might say that it is only *by* myth and autobiography that this anxious concern can take shape.) The "central question" of *Scripts*, Yenser proposes, "is whether humanity can save itself from destruction" (288).

As its beginning suggests, the trilogy will approach this subject only from a slant. The opening lines convey a sense of great urgency:

> Admittedly I err by undertaking
> This in its present form. The baldest prose
> Reportage was called for, that would reach
> The widest public in the shortest time.
> Time, it had transpired, was of the essence.
> Time, the very attar of the Rose,
> Was running out.
>
> (3)

But why this urgency? Time is of the essence in the sense that Time is a central thematic concern of *Ephraim*, but that phrase first means "time is short," or, as the poem puts it, time is running out. In what sense? One of the stories the poem tells, in the present tense, is of its composition from January to December 1974, the year Merrill turned forty-eight; he is hardly an old man, and apparently in good health, so "time was running out" cannot (very rationally) mean he is worried about his time being up before the poem is written. The imperative to reach "the widest public in the shortest time" suggests, rather, that time is running out for all of us. Since Time is defined here as "the very attar of the Rose," and "Rose" leads us to Rosamund Smith, "Perennially youthful" (13), who is linked to the "ancient, ageless woman of the world" (92)—to Earth itself—the lines at least hint at ecological collapse. Or one might think of the "nuclear research" in the lines von Hallberg quotes from section "J"; although "Our instinct first is to deplore [it] and second / To think no more of [it]," the subject nevertheless emerges again, more fully, in "P":

> NO SOULS CAME FROM HIROSHIMA U KNOW
> EARTH WORE A STRANGE NEW ZONE OF ENERGY
> Caused by? SMASHED ATOMS OF THE DEAD MY DEARS
> News that brought into play our deepest fears.
>
> (55)

What compounds their fear is the sense that "when the flood ebbed, or the fire burned low, / Heaven, the world no longer at its feet, / Itself would up and vanish" (56). The image calls to Merrill's mind watching Valhalla burn at the opera on his thirteenth birthday, and he wonders, "How to rid Earth, for Heaven's sake, of power / Without both turning to a funeral pyre?" If anything in *Ephraim* explains its opening urgency, this does, and in turn the opening emphasizes the importance of "P."

And yet, the public threat posed by "P" doesn't really pervade *Ephraim*, whose concern is more to establish the interdependence of heaven and earth (imagination and reality, art and life) than to consider their possible demise. (As early as 1950, however, Merrill is making clear that if earth is heaven we can turn it into hell; "Paradise is *here*, in these rocks, in that white sand!" he writes of Kyoto in "The Beaten Path" [*Recitative* 145], a polished travel diary, in which the title of the next entry reads: "Hiroshima.") As far as this first book of the trilogy goes, the opening lines remain something of a mystery. A mystery, anyway, until we read them in light of *Sandover* as a whole. To "err" is to take the circuitous route Dickinson knows is the way to Truth; having read the entire poem, having considered the dark forces we must hold back in order to save the Greenhouse, we are returned finally to the beginning, with the urgency, and the need for erring, clarified.

These dark forces (whose presence, we realize on rereading, has already clouded *Ephraim*, in "P") move toward the foreground of the poem with the epigraph to *Mirabell*. In addition to suggesting the trilogy's "center of anxious concern, its deep origin," as Berger sees, it also announces that the question of human *will* is close to the heart of Merrill's thinking about this concern. The nuclear scientists "were the first men to see matter yield its inner energy, steadily, at their will," Laura Fermi boasts—but *is* nuclear energy released "steadily"? Can its power be made subservient to human will? Our technocratic culture—more and more caught up in infantile fantasies of omnipotence—has liked to think so.[2] So did the bats, whose destruction resulted from pride in their atomic powers and a corresponding denial of their dependence on earth. Here is Yenser's summary of their confusing history:

> Originally developed in order to serve those centaurs as messengers, they later
> became architects and then physicists, charged by the younger centaurs with

devising atomic weapons powerful enough to blast an increasingly burdensome
population of decrepit immortals down to a convenient size. Having dreamed
up such weapons, the bats overthrew their masters and created their own
civilization—a shimmering network of "SMOOTH PLAINS & LATTICE CITIES"
suspended above Earth. . . . Encroaching vegetation eventually weakened the
moorings, and because they were too proud to lower themselves to repairing
them, the bats finally perished with their antigravitational world. (255)

Fermi liked to think the new powers were docilely at our will, but partly
on the basis of his species' tragic history, Mirabell warns, "THE ATOM
CANNOT BE MAN'S NATURAL FRIEND" (183).

This demonstrated danger of the will helps illuminate why the poem,
especially in *Mirabell*, so often huddles by the safety of the "no accident"
clause, which seemingly puts matters beyond merely human control. Indeed,
in *Scripts* Gabriel reveals that the clause begins in just this motivation: "GOD
CREATED HIS THIRD CHILD & GAVE THE COMMAND: LET / IT SURVIVE AND
LET THERE BE NO ACCIDENT" (473). Berger sees that "the strength of JM
and DJ comes to reside in their being able to provide a space where things
happen"—in the relaxation of the will rather than its assertion—and finds
in the work a "negative prescription for the will" (289–90). And we do see,
for example, that the entire history of our mediums' friendship with MM,
down to the "naps at Sounion," has been strictly plotted. In one sense,
clearly, *Sandover* recoils from the potentially destructive human will that
glowers menacingly, like the Monitor itself, from the epigraph to *Mirabell*.

But, JM knows, "anything worth having's had both ways" (174), and
we can look at the question of will through the other end of the spyglass.
If "no accident," spied at from one end, removes events from human agency,
from the other it restores them there, for the other-worldly powers that
control things are at the same time aspects of JM and DJ. When asked
whether the "trilogy's caps" are "a case of the return of the repressed,"
Merrill responds, "You're probably exactly right there, at least where the
'Grand Design' is concerned" (*Recitative* 70). We might remember here that
Freud also thought there was no accident, that things were charged with
human meaning, interpretable in terms of the unconscious (a synonym for
God, in the Jungian terms JM evokes in *Ephraim*, section "U"); matters
that might appear to occur outside of conscious intention were nevertheless
shaped by the mind. To the extent that psychoanalysis—or poetry or other
ways of making sense—aims at establishing an interplay between conscious
and unconscious (to evoke only one possible pair of terms) parts of the self,
it posits an essential human freedom, and this notion of freedom is finally
at the heart of *Sandover*. If it cautions against an absolute faith in an omnipo-
tent human will, it also imagines we might at least be free enough to save
ourselves.

Whether we will or not remains an open question in *Scripts*. No sooner does DJ imagine that Nature's last "Yes" resolves the issue than the coin of meaning spins again:

> But in fact
> Nature said Yes to man—the question's settled.
> SHE SAYS DEAR BOY EXACTLY WHAT SHE MEANS
> LOOK IT UP "A last resounding Yes."
> LAST? The fête was ending. JM: Or
> Because man won't be hearing Yes much more?
> AH SHE SETS MEANING SPINNING LIKE A COIN.
>
> (492)

Is the X that God B traces with the cup in the final lesson "the mark / That cancels, or the letter-writer's kiss" (493)? The poem makes clear, especially in key moments toward the end, that it is up to us to decide. "We do the judging? Everyone?" asks JM about which way to take Nature's ambiguous "last Yes"; WHA answers, "INDEED." In "The Sermon at Ephesus," Maria warns, "PREPARE TO WEAN / YRSELVES OF THE FATAL DELUSION OF ALLPROV-IDING / HEAVEN. MAN MUST PROVIDE" (496), a lesson God B himself implies in the last lesson: "MY UPRIGHT MAN / FULL OF TIME HE STRUGGLES TO HOLD IT BACK / AND CREATE FOR ME A PARADISE" (494). "I never cared much for the pose of the atheist," Merrill has commented, "though the Angels came round to that, you know, in their way, insisting on man as master of his own destiny" (*Recitative* 70). When God B refers to the "DARK FORCE WE / CONTAIN," his two-sided phrase tells us also what it is that must be mastered; "CONTAIN" locates the force both outside the self (a geopolitical strategy of containment) but also within (to contain one's feelings). The boundary is simultaneously observed and dissolved.

It is because we must "HOLD IT BACK" that *Sandover* is more an anti-apocalyptic work than an apocalyptic one. Drawing on Frank Kermode's description of literary patterns of apocalypse, Berger reads Merrill as an "apocalyptic scribe." An important element of the apocalyptic paradigm, as Kermode describes it, is "a prophetic confidence of renovation" (99), and Berger emphasizes just this element: "According to Kermode," he writes, "certain features remain constant in the works of artists acutely conscious of the End, especially when the End is conceived of as a New Beginning" (283). The biblical Apocalypse promises this sort of redemptive New Beginning, and in general the sense of the "end" is a helpful thing as Kermode describes it, not only because it holds future promise, but because it helps make sense of human life lived in the chaotic middle of things: "Men in the middest make considerable imaginative investments in coherent patterns which, by the provision of an end, make possible a satisfying consonance with the origins and with the middle. That is why the image of the end can never be *permanently* falsified" (17). This underlies Kermode's understanding of imaginative fictions or literary plot:

> . . . The fact that we call the second of the two related sounds *tock* is
> evidence that we use fictions to enable the end to confer organization and
> form on the temporal structure. The interval between the two sounds, between
> *tick* and *tock* is now charged with significant duration. The clock's *tick-tock* I
> take to be a model of what we call a plot, an organization that humanizes
> time by giving it form; and the interval between *tock* and *tick* represents purely
> successive, disorganized time of the sort that we need to humanize. . . .
>
> *Tick* is a humble genesis, *tock* a feeble apocalypse. (45)

In short, "an end will bestow upon the whole duration and meaning" (46).

Kermode's study is imbued with Wallace Stevens, especially "Notes
toward a Supreme Fiction," so it is no surprise that, indirectly, it sheds
much light on *Sandover*. He discusses the "familiar dialogue between credulity
and scepticism" (18) about the apocalypse, for example, and takes as his
critical task to "make sense" of the ways poets "make sense" of our lives, a
phrase that becomes a motif in his analysis, as it will for Merrill. The need
for imaginative paradigms (ways of making sense) to remain alive and useful
even as they are continually revised as "reality" unfolds—Stevens's changing,
pleasurable Supreme Fiction—occupies both critic and poet. Finally, however, Merrill thinks about endings in crucially different ways than Kermode.
That *Sandover* sees the end might come in the rather loud *tock* of a nuclear
explosion profoundly changes how the end is conceived. For Kermode, nuclear weapons are essentially the latest focus for an abiding human sense of
eschatological crisis:

> I don't find it easy to see the uniqueness of our situation. . . . It seems
> doubtful that our crisis, our relation to the future and to the past, is one of
> the important differences between us and our predecessors. Many of them felt
> as we do. If the evidence looks good to us, so it did to them. . . . Other
> people have noticed this, and expressed their feelings about it in images
> different from ours, armies in the sky, for example, or a palpable Antichrist;
> and these we have discarded. But it would be childish to argue, in a discussion
> of how people behave under eschatological threat, that nuclear bombs *are more
> real* and make one experience more authentic crisis-feelings than armies in
> the sky. (95; emphasis added)

But nuclear bombs are not merely another version of the fiction of
armies in the sky (though, as Paul Chilton shows, from their inception one
way we have lived with them is by associating them with God). For one
thing, human action might conceivably prevent nuclear war; what could
prevent armies in the sky (and what good man would want to)? History is
full of natural and man-made catastrophes, but the power to launch the
apocalyptic armies rests now for the first time in human hands. If nuclear
bombs—man-made—are not "more real" than God's armies in the sky
(*especially* in a discussion of "how people behave under eschatological threat,"

and how they ought to), at least the possibility that the bomb/armies might literally drop from the sky is more real, after 1945, than before. Einstein foresaw the difficulty our imaginative paradigms would have keeping pace with a reality that, after it was rendered radically contingent at Hiroshima, changed so profoundly: "The unleashed power of the atom has changed everything save our modes of thinking, and we thus drift toward unparalleled catastrophe" (376).

Modern paradigms do grow out of old ones, as Kermode stresses, but at the same time we need fictions, like Merrill's, to respond to the radical contingency posed by nuclear weaponry, to the fact that "the unleashed power of the atom has changed everything." One way of responding is to rethink our sense of an ending. Kermode powerfully explains, as I've suggested, how the imagined end renders the middle meaningful; but *Sandover* sees that now the end would obliterate rather than bestow meaning. There is no "prophetic confidence of renovation" (crucial to Kermode's "apocalyptic paradigm"), but rather a commitment to contain the dark forces. The end is to be fended off (thus the poem bites its tail), not imagined as redemptive. Yeats exemplifies for Kermode a modern apocalyptic writer, but it never was a matter of holding back the rough beast. *Sandover* does draw on elements of the apocalyptic paradigm, and it is certainly a poem of crisis in Kermode's terms, but finally it sees the end as the end, and not a New Beginning. It is thus an anti-apocalypse: a poem not about a new heaven and a new earth, but about saving the old ones.

This is not to say that as a literary fiction the trilogy doesn't take shape and meaning by virtue of its ending. Indeed, it is a highly patterned poem, quite unlike less shapely, cumulative, virtually endless works like *Paterson* or the *Cantos*. The problem it must thus confront is this: as a literary fiction the poem derives its meaning from its end; but the fiction of the world the poem offers holds that the end wouldn't make sense but rather would annihilate it. The poem is whole; the world has been rendered contingent.

This does not mean, however, that the poem must fail. Its "wholeness," to begin with, is hardly straightforward. Kermode's praise of Sartre's *Nausea* is pertinent here: "Its form has elements of the eidetic, but upon such images are superimposed new images of contingency. Thus the inherited form is made, for a time at any rate, acceptable to those whose life behind the screen of words has not entirely closed their eyes to the nature of the world. The form of *La Nausée* is an instructive dissonance between humanity and contingency" (150). He points out that when "Anny gave Roquentin the kiss which sealed the relationship, she was sitting in a patch of nettles," and claims, "If life were 'like a work of art' this would not occur"; thus, "If the world of words is to have value, if it is to be distinguished from the protective fictions of the *salauds* and the nineteenth-century novelists, the nettles must be there" (149). Much here separates Kermode from Merrill, but we can say that in *Sandover* the human urge to wholeness and the contingency of the world interact, that the nettles are there. Fragments of the lost novel ruffle the surface of *Ephraim*, for example, and much of the bats' story in *Mirabell* likewise pricks the reader. Then, too, key parts of the trilogy *don't* depend on the end for meaning; important lyrical set pieces, like "Samos," are meaningful even lifted from the poem's narrative structure. The end itself is contingent, returning us to the start—stopping us in midphrase—as it fights off finality. (Beginnings, too, are contingent. "Friction made the first thin consommé / Of all we know" [495], Merrill writes after the final lesson, but his description of the origin and history of the world also describes his own childhood. Finally origins remain a mystery, as Maria tells JM, "HUSH ENFANT FOR NO MAN'S MIND CAN REACH / BEYOND THAT HIM & HER" [495].)

It is true that sometimes the nettles seem smoothed over. In the last pages of the coda, life intrudes on art, as at a climactic moment Ephraim's address to the crowded ballroom is interrupted by the doorbell:

> Ephraim has risen. The room dims. His glance
> Lights the chandeliers. A reverence,
> MAJESTY AND FRIENDS—when shatteringly
> The doorbell rings. Our doorbell here in Athens.
> We start up. David opens to a form
> Gaunt, bespectacled, begrimed, in black,
> But black worn days, nights, journeyed, sweated in—
> Vasíli? Ah sweet Heaven, sit him down,
> Take his knapsack, offer food and brandy—.
> He shakes his head. Mimí. Mimí in Rome
> Buried near Shelley. He can't eat, can't sleep,
> Can't weep. D makes to put away the Board,
> Explaining with a grimace of pure shame
> —Because, just as this life takes precedence
> Over the next one, so does live despair
> Over a poem or a parlor game—
> Explaining what our friend has stumbled in on.
>
> (558)

This last scissoring, though, is soon mended, for they do carry on with JM's reading, and Vasíli neatly takes his place in the last empty chair, apparently the previously missing twenty-sixth guest. Art has accommodated life.

And it hasn't. Vasíli's terrible pain over Mimí's death remains vivid, and while he might be diverted by the reading, he won't be too quickly consoled. The poem is neatly rounded off, but Vasíli's grief nettles; time comes full circle even as we're left with the sting of death. The awful but cheerful conclusion defers finality, but also thus defers *to* it, having it both ways.

If the poem, then, is whole, it is also contingent. But just as Merrill knows that he, the artist, is "Two-minded," so is "any atom" (232–33)—nature itself. If the world, that is, is contingent, it is also whole. Though the form-giving world of words may console us, for Kermode (and Sartre) "reality" resists meaning, is finally absurd, and thus the poverty out of which the poem springs is complete: "There are no circles in reality" (149). For Merrill, there *are* circles in reality, as the whole of his work attests; in "Samos" the world is an interconnected web, with language as one of its threads—to "make sense" is to discover as well as to create meaning. Quite futile to absolutely separate the elements of nature, or to separate heaven and earth. But the whole must depend on each part. *Sandover* reminds us that the imagination that makes the earth heaven can also destroy it ( just as, again, "Paradise is here" directly preceded a description of Hiroshima). It is true for *Sandover* as a whole what Yenser writes about its first book: one of its "chief aims is precisely to help to 'CREATE THE MOULDS OF HEAVENLY PERFECTION' and even 'THE ONES ABOVE.' This idea of a world that has the potential of creating the ideal it might become lies at the heart of *Ephraim*" (238). As Yenser connects Ephraim's lecture on the moulds of heavenly perfection, in "Q," to Jung, whom Merrill echoes in "U," the entire trilogy is even more clearly illuminated: "According to Jung the crucial question is 'whether man can climb up to a higher moral level, to a higher plane of consciousness, in order to be equal to the superhuman powers' he possesses. If he fails to do so, man has neither excuse nor future, 'for the dark God . . . has given him the power to empty out the apocalyptic vials of wrath on his fellow creatures' " (239).[3] We are Gabriel as well as Michael, Psyche is Chaos, and we contain—and thus must contain—the dark forces. In this sense the poem's world, like the world's poem, is both whole and contingent, full but unfolding, harmonious but still amassing. Its fiction doesn't falsify the danger; rather, it offers a vision out of which we may yet put things right.

This vision of interdependence—especially its implications for self-hood—is perhaps more deeply political than even the poem's explicitly posed warning and challenge. With it, Merrill stands up against the oppositional thinking that has made the arms race possible. The world is seen as a gameboard for a game with only two players; Third World countries have no interests or identity of their own (no "self") but exist only in relation to the grand "geopolitical" struggle between good (us) and evil (them). (Can it be that we do not generally shorten "Soviet Union" to "S.U." because it is too clearly the mirror image of "U.S."?) If the rhetoric is sometimes softened, if our leaders have learned to stop openly calling the Soviet Union an "evil empire," the absolutist separation of good and evil—which is straight out of Revelation—nevertheless has widespread legitimacy and still underlies our military and foreign policy.

Such thinking depends upon a strict separation between self and other. In this, it is outmoded (because it is literally no longer viable), an inferior fiction that has failed to change. N. Katherine Hayles writes that the "twenti-eth century has seen a profound transformation in the ground of its thought," from "the older paradigm implicit in Newtonian mechanics, the atomistic, 'common sense' perspective we are all familiar with that views the world as composed of objects situated in an empty rectilinear space," to a newer fiction, "catalyzed and validated" by science, that she calls the "field concept" (15, 16). The "distinguishing characteristics" of the field are "its fluid, dynamic nature, the inclusion of the observer, the absence of detachable parts, and the mutuality of component interaction" (15). Because of the "stickiness of the situation, our inability to extricate the object of our descrip-tion from the situation itself," the image she proposes for the field is the "cosmic web" (21), and she shows the range of ways an intuition or awareness of this web informs modern literary strategies. Sometimes (as in Pynchon) the web, which after all is a weapon of prey, may seem to diminish the self. We do see Merrill, in *Ephraim*, feeling that "In neither / The world's poem nor the poem's world have I / Learned to think for myself, much" (85) and, because he is "Imbued with otherness," that "I take up / Less emotional space than a snowdrop" (89). This feeling comes to a head in *Mirabell* 9.1, where JM complains that the middle book is "maddening—it's all by some-one else! / In your voice, Wystan, or in Mirabell's":

> I'd set
> My whole heart, after *Ephraim*, on returning
> To private life, to my own words. Instead,
> Here I go again, a vehicle
> In this cosmic carpool. Mirabell once said
> He taps my word banks. I'd be happier
> If *I* were tapping them. Or thought I were.
> (261–62)

If "all is translation," as Merrill says in another poem, then "every bit of us is lost in it."

"Or found," as "Lost in Translation" also tells us (352). To lose the absolutely private "Newtonian" self isn't necessarily to dissolve away com-pletely. Rather, *by virtue of* one's interconnectedness with things, the self may be found, empowered by its own relativity, by the tension ("friction" or "resistance" in the trilogy) between sameness and difference. "The Green-house [unity] from the start had been / An act of resistance" (453); "Friction made the first thin consommé / Of all we know" (495). "CAN U STILL BE BENT," Wystan answers JM's complaint, "AFTER OUR COURSE IN HOW TO SEE PAST LONE / AUTONOMY TO POWERS BEHIND THE THRONE, / ON DOING YR OWN THING: EACH TEENY BIT / (PARDON MME) MADE PERSONAL AS SHIT?" (262)—but the powers behind the throne are partly those of Merrill himself. And lone autonomy having gone by the boards, they are partly those of David Jackson, too, who in another image of the creative tension between the one and the many calls each speaker in the poem "a changing aspect of the single light" (Jackson 305). As Merrill had put it in "From the Cupola," "Oh but one has many, many tongues!" (150).

The trilogy, then, poses the counterhegemonic fiction of the cosmic web. In *Ephraim* this is largely a matter of an intricate maze of textual interconnections of the sort Yenser follows (236–37) as he shows how every character and landscape, it seems, is a version of Rosamund Smith ("Mrs. Myth" in *Mirabell* 7.6), Earth itself, or Time, or the "naked current" (84), the absolute to which we are drawn and—because the characters are also themselves—from which we are insulated. In *Mirabell* and *Scripts*, it is a matter of the increasing importance of conversation, as a narrative strategy and a way of knowing. Conversation, indeed, may model a way of containing the dark forces. As opposed to the narcissistic denial of the Other basic to absolutist world views, in conversation one voice depends upon its counterpart; the interplay requires both self and other—and *Sandover* locates authority or truth precisely *in* this interplay. Making sense is revealed as a group effort, and an ongoing one. "Mutual endeavor is the indispensable thing" (*Recitative* 59).

For the most part, the current inhabitants of the Greenhouse are thwarting such mutuality. Power is more and more highly centralized (as, for instance, the family farm in the U.S. gives way to corporate agribusiness, mergers concentrate economic and technological power in fewer and fewer hands, highly centralized energy sources replace local ones,[4] and mass-produced fictions homogenize the ways we understand ourselves and the world).[5] Nuclear weapons are perhaps the most extreme example of such concentrations of power, especially as we accumulate them to the incredible degree that we have (and as the U.S. openly states its policy to *use* them in certain circumstances, even against nonnuclear attack). In this accumulation and planned use, the Other is most dramatically suppressed—or made into the devil, the repository for our own dark forces. This leaves us entirely in the clear, with no sense of our own complicity as a nation in what is troubling in the world, with no sense of containing our own darkness. How can you have too many weapons when you are innocent and are fighting the Antichrist? There is only one sanctioned way of seeing things. Authority is located in a single place.

In its reliance on conversation, in its double origin (JM and DJ), in its understanding of the kinship of and distinction between its many, many tongues, *Sandover* locates authority everywhere. If the structure of the otherworld seems hierarchical, almost at times military, the separation of the ranks (as of the two worlds themselves) is always qualified—and the speech of the place is dialogue, not the giving of orders (Mirabell very quickly replaces 40076). Even its God isn't absolute but exists in relation to his brothers in the Pantheon (itself a multiple authority). The trilogy thus describes and embodies a cosmic web that depends upon and transfigures the particularity of the self. "At this point in history," Christopher Lasch writes, "it is essential to question the boundless confidence in human powers that acknowledges no limits, which finds its ultimate expression in the technology of nuclear warfare. But this cannot be done . . . by dissolving the subject-object distinction. . . . Selfhood . . . is precisely the inescapable awareness of man's contradictory place in the natural order of things" (257). We need, that is, poems of two minds, like Merrill's. Without recognizing the world in the self and the self in the world there can be no conversation; without the subject-object distinction there can be no containment.

The trilogy sees that the web, though whole, is seriously at risk. It sounds a warning and enacts a way of making sense of the world out of which the warning might be heeded. If to save the Greenhouse we have need of activists, we also need those who make fictions that can shape how we might act. Even if he still doesn't often read a newspaper or vote, Merrill has given us such a politically useful fiction. "The poet isn't always the hero of a movie who *does* this, *does* that," he knows; "He is a man choosing the words he lives by" (*Recitative* 21). With *The Changing Light at Sandover*, Merrill has chosen at least some of the words by which, if it is not too late, all of us might yet live.

## Notes

1. Quotations from Merrill's poetry before *The Book of Ephraim* are from *From the First Nine*. These include all poems except the trilogy and those from *Late Settings*. Quotations from *The Book of Ephraim*, *Mirabell's Books of Number*, *Scripts for the Pageant*, and "Coda: The Higher Keys" are from *The Changing Light at Sandover*.

2. As Paul Chilton argues, the assumption that nuclear weapons can be controlled is reflected in the practice of naming them after useful and easily mastered tools. The scientists who made it, for example, referred to the first A-bomb as "the gadget."

3. Yenser is quoting Jung, "Answer to Job" (638–39).

4. It is not that centralized energy sources are more economically sound. On the contrary, discussing some problems of the electric power industry, Barry Commoner writes, "A major reason for these economic difficulties is that the present technology of electric-power production is highly centralized" (61).

5. For an analysis of the increasing global cultural homogeneity, see Ivan Illich. He writes, for example: "For two decades now, about fifty languages have died each year; half of those still spoken in 1950 survive only as subjects for doctoral theses. And what distinct languages do remain to witness the incomparably different ways of seeing, using, and enjoying the world now sound more and more alike. Consciousness is everywhere colonized by imported labels" (7–8).

*Works Cited*

Berger, Charles. "Merrill and Pynchon: Our Apocalyptic Scribes." *James Merrill*: *Essays in Criticism*. Ed. David Lehman and Charles Berger. Ithaca: Cornell UP, 1983. 282–97.

Chilton, Paul. "Nukespeak: Nuclear Language, Culture, and Propaganda." *Nukespeak*: *The Media and the Bomb*. Ed. Crispen Aubrey. London: Comedia, 1982.

Commoner, Barry. "A Reporter at Large (The Environment)." *New Yorker* 15 June 1987. 46–71.

Dickinson, Emily. *The Poems of Emily Dickinson*. Ed. Thomas H. Johnson. Cambridge: Harvard UP, 1955.

Einstein, Albert. *Einstein on Peace*. Ed. Otto Nathan and Heinz Norden. New York: Simon, 1960.

Hayles, N. Katherine. *The Cosmic Web*: *Scientific Field Models and Literary Strategies in the Twentieth Century*. Ithaca: Cornell UP, 1984.

Illich, Ivan D. *Toward a History of Needs*. New York: Pantheon, 1978.

Jackson, David. "Lending a Hand." *James Merrill*: *Essays in Criticism*. Ed. David Lehman and Charles Berger. Ithaca: Cornell UP, 1983, 298–305.

Jung, Carl. "Answer to Job." *The Portable Jung*. Ed. Joseph Campbell. Trans. R. F. C. Hull. New York: Viking, 1971. 519–650.

Kermode, Frank. *The Sense of an Ending*: *Studies in the Theory of Fiction*. New York: Oxford UP, 1967.

Lasch, Christopher. *The Minimal Self*: *Psychic Survival in Troubled Times*. New York: Norton, 1984.

Levertov, Denise. "On the Edge of Darkness: What Is Political Poetry?" *Light Up the Cave*. New York: New Directions, 1981. 115–29.

Merrill, James. *The Changing Light at Sandover, Including the whole of The Book of Ephraim, Mirabell's Books of Number, Scripts for the Pageant and a new coda, The Higher Keys*. New York: Atheneum, 1982.

———. *From the First Nine: Poems 1946–1976*. New York: Atheneum, 1982.

———. *Late Settings*. New York: Atheneum, 1985.

———. *Recitative*: *Prose by James Merrill*. Ed. J. D. McClatchy. San Francisco: North Point, 1986.

Smith, Lorrie. "Songs of Experience: Denise Levertov's Political Poetry." *Contemporary Literature* 27 (1986): 213—32.

Stevens, Wallace. *The Palm at the End of the Mind*: *Selected Poems and a Play*. Ed. Holly Stevens. New York: Vintage-Random, 1972.

Von Hallberg, Robert. *American Poetry and Culture, 1945–1980*. Cambridge: Harvard UP, 1985.

Yenser, Stephen. *The Consuming Myth*: *The Work of James Merrill*. Cambridge: Harvard UP, 1987.

# From Polylinguism to Metalinguism: Dante's Language in Merrill's Trilogy[1]

## Andrea Mariani

In both his lyric poems and in the epic-narrative *The Changing Light at Sandover*, James Merrill has often explicitly acknowledged the influence of Dante's language on his poetry, as, for example, in the title of the collection that includes *The Book of Ephraim*: *Divine Comedies*.[2] I begin, then, with a quick review of some of Merrill's most significant references to Dante and his epic.

In the serious *and* facetious tone most typical of *The Changing Light at Sandover*, Merrill, projected in the character JM, and his alter ego DJ, David Jackson, confess to extensive musing on Dante and the system that shapes his *Commedia*: "We'd long since slept through our last talk on Thomist / Structures in Dante . . ." (*Ephraim*, C, 9). And later, acknowledging the centrality of the term *circles* to Dante's work, Merrill confirms that Dante is his primary and most important teacher: "Designs? you whisper with a shamefaced look. / Precisely. Orderings of experience. / From Dante's circles to Kandinsky's" (*Ephraim*, T, 69). In *Mirabell*, after a first, summary description of the trilogy's other world (2.3, 136), a perplexed JM reflects that it all seems a sort of "Warmed-up Milton, Dante, Genesis / This great tradition that has come to grief / In volumes by Blavatsky and Gurdjieff."

For Merrill, then, Dante is one of many voices of a polylingual or, better, polyphonic inheritance;[3] Dante belongs to a tradition Merrill stands before in much the same posture as Dante stands to his tradition when he encounters such predecessors as Guido Guinizelli and Arnaut Daniel. However, given the contrast between the gradual revelation that JM must undergo and the stable structure he recalls in Dante, Merrill's poem sometimes experiences this tradition as wholly inaccessible and at others as a mere historical pattern, part of a specific cultural context or the spirit of a past age: as the poem puts it, the descriptions of hell "In Homer and Dante were needed (underground shelters / from light) by dull animalistic lives for whom truth

This essay originally appeared as "Dal polilinguismo al metalinguismo: Il linguaggio Dantesco nella trilogia di James Merrill" in *Letterature d'America* 5, no. 22 (Spring 1984), 127–60, and is used by permission of Andrea Mariani and the editors of *Letterature d'America*. Translated from the Italian by Guy Rotella.

too / strongly shone" (*Mirabell*, 9.4, 269). The spirits who reveal *Sandover*'s other world display its hell or purgatory only metaphorically: "Doubt is yr HELL JM as YOURS / DJ IS FEAR. HELL IS THE CAVE OF THE PSYCHE."[4]

Nevertheless, as we will see, Merrill's references to Dante are exact: citations, passages, and lines are alluded to with the precision of a poet who has Dante's text nearly by heart and who addresses a reader equally familiar with it. For instance, in *Scripts*, &, 407, when Mother Nature enters the scene, Merrill refers to a depiction in the *Commedia* in order to help the reader picture her, comparing her to Beatrice in the role of "Heavenly Wisdom."

As much or more so than Dante the poet, Merrill also engages Dante the character, both as a pilgrim on an allegorical journey *and* as a man bearing witness to an actual experience. One series of allusions recalls Dante as the protagonist of an experience not unlike Merrill's own: for Merrill, Dante's greatness (like that of Milton, Blake, Yeats, and, by implication, Merrill himself) stems not so much from his having conceived his "grand design" as from his having dared to face "incommensurable subject matter": in Merrill's view, the power of God "STILLD THE TONGUE OF DANTE" (*Mirabell*, 3.3, 155) in the sense that the divine enforcement of silence included a soothing of the poet's anxiety about the task of expressing the inexpressible. Merrill also refers to a Dante who, as the "reporter" of his journey, sometimes needs to be chastized. Like him, JM, too, has moments of weakness: "(This is the point, I later tell DJ, / When Dante would have fainted dead away. / But cloned with minerals, heartsick, eyes red, / I see no way out but to forge ahead)" (*Mirabell*, 6.2, 208). And earlier, in *Ephraim*, I, 29, he had already confessed: "I'd rather skip this part, but courage. . . ." Such passages are transparent allusions to those comforting swoons that save Dante in moments of crisis, as in *Inferno*, III, 133–36, *Inferno*, V, 140–42, and *Purgatorio*, XXXII, 67–70.[5]

But this is not the place for an exhaustive analysis of Merrill's many references to Dante. For now, I conclude my survey by citing this most significant passage: "IN DANTE THE VISION WAS STARLIKE AS HE LOOKD INTO / THE ATOMS EYE HE SAW THE POTENTIAL OF PARADISE" (*Mirabell*, 2.2, 132). Merrill is convinced that Dante, describing the "punto . . . che raggiava lume" [the point . . . that radiated light] in *Paradiso*, XXVIII, 16, is referring to the center of the universe, what Merrill calls the ineffable "red eye of God," that infinitely small and powerful particle of energy upon which, as Beatrice explains, "depende il cielo e tutta la natura" [heaven and all of nature depends] (*Paradiso*, XXVIII, 42). Earlier in Merrill's poem, the "voices" had already explained that during Dante's otherworldly journey a high-born spirit had replaced him in Tuscany in order to enable him to cross the nine heavenly spheres and join in the contemplation of the ultimate well-being of salvation.: "Not otherwise its poet toured the spheres / While Someone very highly placed up there, / Donning his bonnet, in and out through that / Now famous nose haled the cool Tuscan night" (*Ephraim*, M, 45).[6]

After completing his magnum opus, then, Merrill presents himself as another of the many Anglo-Saxon disciples of Italy's greatest poet; he is respectful and reverent but also ready to challenge or even to compete with the maestro, his master-teacher. Unlike Italian poets, Merrill is not discouraged from emulating Dante's text; traversing it with flair, he combs it for semantic possibilities, discovers its internal laws, and—whether by means of great inspiration or stunning talent—imitates its figurative, descriptive power with various and remarkable results.

At first, Pound seems to be the principal model for this sort of reading and rereading, this repetition and reimagining of a received tradition; however, on closer analysis, many more significant mediators appear in the foreground: Milton, Blake, Yeats, Eliot.[7] Merrill's sources are numerous, well articulated, and, in general, very well integrated, sometimes so subtly so as nearly to disappear into the texture of his work. In any case, Merrill is the ablest versifier among the many who have drawn on the tradition in order to manipulate it by means of a playful appropriation of its linguistic prestige. And he counts among his sources not only poets (Wallace Stevens, Robert Lowell, W. H. Auden, the Calderón of the *Autos Sacramentales*, Shelley, Keats), but also prose writers (especially Proust, but Gertrude Stein and Jane Austen as well), not only storytellers but also essayists and filmmakers (Maya Deren), philosophers (Plato, Augustine, Aquinas, Spinoza, Bacon, Bergson), composers (Rossini, Verdi, Wagner, Stravinsky), scientists (Fermi, Einstein, Bohr), and painters (Giorgione, Blake, the impressionists, and—above all—the pointillists).

While I recognize these multiple influences, so far as possible I limit myself here to analysis of the functions of the dialectic between Dante's poetic language and Merrill's, hoping to show that Merrill's encounter with Dante is not limited to producing analogies of content and structure but also enters into the most intimate fabric of the trilogy, subtly penetrating nearly every "cell" of its gigantic organism.[8]

Beyond its numerous references to Dante as poet and character, Merrill's poem also alludes to specific passages in Dante. For instance, in lines near the end of a long and complicated lyric from *Nights and Days*, Merrill discusses issues of lasting literary value: "For his own modest effort to be seen / Against the yardstick of the 'truly great' / (In Spender's phrase) . . . Fearing to overstate, / He (the poet) lets *them* do it—lets their words, I mean, / Enhance his" ("The Thousand and Second Night," [*Nights and Days*] in *Selected Poems 1946–1985*, 101–2[9]). At the level of content, this passage could be said to function to reduce the speaker's burden in claiming comparison to the "truly great," but the passage is more useful at the formal level and is most suggestive when taken other than literally. For the cited lines illustrate Merrill's continuous yielding to the temptation to contextualize quotations, to translate or otherwise intervene in Dante's text. For example, he may do so by conflating fragments from different sources: the phrase "per me va la gente nova" [through—or over—me (the gate of hell in Dante, a bridge in Merrill) the new people go] (*Ephraim*, V, 75), which appears in the section describing the meeting between JM and his imaginary nephew Wendell on the Ponte dell'Accademia in Venice, is a borrowing from Dante.[10] The first part of Merrill's phrase, "per me va" is derived from the line "Per me si va ne la città dolente" [through me you enter the city of woe], from *Inferno*, III, 1; the second part is from the first half of line 73 of *Inferno*, XVI: "la gente nova e i subiti guadagni . . ." [the new people and their sudden wealth].

In *Ephraim*, K, 37, Merrill, like Eliot in *The Waste Land*, prefers to translate a Dantesque image literally. He acknowledges his debt and indicates his source precisely (going so far as to use his citation of the exact line number in Dante as a rhyme): "And in between, / Broad silver wings drone forth our own cloud-backed / Features fainter than pearl / On white brow (*Paradiso*, III, 14)"; actually, Merrill not only translates Dante's "perla in bianca fronte," but also the phrase "d'i nostri visi le postille" from the preceding line (by means of the word *features*) and the adjective *debili* (also in line 14) by means of the comparative "fainter." I don't want to anticipate my conclusion, but it seems that I have already gathered sufficient evidence to refute those who claim that Merrill's debt to Dante is marginal. It may seem marginal to readers who focus only on analogies of structure or content, but to those who engage in a careful close reading of the poem's linguistic dimension, a vast range of significant and signifying indebtedness is revealed.[11]

## I.

## THE NARRATIVE PATTERN

It is obvious that the narrative and ideological content of *The Changing Light at Sandover*[12] can be compared to that of the *Commedia*: a pair of living pilgrims (JM and his companion DJ,[13] the "mind" and the "hand" of the "scribe," respectively) "travel" in the other world by receiving in their home a host of souls of dead friends as well as large numbers of "spirits" who arrive from the obscure depths of other dimensions or as dazzling lights from alternative universes. (There are actually two houses, by the way, one in Stonington, Connecticut, the other in Athens; and there are two rooms, one red, where the conversations occur, the other blue, where they are transcribed.) These spirits want to reveal a message, a message that they insist the poet transcribe and make known by publishing "his" poem—an act for which they establish a deadline which is rigorously adhered to. The means of communication is the Ouija board.

When their adventure begins, the two protagonists are just past thirty years old ("The Rover Boys at thirty," *Ephraim*, C, 9). They start with a sense of bewilderment, of error ("Admittedly, I err by undertaking . . . ," *Ephraim*, A, 3), even of paralysis ("No *headway* through the drafts," as Merrill puts it in "The Will," [*Divine Comedies*] in *Selected*, 275). They are assailed by doubts, not unlike Dante, whose attitude their own recalls: "Ma io, perché venirvi? o chi 'l concede? / Io non Enëa, io non Paulo sono" [But me, why am I the one to go, who agreed to it? / I'm not Aeneas, not Paul] (*Inferno*, II, 31–32). Once they have made a decision to proceed ("I saw my way," *Ephraim*, A, 3), the "entrance" to the other world presents them with a sinister aspect: "the weird / Basalt passage of last winter, / Tunneling black" ("The Will" in *Selected*, 276). This recalls *Inferno*, III, 10–11 ("Queste parole di colore oscuro / vid'io scritte al sommo d'una porta" [I saw these darkly-colored words written above a door]); and in fact, Merrill's term *passage* indicates both a written extract and a threshold, a boundary or limit to be overcome.[14] Like Dante's, JM's and DJ's voyage is made possible by surrender to a higher power or "will," and by the force of love, although, characteristically for Merrill, love in his poem long remains sensual and is only later and by great effort transfigured into a spiritual experience (and even then only partly so): "Leaving to lovers' lips / All further argument" ("The Will" in *Selected*, 277).[15]

As in Dante, Merrill's first "cantica" [or large unit] is the most autobiographical of the trilogy. As such, it is necessarily marked by contingencies, human tensions, and personal idiosyncracies. The long search for an authoritative male figure, a wise and forgiving guide, proceeds through various stages: the seductive and mysterious new friends from the other world (Ephraim first among them) and the figures of departed old friends (Hans Lodeizen, Robert Morse) correspond to Dante's own necessary (and nostalgic) personifications of, in turn, Virgil, Brunetto Latini, Casella, Bonconte, and Forese. In Dante, this search ends in the meeting with Cacciaguida (*Paradiso*, XV–XVII); in Merrill, it ends in *Scripts for the Pageant* in the "paternal" figure of W. H. Auden. Merrill's counterpart for Saint Bernard[16] seems to be Michael, the archangel of light; Beatrice's counterpart is Maria Mitsotáki, who remains human until near the poem's end, when it is revealed that— as the avatar of both Plato and Mother Nature (Psyche, Chaos, Queen M.)— she has been wholly divine from the very beginning.[17]

The other world of Merrill's poem is not subdivided into Hell, Purgatory, and Paradise; on the other hand, there are "infernal" and "purgatorial" moments, elements, and tones in its generally "paradisal" realm, a realm in which there is no lack of hellish or purgatorial ambiguity and contradiction, of lapses and "black holes." For instance, in *Ephraim*, F, 18, the city of Purgatory, Oklahoma, is introduced; there, a crucial scene unfolds in a neutral, liquid atmosphere presented in tones that fall midway between certain flashes of coruscant hellish light and subsequent moments of heavenly luminosity. Moreover, Merrill's suspension of the word "Purgatory" as an end rhyme—so that the identification of the state occurs only after the pause of an enjambment—creates a "suspended" reminder of Dante's poem.

Similarly, the bitter lines "Desires ungratified / Persist from one life to the next" (from "The Kimono," [*Divine Comedies*] in *Selected*, 245) neatly parallel the vexation, grief, and rage of Farinata, whose unsatisfied desire for revenge torments him more than the "bed" of fire on which he lies (*Inferno*, X, 78). And the messages transmitted, even those that come from the highest ranks, can be ambiguous: "I bring equivocal news" (*Scripts*, &, 391); so it is in Dante, too: all doubt is dispersed only with the appearance of Cacciaguida (*Paradiso*, XVII, 19–27).

As in Dante, allegory abounds in Merrill.[18] In fact, a shared taste for pageantry makes entire sections of their respective poems seem comparable.[19] At certain times, in both Merrill and Dante, the "veils" of the mode of presentation lift, making things easier to comprehend than they seem. Both poets admonish the reader about this: "The message hardly needs decoding, so / Sheer the text" (*Mirabell*, 9.9, 275); "Aguzza qui, lettor, ben li occhi al vero / che 'l vel è ora ben tanto sottile / certo che 'l trapassar dentro è leggero" [Turn a sharp eye to the truth here, reader, for the veil is now so very thin that it's easy to see through] (*Purgatorio*, VIII, 19–21).[20]

As in Dante, the souls in Merrill are happy to surrender to God's will and are so resigned to the loss even of their identities that they are willing to sacrifice their very ability to feel. This passage of dialogue in Merrill, "And are you pleased to lose it? PLEASED TO BE / MES ENFANTS AS THEY WANT US," corresponds to the celebrated interchange between Dante and Piccarda in the sphere of the moon: "Voi che siete qui felici, / desiderate voi più alto loco . . .?" [You who are happy here, do you desire a higher place?] (*Paradiso*, III, 64–68). Merrill creates a triadic analogy to the "tre donne benedette" [three blessed ladies] who were concerned about Dante's spiritual condition and called Virgil to help him; that happens when Maya Deren is revealed to be working for Saint Lucy: "*The* St. Lucy? SHES MY BOSS . . . How about Erzulie? BUT SHE IS THE QUEEN / OF HEAVEN Oh, not Mary? Not Kuan Yin? / THEY ARE ALL ONE QUINTESSENCE" (*Ephraim*, R, 64).

Just as in Dante, in Merrill's poem as well the souls of the saved live in eternal joy in the mind of God; Michael puts it this way, "WE RESIDE IN THAT INTELLIGENCE" (*Mirabell*, 9.9, 276). And the master shape of Merrill's Paradiso is, like Dante's, a rose (compare *Paradiso*, XXXI, 1 and XXXII, 120), with the difference that "Dante saw the rose in fullest bloom. Blake saw it sick. / You and Maria, who have seen the bleak, unpetalled knob, must wonder: will it last / Till spring? Is it still rooted in the Sun?" (*Scripts*, Yes, 363). Here, as in many other passages, obvious differences between the two poets result from the ideological distance between them. Merrill, notwithstanding his long approach toward some sort of faith in the course of the poem, subscribes again, at the trilogy's end, to his old skepticism, the skepticism expressed, for example, in "Angel": "I could mention / Flaws in God's world" ([*Water Street*] in *Selected*, 78). A fully Dantesque poet would not share that attitude, nor this one, expressed in a fine pair of lines: "THIS IS OUR PENULTIMATE LESSON THE END OF USEFULNESS / NATURE IS A RUTHLESS FORCE AT ONCE FECUND AND LAZY" (*Mirabell*, 7.3, 288). By the same token, "post mortem piety" is firm in both poets, but in Merrill it assumes a pantheistic coloratura that Dante's theism denies: "OUR STATE IS EXCITING AS WE MOVE WITH THE CURRENT & DEVOTION BECOMES AN ELEMENT OF ITS OWN FORCE" (*Ephraim*, Q, 59).[21]

In much the same way, acceptance of fate itself (after as well as before the "revelations") has well marked limits in Merrill. Dante, from the nearly incomprehensible prophecy of Ciacco early in the poem, to the extremely clear and definitive one of Cacciaguida near its end, must accustom himself to the idea of exile. When Merrill, a *voluntary* exile from New York and the intellectual circles of the Village,[22] considers the threat of dying in a distant land, he firmly locates himself in Stonington and repeats the cry of "The Friend of the Fourth Decade": "I just can't picture dying / On foreign soil" ([*The Fire Screen*] in *Selected*, 141).

All of this shows that to insist on analogies of content alone when comparing Merrill and Dante is to lose ourselves in "una selva oscura" of contradictions. Although Dante has doubts (from the most acute of which arise nobly anguished poetical cries), he is fundamentally a monist: faith in the Absolute is the very shape of his mind. Merrill is torn by dualism.[23] In the deepest heart of the world created by his God (that is, God B, the God of life but also a God of the "second rank") is the "monitor," a negative element, an irreducible "dark power" responsible for those "black holes" that admonish God himself about imperfections in the structure of his creation.

Unlike the monistic Dante, the dualistic Merrill never succeeds in reconciling the contraries of Memory and Forgetfulness, Free Will and Determinism,[24] the Mechanistic and the Organic. And Merrill also differs from Dante in significant ways on intellectual and emotional levels and in terms of content and form. For example, at the intellectual level, Merrill, like any modern poet, has little certain knowledge; his is "a voice crying in the wilderness," like "God B's Song." The "doubleness" provided by his alter ego permits him to express, on the one hand, the classical, stoic attitude "impavidum ferient ruinae" [loosely, fearlessness in the face of ruin], and on the other, *fear*.

At the emotional level, Merrill has incredible hopes and intuits some spiritual realities: free will, a sort of divine mercy, at least a partial indulgence. But this precedence of feeling over intellect is a brief illusion, projected into other places and times, above all in the contexts of other cultures (ancient Greece, the East).[25] Similarly, in Merrill's poem the repressed feminine insinuates itself in nostalgia for the voices (and feelings) of mothers, sisters, female friends and travelling companions. And while Merrill hopes to combine the heroism of refraining from action with the still greater task of replacing action by the writing of poetry itself, he does so while sincerely doubting that his poem can have practical or political value.

Dante's poem has the coherent unity of the medieval world view. Merrill's "duplicitous" poem is—at the level of content—at once rationalistic (empirical almost to the point of agnosticism) and romantic, and—at the formal level—both classical and baroque, mannerist and Alexandrine. For all of its debt to Dante, it could only have been written by a twentieth-century American nourished by seventeenth-century English literature, by French culture from Baudelaire to Valéry to Proust, by German culture from Wagner to Rilke, and above all by both actual and mythic Hellenic experience, the allegory of the mind and the discovery of the senses.

More fruitful analogies of content are to be found in the centrality, in both Merrill and Dante, of certain myths. Myth, however, is not a matter of content alone but rather of the content *and* the form of poetic language, especially when a poem's mythic references are not merely ornamental but are instead the marks of an attempt to connect to myth's condensed realizations of archetypes, those privileged elements of the communicative code.

Let me offer a few examples. The myth of Narcissus, so popular with Dante's teachers, the troubadours, was interpreted by Dante in a sense opposed to the Provençal tradition. Dante the poet alters the myth by presenting Dante the pilgrim as having a nearly antinarcissistic reflex tendency to speculate about who is being reflected, that is, he turns away from the mirror rather than being captured by it or in it (*Paradiso*, III, 16–18). For Merrill, the mirror is, first of all, the surface which reflects the "narcissism" of the poet, for in many ways Merrill's real subject is his own self-projection.[26] In addition, in *Sandover* the mirror is the fragile and mysterious screen which both separates the realm of the living from the realm of the dead and permits reciprocal vision between them. In earlier poems, the mirror is a metaphor for psychoanalytical "intercourse": the conscious mind crosses it in order to explore the unconscious; in the trilogy, it is a symbol of and a means to the partial, progressive communication between two facing worlds. The breaking of the mirror at the conclusion of *Scripts for the Pageant* is equivalent to interrupting the imaginative communication between the two realms forever, but also to the momentary elimination of the barrier between them.

Another obvious point of contact is the two poets' shared tribute to the myth of the phoenix. In Dante the legendary bird, which "more e poi rinasce / quando al cinquecentesimo anno appressa" [dies and is then reborn when it reaches the 500th year] (*Inferno*, XXIV, 107–8), is the emblem of an immortality achieved through repeated self-immolations and periodic resurrections from one's own ashes. In "About the Phoenix,"[27] Merrill adds a dimension to the "magic" of the myth of an eternal cycle of life, death, and rebirth, expanding it to include a suspension between life and death, between sleep (or dream) and waking, almost as though, for the phoenix, as for human beings, the most important phase of the cycle should be the moment between one life and another. In the trilogy, the phoenix is easily transformed into a sign of the workings of karma: it is reborn in a form different from its previous incarnation, while deep down it also preserves certain unchangeable traits. And Merrill also uses the phoenix in its role as the emblem of Venice: the city that, dying, is destined to rise again from its own ruins. Not for nothing is its opera house called La Fenice. There, Stravinsky's and Auden's *The Rake's Progress* had its première; Merrill's friend Robert Morse, who, it is predicted, will become a great composer in his new life, is reborn as Tom, the name of the opera's hero. The opera's cast is slowly regathered in the poem, perhaps for a new performance when the phoenix/Venice rises again.

In *Coda: The Higher Keys*, this same Robert Morse is also a new version of Marsyas, who appears in Dante, too; he will be drawn "de la vagina de le membra sua" [from the womb of his own limbs] (*Paradiso*, I, 21), as a (human) artist who dares to challenge the music of the heavenly spheres. It would be unfortunate if earthly artists, fearing the flaying that punishes the sin of hubris, were to renounce their task.[28]

Another myth Dante and Merrill share is that of Ulysses. In Dante, Ulysses is condemned for his hubristic pride, but because of his "virtute e canoscenza" (virtue and fame), he ends by retracing the route of Adam and attaining to Purgatory (the "montagna bruna" [dark mountain]), of the "nova terra" [new earth] of *Inferno*, XXVI, 133 and 137), on the summit of which is the Garden of Eden. His damnation, then, is somewhat relieved; however, since God doesn't permit human beings a second chance to regain perfect innocence except by Christ's expiation of original sin, he cannot be saved. Ulysses/Merrill, on the other hand, sets sail "for the fixed shore beyond the straits" not out of pride but humbly, in the acceptance of fate itself, of actual origins (the "fixed shore"), of insuperable limits beyond the superable ones.[29] His choice of an obscure and out of the way site (Stonington) is the negation of nostalgia for Eden and the renunciation of certain exquisite pleasures for which there is no longer either time or place. This motif culminates in the second part of the trilogy, with the reception of contradictory messages of salvation and destruction.

The case of Medusa (in the poem of that name) is another sign of Merrill's constant experiments in penetrating *into* myths by drawing new and surprising effects from them. In Dante, the Furies solicit the arrival of their sister: "Vegna Medusa: sì 'l farem di smalto" [Let Medusa come, then we'll turn him to stone] (*Inferno*, IX, 52). In Merrill, Medusa not only petrifies others but turns herself to stone as well, like a self-punishing Niobe.[30] The classical myth gives Niobe the small solace of an inexhaustible source of tears; similarly Merrill grants Midas (whose poor petrified face is frozen in impotence) two eyes able to cry ("Midas among Goldenrod").[31] This same solace, according to cases, Dante grants or denies the souls of Cocytus.

## II.

### Structure and Textual Parallelism

A merely contrastive analysis of parallel structures in the *Commedia* and *Sandover* would be fruitless: divergences and swervings may prove more meaningful than obvious similarities. Therefore, I begin by clearing the field of a misunderstanding that burdens many critics and holds back even the most valuable studies from an adequate appreciation of what is characteristically Merrillian. Notwithstanding its difficulties (especially on a first reading), Merrill's poem—like Dante's, and differently from the poems of Eliot and Pound—aspires to present itself as a perfectly integrated organism: "My narrative / Wanted to be limpid, unfragmented" (*Ephraim*, A, 3).[32] Merrill's models are, precisely, "Dantesque / Or Yeatsian systems" (*Coda*, "The Ceremonies," I, 532), but from this point of view, the parallel with Dante is difficult to sustain, as Merrill admits: "Everything in Dante knew its place. / In this guidebook of yours, how do you tell / Up from down?" (*Mirabell*, 8.8, 256). Yet even so, at the end of Merrill's tour de force one has the sense that the scribe's diligence *has* been rewarded with a coherent, organic result.[33]

Where the three cantiche of Dante's poem are symmetrical, the three sections into which Merrill's poem is divided have asymmetrical proportions. The first (*The Book of Ephraim*) is closest to the *Commedia* in structure: it comprises twenty-six chapters or cantos (one for each letter of the alphabet,[34] with the appropriate letter beginning the first line of each respective section); these cantos are of varying lengths (from a minimum of 75 to a maximum of 150 lines) but generally close to the median of Dante's cantos (130 to 140 lines). Considering the nine poems that precede *Ephraim* in *Divine*

*Comedies* as a kind of prologue, the total number of cantos comes to 35 (the *Inferno* has 34 cantos, of which the first is the general proem) and the total number of lines to nearly 3000, like the *Inferno*.

The second cantica, *Mirabell's Books of Number*, is almost twice as long as the first; it is divided into ten books (identified by the arabic numerals from 0 to 9), each of which is in turn subdivided into five or six chapters, following the listing that appears at the beginning of the poem by way of a prospectus.[35] There are fifty-five chapters in all, and since each book contains approximately 600 lines, each of the subdivisions, again, corresponds to the median length of Dante's cantos.

In the third cantica, *Scripts for the Pageant*, Merrill returns to the "magical" number three. *Scripts* is made up of three sections identified by the terms *Yes*, *&*, and *No*; the first and the last, which mirror and are interchangeable with one another (Merrill does not mean to conclude the poem by denying the hope of salvation), contain eighteen sections (and ten lessons); the middle section, "a bridge that can be crossed both ways," has fourteen sections (and five lessons). The total number of lines is a little less than the sum of lines of the two preceding cantiche, so that the trilogy has the following scheme (the similarities to and differences from Dante's pattern require no further comment):

|  | Sections | Approximate number of lines |
|---|---|---|
| The Changing } Ephraim | 35 (26 + 9) | 3000 |
| Light at San- } Mirabell | 10 (55 chapters) | 6000 |
| dover } Scripts | 50 (25 lessons) | 9000[36] |

At the end of the poem, diverging from the general design of the *Commedia*, Merrill adds his *Coda: The Higher Keys*, of approximately 1800 lines divided into thirteen "sections" and five ceremonies ("final rites"). The total number of lines in the entire poem is close to 19,000, almost doubling the size of its medieval model.

But along with these considerations of the internal proportions and numerical patterns of Merrill's work in relation to Dante's, it is worthwhile (in order to avoid fundamental errors) to stress the difference in the *sense* of its general structure, of its (synchronic) *design* and its (diachronic) *rhythm*. In Dante's case, we have a circular design (in two dimensions) and a spherical design (in three dimensions); in Merrill's case we have a sinusoidal design (in two dimensions) and a spiral design (in three dimensions).[37] The diachronic pulse of Dante's poem is in the direction of infinite expansion (the universe according to traditional physics), while the diachronic pulse of Merrill's poem involves a systole and diastole of expansion and contraction (the universe according to post-Einsteinian physics):

| | **Synchronic or spatial** | **Diachronic or temporal** |
|---|---|---|
| *Dante* | two dimensions: circle<br><br>three dimensions: sphere | infinite expansion |
| *Merrill* | two dimensions: sinusoid<br><br>three dimensions: spiral | expansion/contraction |

If Merrill swerves from Dante's example in these matters, he pays him unequivocal tribute by means of his numerous imitations of clearly Dantesque prosody. First, there is the sonnet, then, more important, the canzone-stanza or sestina (the most luminous example of which is "Samos," the opening poem of the central section of *Scripts*), and finally, of course, the terza rima, or better, "terzina" (although Merrill's use of rhyme in that form is very free and experimental). Terzinas make up "McKane's Falls" ([*Divine Comedies*] in *Selected*, 246–49) but in an unconventional way; they are introduced later, with greater authority and effect, in the phantasmagorical prosody of the trilogy. There, terzinas create a perfect lyric-dramatic balance in three final (or nearly final) passages in each of the three cantiche of Merrill's poem. In them the tribute to Dante is twofold: there is both the general prosodic tribute and the more exact one enacted when Merrill ends each of the three passages just mentioned with the word "stars": it is well known, of course, that the word *stelle* [stars] is the very seal or stamp that closes each of Dante's three cantiche. Here are the Merrill passages: in *Ephraim*, W, 85: "Now early light sweeps under a pink scatter / Rug of cloud the solemn, diehard stars"; in *Mirabell*, 8.8, 256: "As it strikes me, my / Head is in my hands. I'm seeing stars"; in *Scripts*, No, "Venetian Jottings," 506: "Smiles DJ as we link arms, tacitly / Skipping the futuristic coffee-bar's / Debate already under way (ah, me) / On the confusing terms: Dance, Gods, Time, Stars."

Finally, we leave behind similarities of situation and compositional solution and come to an analysis of precise technico-stylistic and linguistic-formal "coincidences"[38] between the two poems. In "After the Fire," Merrill had already spoken of the "Dead flames [that] encircle us, which cannot harm"; in the *Commedia* the flames of the dead cannot harm Dante or Virgil, whether in Hell (for example, *Inferno*, XV, 24–124, throughout the colloquy with Brunetto Latini) or in Purgatory (*Purgatorio*, XXV–XXVI). On Dante's ledge of the lecherous, the spirits of those who loved excessively are, like that "lover's ghost" in Merrill, wrapped in "a sheet of flame"; in Merrill, though, there is a screen of flames that protects from flames, as in *The Fire Screen*.[39]

As is frequently the case in Dante, the souls in Merrill's poem wish to communicate with the living: "Stray souls maneuver / Round the teacup for a chance to glide . . . / To the warmth inside"; it is, above all, human warmth which the spirits want to feel (see *Purgatorio*, V, 25–45, XXVI, 8–15, 18–21, 49–53). The words "sunless shores" from *Ephraim*, K, 38, belong, generically, to the tradition of Homer, Virgil, Dante, and Milton; more specifically Dantesque is the first part of the line: "the sitter *long removed* to sunless shores," which suggests the pain of the dead souls' eternal damnation.

Brief flashes that recall images from the *Paradiso* are especially frequent in Merrill's poem: the phrase "through a sky in flames" (*Ephraim*, T, 71) is worthy of the fiery sky of *Paradiso*, XXVIII and XXIX, for instance. Reading "ITS LIKE A STAR WE ENTER" (*Scripts*, No, 499), one immediately thinks of Dante's "Per entro sé l'etterna margarita / ne ricevette" [the eternal pearl received us into itself] (*Paradiso*, II, 34–35). The words "MICHAEL'S LAUGHTER MADE ALL HEAVEN QUAKE" (*Scripts*, Yes, 302) bring to mind the "riso de l'universo" [the universe's smile] of *Paradiso*, XXVII, 4–5. And finally, the phrase "ALL HEAVEN HOLDS ITS BREATH" (*Scripts*, No, "Finale," 516) echoes the words of Saint Bernard: "Vedi Beatrice con quanti beati / per li miei prieghi ti chiudon le mani" [Look at Beatrice with all those saints; clasping their hands to you, they share my prayer] (*Paradiso*, XXXIII, 38–39).

Also as in Dante, Merrill's characters speak with incredible caution: "Breaking off, the cup stalls round the Board / As who should take a deep breath before speaking" (*Mirabell*, 3.3, 155). And Merrill's use of the subjunctive here ("As who should take . . .") seems especially Dantesque (consider, for instance "Come d'un stizzo verde ch'arso sia . . ." [As which green fire-log should burn] *Inferno*, XIII, 40).[40]

The situation of a spirit who contemplates his own corpse immediately after death (already with partial detachment yet still with some affection) also produces analogous effects in the two poets: "I HEARD A VOICE 'HE'S GONE' / AND LOOKED DOWN AT MY OLD FRIEND: MEAT AND BONE" (*Scripts*, No, "Appearances," 498); compare with that, these words of Bonconte da Montefeltro: "Lo corpo mio gelato in su la foce / trovò l'Archian rubesto . . ." [The raging Archiano found my frozen body at its mouth] (*Purgatorio*, V, 124–25).

The contradictory feelings of JM and DJ, who are doubtful about whether or not to reveal the secrets they have received ("Not tell this secret? / God, how to resist— / And for what other reason were we born? / DJ: The part about our being chosen / Won't sound complacent?"), are homologous to Dante's doubts in the encounter with Cacciaguida (*Paradiso*, XVII, 106–20). The "heavenly" reply in Merrill builds with great effect upon the "high" tone of Dante (*Paradiso*, XVII, 127–35) in this moderately "low" passage in "camp" language: "LET NOT GRACE FILL YOU WITH UNDUE ALARM . . . / REVELATION'S CONSTANT PROCESS CANNOT BE TRUSTED TO THE HACK JOURNALIST" (*Coda*, "Mr. E," 555).

In such passages, and in others treated below, Dantesque language is mixed into Merrill's poem as an irreplaceable ingredient in a very elaborate and personal linguistic recipe; not only as one of many "voices" in a polyphony but also as an "implicit referent," an "additional instrument" to be used on appropriate occasions. In short, we are now on the plane of the metalinguistic.

In the presentation of characters, Merrill wisely displaces Dante's inimitable balance of feeling and morality in favor of a mixture of pathos, irony, and sensuality that is *his* exclusive province. In "Chimes for Yahya" ([*Divine Comedies*] in *Selected*, 252), the figure is "No older or younger than I've pictured you, / No handsomer, no simpler—only kinder." Kindness, courtesy, sweetness of manner and appearance (in Dante, to be *gentile* is also to be *nobile*) distinguish the most beloved souls met in the *Purgatorio*: from Casella, who "soavemente disse" [spoke gently] (II, 85) to Manfredi, who is "biondo . . . e bello e di gentile aspetto" [blond . . . handsome and of noble appearance] (III, 107).[41] I add these two Merrillian descriptions of angels not because Merrill's images correspond exactly to Dante's, but because his technique of presentation is similar and because, whether the desire being expressed is symbolic or actual, the results are remarkably analogous: "A GREAT BEAUTY MY DEARS! A BLAKE! SERENE / MORE THAN HUMAN FEATURES WHITE WINGS TIPPED / BY THE FOUR COLORS" (*Mirabell*, 8.5, 250) and "O IT WAS A FACE MY DEARS OF CALM / INQUIRING FEATURE FACE OF THE IDEAL / PARENT CONFESSOR LOVER READER FRIEND / AND MORE" (*Scripts*, Yes, 286).[42]

On the other hand, one observes a sharp swerve from Dante into an erotic key in this description by Merrill of *"limbs & torso muscled by long folds of / an unemasculated Blake nude. . . . His smile was that of an old friend, so / casual. Hair golden, eyes that amazing / blood washed gold our headlights catch, foxes perhaps / or wildcats . . ."* (*Ephraim*, H, 27).


## III.

### Nodes of Memory

At this point, having offered a brief analysis not only of the different modes of intertextuality and "dialogue at a distance" between the two poets, but also of the relative quality of the results, I would draw the preliminary conclusion that Merrill's best effects are achieved when the opportunity to express analogous situations or feelings leads him to use freely (although with flawless respect and naturalness) the great reservoir of images and technical solutions that Dante offers him: Merrill demythologizes Dante's inimitable work; he approaches it in climactic moments, both making it his own *and* keeping it no less recognizable as what it is. The reader's greatest satisfaction is the discovery of how often Merrill's successes are built upon Dante's achievement.

For instance, Merrill frequently recreates, even in different contexts, an atmosphere very common in Dante, especially in the initial phases of the pilgrimage or in crucial moments of "threshold crossing": "Shall I come lighter-hearted to that Spring tide / Knowing it must be fathomed without a guide? / With no one, nothing along those lines . . ." (*Ephraim*, X, 85). Like Dante the pilgrim, Merrill's protagonist is split between a sense of timidity, inadequacy, and solitude, and a sense of his own mature ability to function independently (a division that recalls Dante's dismissal of "Virgilio dolcissimo padre" [Virgil, dearest father] in *Purgatorio*, XXX, 49–54, and Virgil's replacement as guide by Beatrice).

While such likenesses abound, it should not be ignored that Merrill's emulation of Dante leaves him considerable room for the autonomous expression of his own original poetic language. A dramatic atmosphere of tense suspension between sorrow and relief haunts DJ's meeting with his recently deceased parents: "WE HAVE LIVED & LOVED / & FELT YOUR LOVE LET US GO FORTH ANEW / UNWEIGHTED BY IT" (*Mirabell*, 3.1, 150). In that encounter the echo of a new incommunicability is heard, a stricture against communication between the living and the dead imposed by the laws of the other world and not only accepted but actually desired by the dead themselves. Merrill's passage is akin to this celebrated one in Dante: "Marzïa piacque tanto a li occhi miei / mentre ch'i' fu' di là . . . / Ora che di là dal mal fiume dimora, / più muover non mi può . . ." [Marcia was most pleasing to my eyes while I was in that world . . . Now that she is on the other side of that evil river she can no longer move me] (*Purgatorio*, I, 85–89).

In such tones of precarious (and precious) equilibrium the dialectic between the two cosmic poets attains its finest results. The tender leave-taking of the strange, surviving unicorn, Unice, in Merrill's poem, is presented in a synthesis as delicate as that masterfully created by Dante in describing the apparition of Pia de' Tolomei. Merrill writes, "When you one day come here / Think of your Uni and he will appear" (*Scripts*, &, 430); and Dante has: "Deh, quando tu sarai tornato al mondo . . . / ricorditi di me, che son la Pia" [For pity's sake, when you return to the world, . . . remember me, who am la Pia] (*Purgatorio*, V, 130, 133).

Finally, and representing perfect assimilation of a characteristic Dantesque tonality, there is the splendid opening of the canzone "Samos" in which a sea journey through a night and the following dawn is described with the same finely calibrated touches that we find in more than one of the emotional landscape descriptions in Dante's *Purgatorio*. Merrill writes:

> And still, at sea all night, we had a sense
> Of sunrise, golden oil poured upon water,
> Soothing its heave, letting the sleeper sense
> What inborn, amniotic homing sense
> Was ferrying him. . . .
>
> (*Scripts*, &, 369)

It shouldn't seem too bold to place those lines beside this greatly celebrated passage in Dante:

> Era già l 'ora che volge il disio
> ai navicanti e 'ntenerisce il core
> lo dì c'han detto ai dolci amici addio . . .

[It was already the hour that turns sailors' longings homeward, filling their hearts with feeling for the day they said goodbye to their sweet friends] (*Purgatorio*, VIII, 1–3).

In anticipation of the objection that I have largely limited myself to parallels of tone, shading, and atmosphere which permit only limited verbal verification (since they depend considerably upon the sensibility of the reader, or on a lesser or greater familiarity with Dante's text), let me go on to discuss a series of similarities which, it seems to me, *can* be justified by unequivocal linguistic relationships. For example, it seems clear that the double meeting of JM and DJ with W. B. Yeats imitates Dante's meeting with Virgil. Merrill's homage here is expressed in two ways, as if the speaker, dividing himself, took his starting point from Dante's lines and then displayed his ability to develop his material in different ways. JM's invocation ("O please, Mr. Yeats, you who have always / Been such a force in my life!" [*Scripts*, No, 492]) recalls Dante's words to Virgil, "'l lungo studio e 'l grande amore / che m'ha fatto cercar lo tuo volume" [the long study and the great love with which I have searched your book] (*Inferno*, I, 83–84), while in these words spoken by Auden: "MAITRE, I HAVE EVER HEARD: THE GOLDEN METER IN YOUR WORD, AND KISS YR HAND," the term "Maitre," even though in French, is enough to send the reader back immediately to this passage in Dante: "Tu se' lo mio maestro e 'l mio autore . . ." [you are my master and my author], from *Inferno*, I, 85.

Similarly, these lines by Merrill, "And what was the sensation / When stars alone like bees / Crawled numbly over it?" (*Ephraim*, L, 42) correspond to these by Dante, "Sì come schiera d'ape che s'infiora / una fiata e una si ritorna" [Like a swarm of bees that is at the flowers one moment and at the next returns] (*Paradiso*, XXXI, 7–8). And this Merrill passage: "Then when the flame forked like a sudden path" ("Log" [*Braving the Elements*] in *Selected*, 189) is similar to these in Dante: "la fiamma cornuta" [the horned flame] (*Inferno*, XXVI, 68) and "lo maggior corno de la fiamma antica" [the larger horn of the ancient flame] (*Inferno*, XXVI, 85).

I do not want to claim that in every case cited the intrinsic quality of Merrill's verse matches the high level of Dante's, but much pleasure comes from tracking the "how" of the process we are following: Merrill's way of assimilating Dante's language to his own. In any case, my interest is not so much in declaring judgments of value as in confirming connection, that is, in showing that in Merrill Dante's language expands into a "metalanguage" that underlies much of the explicit language of Merrill's poem, where its resonance enriches the trilogy's semantic gifts and amplifies its range. My point is not that Merrill's poem can be read as an imitation of the *Commedia*, but rather that Merrill's language surely reveals itself as a much wiser and more articulate instrument when it is heard against the background of Dante's complex and varied orchestration.

Another concrete example: the valence of meaning of these simple lines, "We've wanted / Consuming passions; these refine instead" (*Ephraim*, 0, 50), is greatly increased when they are read against, or better, by the light of *Purgatorio*, XXVI, 148: like the fire that punishes the "inconsummate" souls of the passionate on the highest ledge of Purgatory, the flames of passion do not so much *consume* as *refine* Merrill's characters; and, of course, there is also Arnaut Daniel, who "s'ascose nel foco che li *affina*" [hid himself in the fire that *refines* them].

A similar effect occurs in the discourse of *Scripts*, &, 407: "The sense / Through walls of a concentric audience, / Rank upon blazed petaled rank arisen," where Merrill has skillfully condensed the series of images (*Paradiso*, XXXII, 1–36) which Dante uses to describe the ranks of the saints (seated in concentric rows of high-backed chairs) so that the general impression is of a rose with innumerable petals. Without the support of Dante's passage, Merrill's lines might still be stimulating, but they would be less clear.

In the case of these lines, "Dante saw the letter M / Become an eagle of ruby souls / Which sang to him" (*Scripts*, Yes, 299), my concern is less with the general reference to the "spiriti giusti" [just spirits] of the sphere of Jupiter (*Paradiso*, XVIII, 91–95) than with the extremely effective phrase "ruby souls," which crisply translates the words "rubinetto in cui / raggio di sole ardesse" [a ruby in which a sunray burned] form *Paradiso*, XIX, 4–5. Similarly, in the previously cited passage from *Mirabell*, 2.2, 132 ("In Dante the vision was starlike"), we recognize and admire the compression of a whole series of Dantesque images, in disheveled order, so to speak, but with a resulting effect of rare incisiveness. And it is clear in this four-line excerpt that Merrill is again conflating several passages, this time from *Paradiso*, XXVIII, 22–27, 41–45, 94–102:

> That uncanny shining tininess
> Ringed with decelerating zones of light
> (*Paradiso* XXVIII) on which, says Beatrice,
> The heavens and all nature are dependent.

It would be easy enough to identify additional nodal passages from the *Commedia* that enter into and revivify Merrill's poem. I cite just two: the first approach of Virgil (*Inferno*, I) and the dramatic, brusquely interrupted interchange with Cavalcante Cavalcanti (*Inferno*, X). The first produces these results in Merrill: the exhaustedly expressed and fractured invocation (in which the accent is placed on the central vowel *O*) of the spirit who first makes contact with JM and DJ ("HELLP O SAV ME," *Ephraim*, B, 6) recalls, phonetically, the words "Non *omo, omo* già fui" [I am not a living man, I *was*] of *Inferno*, I, 67 (the spelling out of "help" as "HELLP"—especially since we know that Merrill is an enthusiast of puns—fuses the plea for assistance ("help") with the imprecation "hell" in the desperate cry of a spirit who is at that very moment dying in a fire).[43] Also, the passage that precedes the first words spoken by Yeats ("If an old man's speech / Stiff from long silence . . .," *Scripts*, No, 486) explicitly alludes to *Inferno*, I, 63, where Virgil is described as one "chi per lungo silenzio parea fioco" [who seemed hoarse from long silence].[44]

As for the second nodal passage, in it the power of Dante's language comes from the abrupt excitement created by the broken speech rhythms of Cavalcanti, who, in his intensely human love for the son whom he believes and hopes is still alive, has fallen into the error of the damned: "Di subito drizzato gridò: 'Come? / dicesti "elli ebbe"? non viv'elli ancora? / non fere li occhi suoi lo dolce lume?' " [Suddenly he straightened up and shouted: "What? / You say, 'he did'? isn't he still alive? / doesn't the sweet light still strike his eyes?"] (*Inferno*, X, 67–69). Merrill likes this effect so well that he reproduces it many times, most frequently when conveying misunderstandings in conversations between the living and the dead. For instance, in *Ephraim*, G, 25, the interruption "Stop, oh stop!" at the end of the line— a violent break intensified by the parenthetical address with which the next line begins ("Ephraim, this cannot be borne")—is Merrill's version of the "Come?" left hanging in Dante's rhyme (the rhyme *come / lume* is a rare example of imperfect or slant rhyme in Dante; perhaps it offers a precedent for Merrill's frequent use of the same technique). A clinching example is the sequence of dramatic questions in *Mirabell*, 2.4, 137, where DJ asks the voice then addressing them to clarify the sense of some words with potentially ominous import: "In solitude? Why? Where will I— / This operation—does he mean I'll die?"

## IV.

### "EXPANDED LANGUAGE AND THE POETRY OF SILENCE

I close with an observation that proceeds from and partly surpasses those made so far. As I have stressed, Dantesque language, much of it metalanguage, offers Merrill a way to demonstrate mastery of his own language, an "expanded" language that surpasses the limits of any single poetic one. But beyond even that, Dante's language offers Merrill an exemplary and well-tested instrument for producing those effects of silence which serve as the unique sign for expressing the profundity of certain feelings, the elation of certain visions.

In this sense, the Dantesque model functions splendidly as a "legitimization of not speaking," a poetics of silence. The *Commedia* begins with the struggling articulation of words by the wise and sad spirit Virgil, who recovers the use of his own voice after centuries of silence and must overcome the gulf between life and death; it concludes (at that moment when the pilgrim loses himself in the contemplation of God) with an insistent confession of the poet's powerlessness to versify such dumbfounding material. Even restricting ourselves only to the last canto of the *Paradiso*, we find many relevant passages: "il mio veder fu maggio / che 'l parlar mostra, ch'a tal vista cede, / e cede la memoria a tanto oltraggio" [what I saw was more than speech could show; speech fails before such extreme experiences, and so does memory] (lines 55–57), "quasi tutta cessa / mia visïone" [my vision is almost ended] (lines 61–62), "così la neve al sol si disingilla, / così al vento ne le foglie levi / si perdea la sentenza di Sibilla" [so the snow unseals itself in the sun, so the wind lifts the leaves and scatters the Sybil's meaning] (lines 64–65), "un punto solo m'è maggior letargo . . ." [that single moment makes me more forgetful] (line 94), "Oh quanto è corto il dire e come fioco / al mio concetto!" [How feeble my speech is, how short of my conception!] (lines 121–22), "ma non eran di ciò le proprie penne" [but my own wings weren't up to that] (line 139), and, finally, "A l'alta fantasia qui mancò possa" [I lacked the power for this high fantasy] (line 142). Surrender to love's power concludes the journey, as it had begun it, and (since the poet can never hope to describe his "return" from such heights) only silence follows the song of the saints.

Merrill's poem begins with the hesitant stammer of a porcelain cup on a Ouija board, with the exhausting spelling out of the dictated letters, and with the timid transcription of the first uncertain steps of a long voyage. After numerous expressions of powerlessness like those cited in Dante, it concludes at first with an immensely hesitant passage presenting the voice of God (and his "willful" act of love for humanity). That voice resounds in the astral silence inhabited by the other gods of the Pantheon, who do not reply:

> HERS HEAR ME I AND MINE SURVIVE
> SIGNAL ME DO YOU WELL I ALONE IN MY NIGHT
> HOLD IT BACK HEAR ME BROTHERS I AND MINE
> (*Scripts*, No, 517)

Supreme love, then, as in Dante—and silence. But Merrill's poem has a second, *final* conclusion (*Coda*, "The Ballroom at Sandover," 559) in which its author reads the fruits of his twenty years of labor to an assembly of "great souls." Even in this final scene, much is beyond words. In the act of taking refuge in the closed circle of his own private universe (the "absolute discretion of our circle") Merrill finds a way both to *speak* and *not to speak* ("words unspoken"), a speech that for all it can say is unable to say everything: was the poem written for the dead? will it please the living?[45]

Because of his medieval context, Dante has more faith in the Absolute than Merrill does, and therefore more faith in the communicability of his message. For his part, Merrill doubts his power to communicate from the time he begins his poem until his recitation of it at the trilogy's end; and yet he must have some faith, for among so many dead listeners there are at least three living ones: the poet/character himself, DJ, and their friend Vasíli, whose wife, recently dead, is "on the other side." The couple's love is still intensely alive; it is kept so by the poem itself, the sole bridge between the two dimensions.

Both in Dante and in Merrill, then, the highest achievement of poetry is limited by the inexpressible. As their poems end, their poetic language yields to the metalanguage of devotion and mute homage, to a suspenseful and reverent adherence to the mysteries of this world and the next. In the light of those ideas, let us read again one of Merrill's most beautiful lyrics:

> Hans, there are moments when the whole mind
> Resolves into a pair of brimming eyes or lips
> Parting to drink from the deep spring of a death
> That freshness they do not need to understand.
> These are the moments, if ever, an angel steps
> Into the mind . . .
> There are moments when speech is but a mouth pressed
> Lightly and humbly against the angel's hand.[46]

*Notes*

1. For other aspects of Merrill's poetry, see the following works by the author: "James Merrill," in *Novecento Americano*, ed. Elémire Zolla (Rome: Lucarini, 1982) vol. 1, 13–32; "Il luogo esotico nella poesia di James Merrill," in *L'Esotismo nella Letteratura Angloamericana*, ed. Elémire Zolla (Rome: Lucarini, 1982), vol. 3, 135–60; and "James Merrill: dalla lirica pura al saggio poetico," in *Conoscenza Religiosa*, no. 2 (1983), 148–54. See also "James Merrill," in *In Forma di Parole*, ed., B. Tarozzi, 5, no. 2 (April–June 1984), 247–73. Passages from Dante in this essay are from l'Edizione Nazionale della Società Dantesca Italiana, 4 vols., ed. G. Petrocchi, (Milan: Mondadori, 1967).

2. The term "lyric" (or "earlier") refers to poems from the collection preceding the *Sandover* trilogy; the term "epic-narrative" refers to the trilogy itself. Citations are to the Atheneum one-volume edition of 1982 and use these abbreviations: *Ephraim*, *Mirabell*, *Scripts*, and *Coda*, followed by section or canto indications and by page numbers for the 1982 edition.

3. See Edmund White, "On James Merrill," in *American Poetry Review*, 8, no. 5 (1979), 9–11, especially 10.

4. See *Ephraim*, M, 45: "The dogma of his day / Calls for a Purgatory, for a Hell, / Both of which Dante thereupon / . . . invents."

5. Beatrice, too, is not only a figure or poetic pretext ("a kind of music personified in female form" in the extract cited) but also an actual historical personage, a "dense" spirit, "perfect," destined to return—as avatar in a series of visits—to lead other worthy men to salvation. See *Ephraim*, Q, 59. Other explicit references to Beatrice occur in *Scripts*, Yes, 354, and No, 479.

6. See Ross Labrie, "James Merrill at Home: An Interview," in *Arizona Quarterly* 38, no. 1 (Spring 1982), 19–36; especially 35–36.

7. For Merrill's first encounter with Dante in the epigraph of Eliot's "The Love Song of J. Alfred Prufrock," see James Merrill, "Divine Poem: Dante's Cosmic Web," in *New Republic*, November 29, 1980, 29. See also Andrea Mariani, "Yeats in Merrill: maschera e figura," in *Yeats oggi*, ed. Carla de Petris (Rome: A.B.E.TE., 1993) 89–105.

8. The significance of Dante's example is so clearly carried forward and so thoroughly involved in the operations of Merrill's poem that many critics suggest that the entire trilogy should be called *Divine Comedies*. In fact, Merrill himself reveals that he was in the habit of referring to the 1976 collection which includes *Ephraim* as "my Comedy" and that David Jackson suggested that he use the plural. See the interview conducted by Helen Vendler, "James Merrill's Myth" in *New York Review of Books*, May 3, 1979, 12.

9. Citations from the following works are drawn from: James Merrill, *Selected Poems 1946–1985* (New York: Alfred Knopf, 1992). The title of the poem cited is followed by the title (in parentheses) of the work in which it first appeared.

*Country of a Thousand Years of Peace* (New York: Atheneum, 1959)
*Water Street* (New York: Atheneum, 1962)
*Nights and Days* (New York: Atheneum, 1966)
*The Fire Screen* (New York: Atheneum, 1969)
*Braving the Elements* (New York: Atheneum, 1973)
*Divine Comedies* (New York: Atheneum, 1977)

10. The passage has, as an intermediary "source" between Dante and Merrill, the famous line 63 of "The Burial of the Dead" section of Eliot's *The Waste Land*, which describes the crowd crossing London Bridge by borrowing a line from Dante.

11. See especially Rachel Jacoff, "Dante and Merrill," in *James Merrill: Essays in Criticism*, ed. David Lehman and Charles Berger (Ithaca: Cornell University Press, 1983). This is the best collection of essays on the author; for ease of reference it is cited here as

Lehman and Berger. Fully engaged, if not always wholly convincing in its conclusions, is Judith Moffett's *James Merrill: An Introduction to the Poetry* (New York: Columbia University Press, 1984), cited as Moffett. See also Ross Labrie, *James Merrill* (Boston: Twayne, 1982). Dante's influence is recognized as fundamental by Moffett, Peter Sacks ("The Divine Translation: Elegiac Aspects of *The Changing Light at Sandover*," in Lehman and Berger, 159–85), David Lehman himself ("Introduction," in Lehman and Berger, 18; and "Elemental Bravery: The Unity of James Merrill's Poetry," in Lehman and Berger, 23–60), Michael Harrington ("Paradise or Disintegration: James Merrill's Unique Search for New Myths," in *Commonweal*, November 4, 1983, 585–89), and J. D. McClatchy ("Lost Paradises," in *Parnassus*, Fall–Winter, 1976, 305–21). Other essays take an opposing view, tending to give more importance to differences from Dante than to similarities with him: David Kalstone ("'Persisting Figures' : The Poet's Story and How We Read It," in Lehman and Berger, 125–44), Richard Sáez ("At the Salon Level: Merrill's Apocalyptic Epic," in Lehman and Berger, 211–45), Henry Sloss ("James Merrill's *The Book of Ephraim*," in *Shenandoah*, 17, no. 4 (Summer 1976), 63–91 and 18, no. 1 (Fall 1976), 83–110), and Robert Mazzocco ("The Right Stuff," in *New York Review of Books*, June 16, 1983, 41–46).

12.    The most effective summary of the trilogy's plot and ideological content is in the Moffett monograph cited above, especially 152 ff.

13.    JM and DJ indicate James Merrill and David Jackson as *characters* in the epic. Whether as the *mind* or the *hand* of the scribe, they are even more reluctant than the pilgrim-poet in Dante to face up to their "vision"; see, for example, *Mirabell*, 6.8, 218–19 and 7.1, 224. Even though DJ is defined as the hand, he cannot confidently be considered the "passive" member of the couple who merely transcribes messages *mechanically*; see Sáez, 313n6.

14.    In "Dreams about Clothes" ([*Braving the Elements*] in *Selected*, 231–32), Merrill had implored "Art" [both the name of a dry cleaner and the elevated abstraction] to assist him in a moment in which he felt the desire to turn to the Divine: "Won't you as well forgive / Whoever settles for the immaterial?" (232).

15.    Reread from this perspective, this line from the lyric "Dream (Escape from the Sculpture Museum) and Waking" ([*The Country of a Thousand Years of Peace*] in *Selected*, 49–57) is clearly Dantesque and pertinent to present considerations: "Now that my life has lost its way" (49). Note that it is not (as in Dante) the "way" (as subject) that is "lost" by a complement of the implied agent (the poet); here, "way" is the object of the transitive verb "lose," the subject of which is not the poet but "my life." The effect is a crossing of Dante with the Gospel passage in which Christ asserts: "I am the *way*, the *truth*, and the *life*." However, as in Dante, at the end of the lyric a clear light of hope illuminates an atmosphere that until then was neutral and distressing, as in Alain Resnais's *Last Year at Marienbad* or in certain works of Robert Frost. See *Inferno*, I, 16–18: "vidi le sue spalle / vestite già de' raggi del pianeta / che mena dritto altrui per ogni calle" [I could see the back (of the hill) already dressed with the rays of the star that guides others along their proper paths].

16.    See *Scripts*, 5, 425: "Who else spread wings above you when God B / Sang in Space? OUR ST. BERNARD JM who— / Isn't it St. Bernard—helps Dante see / Our Lady? AH THE PATTERN BLEEDING THROUGH. . . ."

17.    I do not agree with those critics who complain about the scarcity of female figures in Merrill's poems, attributing it to his homosexuality. If it is true that at the end of the trilogy Maria Mitsotáki will reveal herself as an avatar of Plato, it is also true that she continues contentedly to play her role in female garb until the end. If it is true that Erzulie, queen of the sky (and one with the Virgin Mary and Kuan Yin) is fundamentally androgynous (as are "the blessed Luca Spionari," Unice, the centaur, and all the Archangels), it is also true that Nature (Psyche, Chaos) remains not only a character but also an irreducibly female symbol, sister of God B, as powerful as he is, his complement, and indivisible from him. Finally, it should not be forgotten that the poem ends, most aptly, with the moving inclusion of a tender *marital* love, that between Vasíli and Mimí, and that that love alone surmounts

the barrier between the worlds of the living and the dead. Also, the poem has fleeting but still important appearances by Maya Deren, Gertrude Stein, Alice B. Toklas, Maria Callas, and the nine muses. See Jacoff, 150.

18. As it were precociously, in "To a Butterfly" ([*Water Street*] in *Selected*, 79–80), the poet had already confessed his fatigue in confronting his "professional obligation" to see everything metaphorically: "How tired one grows / Just looking through a prism: / Allegory, symbolism. . . ." (79).

19. The "minimasque" at the end of *Mirabell* recalls the grand allegory at the end of the *Purgatorio* (see particularly *Purgatorio*, XXXII), but Merrill's spirits insist that the whole of life after death is "an unfailing surprise for the dead" (*Mirabell*, 9, 259–61).

20. Many critics affirm, justly I think, that Merrill is a much less difficult poet than he seems at first reading.

21. See Sloss, 99–109.

22. For the choice of Stonington and the abandonment of Greenwich Village, see Eve Ottenberg, "Into the Mystic with James Merrill," in *Village Voice*, February 25, 1980, 31, 46, 71; the definitive farewell to New York belongs not to 1955 (the year of the move to Connecticut) but to 1971 (the year of the destruction of the building in which Merrill was born and in which he lived for almost thirty years).

23. Compare Stephen Yenser, "The Names of God: *Scripts for the Pageant*," in Lehman and Berger, 265 and 274–75.

24. Compare *Paradiso*, XVII, 37–42: "La contingenza, che fuor del quaderno / de la vostra matera non si stende / tutta é dipinta nel cospetto etterno; / necessità però quindi non prende / se non come dal viso in che si specchia / nave che per torrente giù discende" [Contingency, although it does not extend beyond the painting in which your material world is depicted, is nonetheless painted on the face of eternity; but it no more acquires necessity from this than a ship going downstream does from the eye in which it is reflected].

25. See, above all, "Yànnina" in *Divine Comedies*, 25 ff.

26. Merrill has often been scolded for "narcissism"; see, for example, Vernon Shetley, "Take But Degree Away," in *Poetry*, February, 1981, 297–302 and Robert von Hallberg, "James Merrill: Revealing by Obscuring," in his *American Poetry and Culture* (Cambridge: Harvard University Press, 1985), 93–116. However, the best analyses of this myth in Merrill's poetry are in John Hollander, "A Poetry of Restitution," in *Yale Review*, 70, 2 (1981), 161–86; Sáez, 234; and Jacoff, 158. Finally, it should also be recalled that while completing composition of the trilogy, Merrill privately printed *Ideas, Etc.* (New York: Jordan Davies, 1980), in which these lines appear in the poem "Think Tank": "The harlequin all menace and greed / Made fitful mincemeat of the mirror kissed."

27. See "About the Phoenix" (*The Country of a Thousand Years of Peace*) in *Selected*, 45–46. The lyric that immediately follows it ("Voices from the Other World" in *Selected*, 47–48) is the first piece to indicate contact with the world of the dead.

28. See "Marsyas" ([*The Country of a Thousand Years of Peace*] in *Selected*, 41), in which the "better maker" is perhaps Wallace Stevens but may also be Ezra Pound. On the myth of Marsyas in Merrill, see also Sacks, 178.

29. "The Thousand and Second Night" (*Nights and Days*) in *Selected*, 92–102. Moffett sees Merrill's acceptance of homosexuality in the poem as moving his work in the direction of a poetry less burdened by a sense of guilt.

30. See "Medusa" in *First Poems* (New York: Knopf, 1951), 10.

31. See "Midas among Goldenrod" in *The Country of a Thousand Years of Peace* (New York: Atheneum, 1959), 28.

32. Compare David Bromwich, "Answer, Heavenly Muse, Yes or No," in *Hudson Review*, 32 (1979), 455–60. Although Bromwich's judgment of *Ephraim* and *Mirabell* is substantially positive, he thinks that the style (and especially the structure) of the work has

more in common with the fragmentariness of *Paterson* and the *Cantos* than with the ideological coherence of *Notes Toward a Supreme Fiction*.

33. "I keep rereading, discovering new meanings and connections each time. It's a perfectly spell-binding poem." Thus, Merrill, in the interview with Ottenberg. The other of the poem's *two* authors, David Jackson, offers the same final impression: "Yes, it all falls into place" (J. D. McClatchy, "D. J.: A Conversation with David Jackson," in *Shenandoah*, 30, 4 (1979), 23–44).

34. In this sense, the most important analogue is with Homer; the "books" of the *Iliad* and the *Odyssey* were identified by the Alexandrian grammarians with the twenty-four letters of the Greek alphabet.

35. See "Contents," 95.

36. Note the presence of the "magical" progression in the approximate number of lines: 3–6–9.

37. This disagrees with Jacoff, who proposes a different interpretation of the poem's structure; see 153.

38. I use the term *coincidences* deliberately. As in Dante, so in Merrill, *fortuitous* coincidences don't exist. In Merrill there is a "NO ACCIDENT" clause (revealed half-way through the poem but running throughout it). On this point, Merrill agrees with Jung, another of his primary sources: "Among the many prospective patrons for this poem—Plato, Dante, Proust, Stevens, or Auden—it is Jung who presides, especially the later stage of *Answer to Job* and *Memories, Dreams, Reflections*" (J. D. McClatchy, "Lost Paradises," 312 and 313. See also William Harmon, "The Metaphors and Metamorphoses of M," in *Parnassus* 8, 2 (1980), 29–41, especially 30.)

39. Like the word *fire* in Merrill, *fuoco* is one of the fundamental "complex words" of Dante's poem. In this connection, see the excellent and careful discussion by D. Consoli in the *Enciclopedia Dantesca*, ed. U. Bosco (Rome: Treccani, 1970–1978), vol. 3, 73–75.

40. Also similar to *Inferno*, XIII, 40–42, is *Ephraim*, H, 27: "A voice not his, less near, / Deeper than his, now limpid, now unclear."

41. Compare *Ephraim*, E, 15: "He remained / Sweetness itself."

42. See, in Dante, "Poi d'ogne lato ad esso m'apparìo / *un non sapeva che bianco*" [Then from every side there appeared to me *a whiteness I had never known before*] (*Purgatorio*, II, 22–23) and "Ben discernea in lor la testa bionda; / ma ne la faccia l'occhio si smarria" [I made out their blonde heads clearly; but their faces blurred my sight] (*Purgatorio*, VIII, 35–36). The observer's reaction to the indescribable beauty of a heavenly being in Merrill is analogous: "THE VOICE A MAN'S BUT O! / MELODIOUS & RAVISHING WE WEPT / IN OUR RED ROBES . . ." (*Mirabell*, 8.5, 250).

43. As Harrington observes, in German *hell* means "light" (588). All at once and confusedly the desperate spirit asks for help, curses, and surrenders himself to the *light* of the fire and of the life after death; something similar happens with all of Merrill's spirits when they die.

44. Immediately thereafter, Mother Nature comments, in a tone mixing amiability with irony: "NOT RUSTY, AFTER ALL, GOOD YEATS."

45. In his essay "Breaking the Mirror: Interruption in Merrill's Trilogy" (Lehman and Berger, 186–210), Willard Spiegelman interprets the entire poem as a following out of attempts to speak and not speak, understand, and allude. Interruptions, omissions, censorings (especially self-censorings), the substitution of questions for answers, evasions of questions, all these are, in effect, a further guarantee of the closeness of Merrill's poem to certain devices in Dante's. See also, Robert von Hallberg, "James Merrill: Revealing by Obscuring," in *Contemporary Literature* 21, 4 (1980), 549–71. Merrill's poetics is also in some ways akin to that of *dhvani*: see Ànandavardhana Dhvanyaloka, *I principi dello Dhvani: la teoria indiana del non detto poetico*, ed. V. Mazzarino (Turin: Einaudi, 1983). See also Elémire Zolla, "Mystical Silence and Poetry," in *Studies in Mystical Literature* I (1980), 14–40.

46. "A Dedication: for Hans Lodeizen," in *The Country of a Thousand Years of Peace*. This is not the place for an excursus on the "poetic silence" that runs through the Judeo-Christian tradition (in the classical tradition, divinity only becomes "unspeakable" with Neoplatonism). Some examples of the superhuman silences of the infinite do come to mind, however: the silence that concludes the experience of Hamlet, the exclamation of Moses before the burning bush in Schoenberg's *Moses and Aaron* ("Oh, word, you fail me"), the "free flight into the wordless" in Whitman ("A Clear Midnight"; see E. Carr, *Hundreds and Thousands* [Toronto: Clarke-Irwin, 1978], 54), the visions of divinity and truth that dazzle Oedipus and pilgrims to Mecca, those who are rendered mute by epiphanic experience (such as Dylan Thomas), the substitution for prayer of the mantra's concentrated litany of pure meaningless sound, and the mute humility of the publican in the corner of the temple. For connections between Merrill and Hebraic culture, I suggest the "silent listening" of Edmond Jabès (in his *Le Parcours* [Paris: Gallimard, 1985]). I think, too, of the theory of the ineffable in Schumann, in which the Apollonian is wedded to the Dionysian, and of the landscapes of absence of Caspar David Friedrich, which correspond to luminism in America. In modern music, there is the plausible paradox of John Cage's musical silence; in painting, those blank canvases on which only the spectator's shadow is projected. Merrill's poem could be, then, an enormous, hypertrophied production of the poet's "I," and the unsayable not so much a limit confronting the artist as a projection of his narcissism.

# Writing on the (Sur)face of the Past: Convivial Visions and Revisions in the Poetry of James Merrill

JEFF WESTOVER

> The pretty song, rising one will never know how, from a palimpsest memory.
> —William Cory, *Extracts from his Letters*
> *and Journals 1838–92* (1897), 308.

In art as in life, the past is a presence to be faced. James Merrill acknowledges this double necessity in his writing, often representing his relationship to his poetic predecessors in terms of his difficult yet reconciling relationship to his real parents. In fact, the characterizations of WHA (W. H. Auden) as "father of forms" and MM (Maria Mitsotáki) as "Maman" in *The Changing Light at Sandover* epitomize the mythopoeic importance of parenthood to Merrill's poetry as a whole, showing how his permutations of parental metaphor reflect the complex conviviality of his relationship to prior writers. In the tropic arc of Merrill's art, parental relations become poetic relations.

The shadow cast by the poet's financier father provides both the subject matter of many lyrics and an apt vehicle for expressing Merrill's sense of place in literary history, as in "Arabian Night," one of the shorter poems in *The Inner Room*. The speaker impersonally (yet narcissistically, too) gazes into a mirror, meditating on his reflection. The poem opens with a question, but since its syntax sprawls throughout the entire first stanza, that question strikes one first as an objective description and next perhaps as a kind of reverent invocation:

> Features unseen embers and tongs once worried
> bright as brass, cool, trim, of a depth to light his
> way at least who, trusting mirages, finds in
> them the oasis . . .[1]

The syntax suspended at the end of this first quatrain finds its resolution in the first three words of the second stanza: "what went wrong?" The trochaic

This essay was written specifically for this volume and is published here for the first time by permission of the author.

stresses falling on the interrogative pronoun and predicate adjective presage the question mark that punctuates this terse clause, while the alliterative and rhythmic energy of the question itself stages the drama at the heart of the entire poem. Something troubles the speaker, who, unlike the witch in "Snow White," seeks insight from a reflection.

While at first "No reply" seems to be forthcoming, suddenly

> Then ("there" of course, also) insight's
> dazzle snaps at gloom, like a wick when first lit.

In the instantaneous light of this specular epiphany, the speaker discovers that the perceived "stranger / kindles to father / / . . . whose traits [and *straits*?] . . . / / solve the lifelong riddle: a face no longer / sought in dreams but worn as my own" (14).

The poem describes a narcissistic vision with an eerie "twist," then, for the face found in the mirror both does and does not belong to the poem's speaker. The image that he sees reproduces the face of his father, so that a fusion of father's and son's face magically occurs:

> Aladdin
> rubs his lamp—youth?   age?—and the rival two beam
> forth in one likeness (14).

The "dazzle" of this poem is paradoxical. It consists at once in the speaker's recognition of his father's features in the lineaments of his own— so that a sense of unexpected familiarity invests his vision—and in the speaker's distanced or alienated relationship to those very features. Though "worn as my own," the face the poet finds reflected in his mirror seems to belong to someone else. The pun on the past participle of that deceptively simple adjective phrase suggests that the poet both wears his father's features like a mask, and that the aged features of his own face match those of his once elderly and now dead father.

The resulting sensation is uncanny, or, in the term Freud favored, *unheimlich*, since the recounted experience partakes alike in a domestic familiarity and a startling transformation.[2] Aladdin's alchemy may culminate in the soothing rhythms of the poem's harmonious closing sentence ("and the rival two beam / forth in one likeness"), but the *unheimlich* character of that alchemy lingers. In fact, the climactic vigor issuing from the enjambment of the last sentence (which includes the trochaic stress on *forth* in the phrase "beam / forth," so that the sparkling immediacy of the vision is rhythmically patent) reflects the eerie ambiguity of the mirror's glassy revelation. On the one hand, the phrase—composed as it is of two brief monosyllables—is strikingly spare. On the other hand, however, its pristine simplicity is complicated by the haunting "lifelong riddle" the poet alludes to at the beginning of the same stanza. The poem resolves the riddle through its ritualistic conflation of father and son, but such resolution requires a conciliatory acceptance on the son's part.

The uncanny quality of "Arabian Night" derives from its Oedipal undertone. The fact that the paternal face the speaker sees "solves the lifelong riddle" demonstrates the speaker's acceptance of his relationship to his father—so that the poem finally celebrates a genuine reconciliation between father and son. This surprised and deliberate adoption of an ambivalent yet harmonizing stance characterizes not only "Arabian Night" but Merrill's poetry in general. In fact, the persona Merrill assumes here can be read as an emblem for his poetry as a whole: in both his lyrics and *The Changing Light at Sandover*, Merrill routinely wears a "face" as a means of situating his poetry with respect to his *literary* as well as his familial forebears. As in "Arabian Night," Merrill's attitude towards his poetic predecessors is conciliatory and convivial rather than slavish or antagonistic.

To put it another way, as against Harold Bloom's thesis that every strong poet must symbolically kill his father, Merrill "faces up" to his predecessors by embracing them. Implicit in the gesture is a collegial view of the poet's relation to his precursors. Merrill "faces down" the potential threat posed by the example of the past without engaging the poetic figures of that past in some murderous Oedipal struggle. Although Merrill quite overtly addresses the Freudian model of male maturation in several of his poems—including "Scenes of Childhood," "Five Old Favorites," and, most emphatically, "The Broken Home"—he also subtly subverts and recasts that model. Rather than simply overthrowing the figure of the father, the poet simultaneously fends off and incorporates him, accepting the necessary presence of the past while presenting his poetry as an elegant overlay upon the texts of that past (just as the speaker of "Arabian Night" sees his father's features underlying his own). The more specifically textual model of the palimpsest better suits Merrill's poetic attitude towards the past than Bloom's Freudian one because it reflects the glimmering persistence of history between the very lines of the various texts that the contemporary poet produces. The living poet makes his mark on the face of his predecessors' pages.

Traces of the palimpsest-image appear in the pre-*Sandover* lyrics "The Broken Home," "Friend of the Fourth Decade," and "Lost in Translation," as well as in section X of *The Book of Ephraim*. In "The Broken Home," the speaker's vision of a living family portrait behind the glass of the window near which they sit functions as an "undertext." In this case, however, the palimpsest appears rather as a pentimento, for the poet's opening description is plainly painterly:

> I saw the parents and the child
> At their window, gleaming like fruit
> with evening's mild gold leaf.[3]

This "image that, gilt and framed, seems to have come as much from medieval religious painting as from contemporary life"[4] prompts the memories that unfold throughout the remainder of the poem. The poet implicates this initial picture in the subsequent narrative, so that its shimmering image underlies what follows. The image fittingly signals the past's inescapable presence, for it reappears in the poem at precisely the moment when the poet glimpses the "blue gaze" of his father's eyes "Through the smoked glass of being thirty-six" (*Selected*, 109). Finally, the window at the beginning of the poem corresponds to the "window onto the past" of the poem's closing stanza:

> Under the ballroom ceiling's allegory
> Someone at last may actually be allowed
> To learn something; or, from my window, cool
> With the unstiflement of the entire story,
> Watch a red setter stretch and sink in cloud (*Selected*, 112)

In "The Friend of the Fourth Decade," the poet's "Friend" tells how he has taken to soaking his postcards, performing a ritual of erasure that renders "The text unreadable," the verso of each card's picture "Rinsed of the word" (*Selected*, 139). The friend clearly reflects his desire to rid himself of the burden of the past through the exclamations of relief that punctuate the description of his rite. He speaks with delight at having "a lighter / Heart than I have had in many a day" and of feeling "Absolved . . . / By water holy from the tap, by air that dries, / Of having cared and having ceased to care" (*Selected*, 139). When the poem's narrator—the *first* "I" of the poem—tries the postcard experiment himself, however, the results are significantly different: "I watched my mother's *Dearest Son* unfurl / / In blue ornate brief plungings-up," he reports. But despite his best efforts, the narrator discovers that "the message remained legible, / The memories it stirred did not elude me." That the message on the postcard is written by his mother demonstrates Merrill's perception of his relationship to the past as being specifically familial. It seems "NO ACCIDENT" that the memory persists in the life and work of the writer: "Certain things," the poet finds, "die only with oneself" (*Selected*, 140). In other words, the poet consciously acknowledges that his own harbingers of the past necessarily persist; traces of the writing of others remain in the writing of the poet himself. The words on the postcard underwrite those of the poem.

The image of the palimpsest appears again in "Lost in Translation," in the form of "that long-term lamination / Of hazard and craft" (*Selected*, 280) that lies behind the puzzle pieces comprising the poem's central metaphor. One prior text contributing to such lamination, leaving its complex traces in the poem, is Valéry's "Palme," in the original or in Rilke's translation. These two texts—the second already a version of the first—underwrite "Lost in Translation." Untranslated phrases from both even stud Merrill's poem, and many details derive from Valéry's text or Rilke's translation of it.[5] Alan Nadel reads "Lost in Translation" as a response to *The Waste Land*, adding yet another layer to Merrill's laminations. Noting that Eliot's famous line, "These fragments I have shored against my ruins," once read, "These fragments I have spelt into my ruins," Nadel aligns Eliot's draft-version of the line with the translated language and Ouija letters of Merrill's poems: "with the publication of 'Lost in Translation' and *Book of Ephraim*, Merrill begins to spell out what Eliot had erased. . . ."[6]

"Lost in Translation" suggests that the work of the poet is "above all to be the inventive recipient, scribe, or surface of a message received from elsewhere. . . ."[7] The layered texts that lie behind "Lost in Translation" thus leave their mark—their overt and covert traces—on the *text*ure of the new poem Merrill produces.

Like "The Broken Home," section X of *The Book of Ephraim* combines hints of a saintly son's Oedipal complex with the organizing image of a pentimento. The chapter begins by referring to Giorgione's famous painting:

> X rays of *La Tempesta* show this curdling
> Nude arisen, faint as ectoplasm,
> From flowing water which no longer fills
> The eventual foreground. Images that hint
> At meanings we had missed simply by looking.[8]

Looking does not reveal the missed images here because those images lie beneath the paint of the final picture. While (as the word *pentimento* suggests) the artist repented of his first sketch and finally decided on something different, the images he initially drew form an invisible underpinning (or "underpainting") to the finished painting. The relation between these layers is analogous to the layered texts forming a palimpsest. Merrill interweaves the legend of St. Theodore, which he derives from the stratified texture of "Giorgione's palimpsest painting,"[9] into the several "stories" of his poem. He identifies the nude woman in the painting as Theodore's mother, and he alludes to the Oedipal legend associated with the saint, elaborating this scenario as an elliptical continuation of his own narrative. The complexity and uncertainty of Giorgione's subject matter is epitomized in the very layers of his painting. In his role as maker of fictions, Merrill "draws" on those layers, relying on them as an introduction to the subject of his own mother:

> All of which lights up, as scholarship
> Now and then does, a matter hitherto
> Overpainted—the absence from these pages
> Of my own mother. Because of course she's here
> Throughout, the breath drawn after every line,
> Essential to its making as to mine . . . (*Sandover*, 83–84).

Merrill explicitly figures his writing as an act of "painting over" (which incidentally recalls his earlier characterization of his writing, in section A of *Ephraim*, as "word-painting"). One immediate meaning of "matter . . . / Overpainted" in the context of the passage above is "Matter elided" (*Sandover*, 86). In other words, the text that Merrill writes over the face of the past, while it virtually erases that past, points beyond itself to a significant absence, to an underlying, other text—the splintered meanings of which persist in the language of his own work.

The marked Oedipal undertones in "The Broken Home,"[10] section X of *Ephraim*, and "Lost in Translation" (a poem about a child in love with his motherly governess) may prompt but do not ultimately permit a Freudian interpretation, for Merrill combines such undercurrents with a reconciling attitude toward the past. In X, the element elided is also consciously welcomed and embraced. The figure of the mother forms the matrix of the poem: "she's here / Throughout, the breath drawn after every line, / Essential to its making . . ." (*Sandover*, 84). The poet lauds and accepts the mother instead of rejecting her and assuming the authoritarian position of "the Father." Just as he reconciles himself to the presence of his father's features in the lineaments of his own in "Arabian Night," so he accepts his mother's mythical ubiquity in section X.

Nonetheless, while Bloom's agonistic scheme of poetic influence would force a misreading of the communal vision of Merrill's lyrics and of *Sandover*, there are aspects of the final stage of that scheme that do seem to apply to Merrill's trilogy. Bloom calls this final stage the *apophrades*, "the dismal or unlucky days upon which the dead return to inhabit their former house." He maintains that the *apophrades* necessarily "come to the strongest poets, but with the very strongest there is a grand and final revisionary movement that purifies even this last influx."[11] It is tempting to interpret Merrill's epic as one extended train of *apophrades*.[12] Bloom's observation that "Perhaps all Romantic style . . . depends upon a successful manifestation of the dead in the garments of the living, as though the dead poets were given a suppler freedom than they had found for themselves"[13] can seem a commentary on the specific characterizations in *Sandover*, with its constant interactions between the living and the dead.

Ultimately, however, Bloom's theory *is* incompatible with Merrill's poem. For, despite the claims to greatness that the poet clearly makes in the text of *Sandover*, and despite the fact that he occasionally measures the success of his poetry against what he considers to be the failures of his influential forerunners, Merrill insists on maintaining a place for those poets at the inviting table that his own poem embodies. "His is a style," writes J. D. McClatchy, "extremely composed and sociable."[14] *Sandover* "dramatizes poetic influence, verging on possession, and yet it does not follow the tragic logic of Bloom's violent battle of souls. . . ."[15] Bloom argues that "the strong poet's love of his poetry, as itself, must exclude the reality of all other poetry, except for . . . the initial identification with the poetry of the precursor."[16] Merrill, however, includes other poetic presences in his poem without compromising his own art.[17]

T. S. Eliot's "Tradition and the Individual Talent" provides a more useful context for discussing the generosity that suffuses *Sandover* than Bloom's psychoanalytic model, especially in terms of the poem's several important parallels to Dante's *Commedia*. Eliot insists that the contemporary poet must write with a "historical sense" characterized by "a perception, not only of the pastness of the past, but of its presence" as well.[18] The presence of the past that Eliot describes is as fundamental a characteristic of Merrill's trilogy as it is of the *Commedia*. Indeed, "The very fact that communication with the dead forms the foundation of the entire trilogy asserts the importance of tradition and demonstrates how much Merrill values listening to the dead and giving them voice."[19] Merrill explores, for example, the relationship between his own historical moment and the literary tradition that he creatively revises as thoroughly as Dante did in his own trilogy. In the *Commedia*, Dante dramatizes the kind of relationship between the poet and the past that Eliot advocates by casting himself as an inquisitive pilgrim who interviews the dead as he winds his way through the three tiers of the universe. Merrill similarly fictionalizes himself in *Sandover*, giving an extended account of the exchanges between "JM" and his partner "DJ" with both the disembodied dead and a mysterious host of swarming spirits.

Dante's poem and Eliot's essay, then, provide useful models for understanding Merrill's vast poem. The vision Eliot defines helps one to see Merrill's poetic report of his extended conversations with the dead as a lively dramatization of JM's study and assumption of their wisdom; it also provides a way for Merrill's readers to interpret his poem itself in terms of Tradition. For Eliot's vision of the possible relationship between a poet and the poet's impressive predecessors is sociably collegial rather than threateningly competitive. (It is precisely such convivial humility on the part of the pilgrim Dante, for example, that Merrill singles out for praise in a recent bit of prose: "Whatever Dante sees and hears he bears in mind, he takes to heart. It is his self-confessed frailty, his need for guidance, that draw us to him. . . ."[20]) In Eliot's view, the dead exert a fostering influence upon the living poet—an influence which nurtures the poet's creative potential.

Along these lines, Merrill's claim that "Dante's conceptual innovations . . . refigure rather than refute the thought that preceded them"[21] can be applied to his own innovations in *Sandover*, where the poet sings in several voices not his own.[22] As Rachel Jacoff remarks, Merrill's "cultivation of other voices, other visions, is part of the poem's theme as well as its procedure. It is the literary form of its human sense of community and yet another link the poem forges between the living and the dead."[23] Merrill and Dante alike people their poems with a procession of guides and literary celebrities (including, in Merrill, W. H. Auden, T. S. Eliot, Wallace Stevens, W. B.

Yeats, Alexander Pope, and Maria Mitsotáki; and, in Dante, Homer, Horace, Ovid, Lucan, Virgil, Statius, and Beatrice). The crucial importance of these figures for the two poets lies in the development and celebration of their own work. The voices and influence of the dead suffuse both poems and give to each a depth and resonance that is as social as it is personal, as historically conscious as it is deliberately contemporary.

In fact, it is precisely Merrill's use of dialogue in *Sandover* that functions as the palimpsestic "undertext" to that poem, as Merrill's and David Jackson's references to the Ouija transcripts testify.[24] "The upper-case messages, placed as they are in a larger poem that includes them in its history of the events, function as a text-within-the-text, and have the corresponding power over JM that any text has over a reader."[25] In *Sandover*, the historical texts that underlie Merrill's whole body of poetry actually speak through the fictionalized figures of the dead. As the source material for *Sandover*, the Ouija transcripts form a repository of letters analogous to Eliot's Tradition, in which the transcripts might be said to represent the sum of the great literary texts gathered from the past. Merrill contributes to a vast historical palimpsest when he inscribes his new text on the complexly marked surface of this already existing script.

It is significant that Merrill's use of voice usually occurs within the context of conversation because "in conversation one voice depends upon its counterpart; the interplay requires both self and other—and *Sandover* locates authority or truth precisely *in* this interplay. Making sense is revealed as a group effort, and an ongoing one."[26] The priority of conversation in the bulk of Merrill's trilogy reflects his communal perspective.

Such a perspective, moreover, extends to the community of the past. For by resorting to so wide a variety of voices—by making his poem genuinely polyphonic[27]—Merrill is also drawing on one more poetic device in order to celebrate his dialogue with the past, his existence within Eliot's living Tradition. The poet consciously opts for a position that distinguishes him from his poetic precursors at the same time that he locates himself within their community, emphasizing his dependence as an artist on the Tradition that he hopes his work will join. Merrill's poem exemplifies Eliot's sense of "conformity between old and new,"[28] particularly in its final sequence ("The Ballroom at Sandover"), when the poet prepares to read his poem to the august company of the dead before him—which pointedly includes Eliot himself. The poem's final scene combines the worlds of the living and the dead, fusing the past with the present by ending with its initial word: "For *their* ears I begin: 'Admittedly . . . ' " (*Sandover*, 560). The broad sweep of the poem's circle thus encompasses the bright point of the present and literally enacts Ephraim's description of heaven as "THE SURROUND OF THE LIVING" (*Sandover*, 59).

Although of a different order than the poetic method of the *Commedia* and Eliot's critical position, Linda Hutcheon's insights about intertextuality also reveal much when applied to Merrill's epic-length poem. According to Hutcheon, intertextuality situates "the locus of textual meaning within the history of discourse itself," an interpretive view that is tellingly akin to Eliot's insistence upon "the importance of the relation of the poem to other poems by other authors" and of his "conception of poetry as a living whole of all the poetry that has ever been written."[29] Indeed, "a literary work can actually no longer be considered original, [for] if it were, it could have no meaning for the reader. It is only as part of prior discourses that any text derives meaning and significance."[30] In *Sandover*, this dialectical contextualization takes the form of an "interface . . . of upper and lower case."[31] Though in the following passage the character JM in *Sandover* wants to retain his sense of individual intentionality and accomplishment despite the impositions of history and prior texts, the poet Merrill reveals his recognition of authorial originality as a fiction, exposing it as such in his handling of the exchange between JM and WHA on just that subject. JM first exclaims:

> And maddening—its all by someone else!
> In your voice, Wystan, or in Mirabell's.
> I want it mine, but cannot spare those twenty
> Years in a cool dark place that *Ephraim* took
> In order to be palatable wine.
>
> . . . . . . . . . . . . . . . . . . . . . .
>
>                       I'd set
> My whole heart, after *Ephraim*, on returning
> To private life, to my own words. Instead,
> Here I go again, a vehicle
> In this cosmic carpool. Mirabell once said
> He taps my word banks. I'd be happier
> If *I* were tapping them. Or thought I were (*Sandover*, 261).

As this passage suggests, "Textuality itself, as 'flesh made word,' unseats the author's mastery over writing."[32] WHA recognizes this fact, bluntly but gently observing that JM's complaints are inconsequential:

>                 THINK WHAT A MINOR
>     PART THE SELF PLAYS IN A WORK OF ART
>     COMPARED TO THOSE GREAT GIVENS   THE ROSEBRICK
>         MANOR
>     ALL TOPIARY FORMS & METRICAL
>     MOAT ARIPPLE! FROM ANTHOLOGIZED
>     PERENNIALS TO HERB GARDEN OF CLICHES
>     FROM LATIN-LABELED HYBRIDS TO THE FAWN
>     4 LETTER FUNGI THAT ENRICH THE LAWN,
>     IS NOT ARCADIA TO DWELL AMONG
>     GREENWOOD PERSPECTIVES OF THE MOTHER TONGUE

ROOTSYSTEMS UNDERFOOT WHILE OVERHEAD
THE SUN GOD SANG & SHADES OF MEANING SPREAD
& FAR SNOWCAPPED ABSTRACTIONS GLITTERED NEAR
OR FAIRLY MELTED INTO ATMOSPHERE?
AS FOR THE FAMILY ITSELF MY DEAR
JUST GAPE UP AT THE CORONETED FRIEZE:
SWEET WILLIAMS & FATE-FLAVORED EMILIES
THE DOUBTING THOMAS AND THE DULCET ONE
(HARDY MY BOY WHO ELSE & CAMPION)
MILTON & DRYDEN OUR LONG JOHNS   IN SHORT
IN BED AT PRAYERS AT MUSIC FLUSHED WITH PORT
THE DULL THE PRODIGAL THE MEAN THE MAD
IT WAS THE GREATEST PRIVILEGE TO HAVE HAD
A BARE LOWCEILINGED MAID'S ROOM AT THE TOP (*Sandover*, 262).

JM's response—"Stop! You've convinced me"—indicates his thorough "acceptance of the inevitable textual infiltration of prior discursive practices" in his own encyclopedic poem.[33] "Literary history is represented here as the garden around the manor, and literary figures as parts of, or occupants within, the actual building."[34]

Numerous echoes and allusions to the work of earlier poets in *Sandover* illuminate Merrill's amiable relationship to the literary past, demonstrating one way the poem "negotiates an eclectic textuality through a poetics open to the errancy of its own verbal process."[35] One such allusion occurs near the end of the second book of the epic:

Here where the table glistens, cleared, one candle
Shines invisibly in the slant light
Beside our nameless houseplant. It's the hour
When Hell (a syllable identified
In childhood as the German word for *bright*
So that my father's cheerful, "Go to Hell,"
Long unheard, and Vaughan's unbeatable
"They are all gone into a world of light"
Come, even now at times, to the same thing)—
The hour when Hell shall render what it owes (*Sandover*, 274).

This passage is an especially good example of the intertextuality discussed by Hutcheon because it is so exact; the quotation is verbatim. And yet the changes that Merrill works on the line—his imaginative variation on the theme—is truly, even magically, extraordinary. Merrill's treatment of the text from Vaughan demonstrates an unabashed admiration of that poet (whose line is "unbeatable") at the same time that it serves as a basis for subverting the traditional conception of "Hell." The intertextuality proper to *Sandover* thus demonstrates the poem's unique link with the past. For it is in the very midst of the poem's festive remembering that Merrill's elegant and witty originality most clearly manifests itself. In fact, the momentary "variation on a theme" that this passage represents might be said to symbolize the relationship between Merrill's poetry and literary history in general.

As Hutcheon's paradigm suggests, the "intertextuality" of Merrill's magnum opus is sometimes parodic and subversive—as when Yeats is playfully ridiculed by DJ when he wonders whether the lump in his hand might be "Yeats raising a molehill?" (*Sandover*, 220). But the allusions are not in every case subversive: because Merrill's relationship to the past is so warmly congenial rather than slavishly reverent or arrogantly condescending, the allusions in *Sandover* can function in the way allusions do in much of English poetry before his. That is, the allusions in *Sandover* illuminate a passage, providing historical and social contexts for a particular scene and amplifying the meaning of a specific event or conversation. The function of allusion is complex, for, as Hutcheon notes, parody does not preclude reverence for or admiration of that which is parodied: "to parody is not to destroy the past; in fact to parody is both to enshrine the past and to question it."[36] Hence Merrill's superimposed text both challenges and celebrates its palimpsestic undertext.

As I have suggested, Merrill's conviviality is evident not only in *Sandover* but also in the lyrics that have followed it. The *Gemütlichkeit* of *Sandover*'s after-dinner ethos—the sweet hum of its postprandial pleasantries—extends in an obvious way to "From the Cutting Room Floor," for example. Here, JM makes up for certain significant absences in his audience at the close of the epic, trotting out William Carlos Williams and passing along word from Whitman, chatting with Marianne Moore and alluding to Frost. The only comic stab is at that "POOR BLOATED BOBBY,"[37] the eternally returning ghost of Elvis Presley.

"From the Cutting Room Floor" continues *Sandover*'s conversational celebration of the dead while distinguishing the living poet from their company by singling out his ability to revise. As Michael explains, the famous dead "HAVE HAD THEIR DAY (& SAY). THEREFORE / CHANGE AND CHANGE, O SCRIBE!" The commanding impact of the angel's last injunction—"CHANGE! / REVISE, RISE, SHINE!" (*Settings*, 67)—indicates that "revision not creation . . . constitutes poetry as poetry."[38] The living poet composes his poem over the "DIMWIT FACES" (*Settings*, 67) of the dead, applying his new text as a finishing *gloss* upon their old.

Samuel Schulman detects in Merrill's earlier lyrics and in *Sandover* a "strong impulse toward . . . the dispersal of the self."[39] He views this tendency as a form of extroverted sympathy in a Whitmanian vein.[40] Such "outgoing" conviviality appears in post-*Sandover* poems as well. For example, in "Clearing the Title," an extended lyric full of images and verbal echoes recalling *Sandover*, the poet affably emphasizes the shared origin of the epic: "*Our* poem now," Merrill insists in an address to "DJ"; "It's signed JM, but grew / From life together, grain by coral grain" (*Selected*, 290). In these and similar lines, "Merrill implies that a poem always belongs to and is already signed by another."[41]

The Dantescan echoes of the following passage provide the proper historical context for understanding Merrill's conviviality because it demonstrates his continuing warmth towards his poetic forebears:

> Earth visible through floor-cracks, miles or inches-down,
> And spun by a gold key-chain round and round . . . (*Selected*, 292).

The quotidian domesticity of Merrill's mesmeric key-chain echoes Dante's heavenly view of the earth as a diminutive planet, seen as a celestial threshing-floor in the *Paradiso* (XXVII, 76–87).

In "Bronze" and "Losing the Marbles," Merrill turns to sculpture as a representative emblem for art, finding in the Greek artistry at the center of both poems a heritage that is at once—like the uncanny recognition of his father's face in the lines of his own in "Arabian Night"—threatening and inspiring. The moment in "Bronze" when the Greek statues speak is an instance of parodic satire at the same time that it reflects a feeling of genuine awe in the face of the past. The bronze warriors deliver their peremptory final remark—"We have done"—as both a supercilious boast and a curtly snide dismissal. Their terse valediction dares posterity to match their splendid prowess but scorns its very ability to do so.

Yet the poet is not altogether nonplussed—or "outfaced"—by the warrior glory of these ancient and only recently recovered figures. He responds with plausible optimism to their clipped, oracular harangue as a challenge to be seriously faced, at once acknowledging the limitations and potential of the past.

> Let's do. From the entropy of Florence, dead
> Ends, wrong turns, *I told you so*'s, through rings
> First torpid then vertiginous, our route
> Leads outward into the bright spin of things. (*Selected*, 321)

The historical and the personal merge in the language of this passage (as so often in *Sandover*), so that the poet's dizzying vision as he steps toward "the bright spin of things" assumes a broader field of reference than the merely personal and functions as the point at which past and present meet.

"Losing the Marbles" (from *The Inner Room*) continues Merrill's patronage of "the groggy treasures of the Glyptothek" ("Bronze," *Selected*, 322) as a source for his simultaneously reverent and irreverent parody of artistic tradition. The poem begins with the loss of a calendar, reflecting a displacement of time: "Ten whole months mislaid. . . ." The poet chalks this loss up to the aging process, so that when he writes, "Another / Marble gone"

(*Inner Room*, 84), he alludes not only to the theft of a Greek statue—a loss to a particular society—but to the personal losses wrought by time's scoring of the memory. Hence the speaker fuses the degradations of an entire culture's history with the decimations of his personal past: this is Merrill's method of preserving yet renewing the values posed by the past, posed either as overwhelming threats to the present or potential inspirations to the creation of new art.

Dual reference to both the individual experience of growing older and to the repeated rapes of Greek culture continues throughout the first "movement" of "Losing the Marbles." Merrill maintains such polysemy by marrying the language of personal experience to an often equivocal use of clear and simple descriptions. For example, the speaker puns, "These dreamy blinkings-out / Strike me as grace, if I may say so, / Capital punishment, / Yes, but of utmost clemency at work" (*Inner Room*, 84). Three lines prior to this, the poet quotes a line verbatim from Dylan Thomas's famous villanelle in order to "correct" its sentiment:

> Here in the gathering dusk one could no doubt
> "Rage against the dying of the light."
> But really—rage? (So like the Athens press
> Breathing fire to get the marbles back) (*Inner Room*, 84).

In the pitiful midst of its latter-day state, Greece undergoes a twilight demise—a kind of cultural *Dämmerung*. Merrill's persona strikes an ironical pose, belittling the fiercely nationalist rhetoric of the "Athens press" and asking in a politely condescending tone, "But really—rage?"—as though the bloated political cant of the newspaper obscuring the issue at stake negated the underlying legitimacy of the complaint itself. At the same time, however, the poet generously identifies himself with the Greek government through the metaphor signaled in his poem's title. Like the state, the poet also faces the loss of "marbles," though of a more invisible sort.

The second section of "Losing the Marbles" records the watery decimations of a manuscript. The manuscript itself is represented in the poem's third section, which functions as a palimpsest-version of section five. In other words, the section figuratively (and perhaps literally) underlies that of the fifth. The poem appears to dramatize the process of reconstruction necessary to "complete" the flawed text, calling attention to the (inchoate) structure that underwrites the fifth section and perhaps, by extension, the "whole" of the poem. Such an imperfectly "finished" text acknowledges its underlying sources by permitting intermittent glimpses of them. The fragmentary manuscript represented in the typography of section three thus serves as an emblem for the influence exercised by prior texts (i. e., their "bearing" [*Inner Room*, 87]) upon the process of contemporary composition. The dialectical tension between the third and fifth sections of the poem puts the past under erasure at the same time that it partially unearths it. In one and the same gesture, the poet asserts and surrenders his authority, exposing and celebrating the permeating presence of past texts within his current one. Merrill's poem thus resembles a modern city built atop the thickly layered strata of now buried civilizations.

For Merrill, the past both literally and figuratively underwrites his work as a poet. The metaphor of the palimpsest illuminates that work by foregrounding Merrill's keen sense of the persisting relevance of the past in the language of his own poetry. The poet reconciles himself to the claims of his family and his personal past in such poems as "The Broken Home," "The Friend of the Fourth Decade" and "Lost in Translation," while the intricate parallels between *Sandover* and the *Commedia* extend a similar acceptance to the larger family of Merrill's poetic progenitors. The treatment of family "themes" in the post-*Sandover* poems "Clearing the Title," "Bronze," and "Arabian Night" consequently resonates beyond the particular family attachments of the poet. In the same way, the poet's reference in "Losing the Marbles" to "our old poets" (*Inner Room*, 89) demonstrates his congenial solidarity with "past masters" in the art of poetry. By availing himself of their insight and by remaining conscious of its impact on his own artistry, Merrill "creates" an art that acknowledges its resemblance to the family of its predecessors at the same time that it consistently makes that family new.

*Notes*

1.  James Merrill, *The Inner Room* (New York: Knopf, 1988), 14. Hereafter cited in the text as *Inner Room*.

2.  Sigmund Freud, "The 'Uncanny'," in *The Standard Edition of the Complete Psychological Works of Sigmund Freud*, trans. James Strachey, vol. 17 (1955; repr. London: Hogarth Press; Toronto: Clarke Irwin, 1978) 224–26, 241.

3.  James Merrill, *Selected Poems: 1946–1985*, (New York: Knopf, 1992), 109. Hereafter cited in the text as *Selected*.

4.  While Vernon Shetley sees a "medieval . . . painting," (76) Richard Sáez finds a "renaissance portrait" that the poet "explodes . . . into a darkly shaded canvas of manneristic tension" (172). In any event, both critics consider the description to be very much like a painting. See Richard Sáez, "James Merrill's Oedipal Fire," *Parnassus* 3 (1974), 159–84; and Vernon Shetley, *After the Death of Poetry* (Durham: Duke Univ. Press, 1993).

5.  Stephen Yenser, *The Consuming Myth: The Work of James Merrill* (Cambridge: Harvard Univ. Press, 1987), 30.

6.  Alan Nadel, "Replacing the Waste Land: James Merrill's Quest for Transcendent Authority," *College Literature* 20, no. 2 (1993), 170–71.

7.  Jeffrey Mehlman, "Merrill's Valéry: An Erotics of Translation," in *Rethinking Translation: Discourse, Subjectivity, Ideology*, ed. Lawrence Venuti (New York: Routledge, 1992), 86.

8.  James Merrill, *The Changing Light at Sandover* (New York: Knopf, 1992), 83. Hereafter cited in the text as *Sandover*.

9. Willard Spiegelman, *The Didactic Muse: Scenes of Instruction in Contemporary American Poetry* (Princeton: Princeton Univ. Press, 1989), 206.

10. See Sáez, 172–73, and Shetley, 80.

11. Harold Bloom, *The Anxiety of Influence* (New York: Oxford Univ. Press, 1973), 141.

12. Timothy Materer, "The Error of His Ways: James Merrill and the Fall into Myth," *American Poetry* 7, no. 3 (1990), 72.

13. Bloom, 143.

14. J. D. McClatchy, "Encountering the Sublime," *Verse* 5, no. 2 (1988), 53.

15. Philip Kuberski, "The Metaphysics of Postmodern Death: Mailer's *Ancient Evenings* and Merrill's *The Changing Light at Sandover*," *ELH* 56 (1989), 244.

16. Bloom, 143.

17. Materer, 72.

18. T. S. Eliot, *Selected Essays*, (New York: Harcourt, Brace, and World, 1964), 4.

19. Lynn Keller, *Re-making It New: Contemporary American Poetry and the Modernist Tradition* (New York: Cambridge Univ. Press, 1987), 220.

20. James Merrill, "Introduction," in *Dante's Inferno: Translations by Twenty Contemporary Poets*, ed. Daniel Halpern (Hopewell, N. J.: Ecco, 1993), xiii.

21. James Merrill, *Recitative: The Prose of James Merrill*, ed. J. D. McClatchy (San Francisco: North Point Press, 1986), 87.

22. Helen Vendler, *Part of Nature, Part of Us* (Cambridge: Harvard Univ. Press, 1980), 226.

23. Rachel Jacoff, "Merrill and Dante," in *James Merrill: Essays in Criticism*, ed. David Lehman and Charles Berger (Ithaca: Cornell Univ. Press, 1983), 155.

24. See J. D. McClatchy, "*DJ*: A Conversation with David Jackson," *Shenandoah* 30 (1979), 35–37; David Jackson, "Lending a Hand," in *James Merrill: Essays in Criticism*, ed. David Lehman and Charles Berger (Ithaca: Cornell Univ. Press, 1983), 298–305; Merrill, *Recitative*, 49, 52, 57, 64, 66–67; and C. A. Buckley, "Exploring *The Changing Light at Sandover*: An Interview with James Merrill," *Twentieth Century Literature* 38 (1992), 420–21.

25. McClatchy, "Sublime," 52.

26. Lee Zimmerman, "Against Apocalypse: Politics and James Merrill's *The Changing Light at Sandover*," *Contemporary Literature* 30 (1989), 384–85.

27. Charles Berger, "*Mirabell*: Conservative Epic," in *Modern Critical Views: James Merrill*, ed. Harold Bloom (New York: Chelsea House, 1985), 183.

28. Eliot, 5.

29. Linda Hutcheon, *The Poetics of Postmodernism* (New York: Routledge, 1988), 7.

30. Hutcheon, 126.

31. McClatchy, "Sublime," 54.

32. Walter Kalaidjian, *Languages of Liberation: The Social Text in Contemporary American Poetry* (New York: Columbia Univ. Press, 1989), 102.

33. "There's always a lurking air of pastiche that, consciously or unconsciously, gets into your diction," Merrill has remarked. "That doesn't bother me. . . . No voice is as individual as the poet would like to think." *Recitative*, 80. Compare as well the poet's epigrammatic statement in his recent memoir: "Freedom to be oneself is all very well; the greater freedom is not to be oneself." *A Different Person* (New York: Knopf, 1993), 129.

34. Jeffrey Donaldson, "Going Down in History: Richard Howard's 'Untitled Subjects' and James Merrill's *The Changing Light at Sandover*," *Salmagundi* 76–77 (1987–88), 194.

35. Kalaidjian, 109.

36. Hutcheon, 126.

37. James Merrill, *Late Settings* (New York: Atheneum, 1985), 65. Hereafter cited in the text as *Settings*.

38. Richard A. Grusin, "Thirteen Ways of Reading the Ouija Board: James Merrill and the Question of Authorship," *Verse* 5, no. 2 (1988), 31.

39. Samuel Schulman, "Lyric Knowledge in *The Fire Screen* and *Braving the Elements*," in *James Merrill: Essays in Criticism* ed. David Lehman and Charles Berger (Ithaca: Cornell Univ. Press, 1983), 105.

40. Schulman, 98.

41. Grusin, 25.

# Braving the Elements

## J. D. McClatchy

The news that James Merrill had died last month in Arizona at the age of sixty-eight, of a sudden heart attack, caused a palpable shock in the literary world. Spontaneous tributes and readings sprang up all around the country. Disbelieving letters and phone calls crisscrossed the circle of professional writers. Not since a starry chapter closed in the nineteen-seventies with the deaths of W. H. Auden, Robert Lowell, and Elizabeth Bishop has the loss of an American poet been as momentous, or as widely acknowledged to be so.

That is in part because, however compelling Merrill's ambitions or demanding his methods, his readers always felt a sort of intimacy with him. For fifty years, the poet had used the details of his own life to shape a portrait that in turn mirrored back to us an image of our world and our moment. When his sixth book of poems, "Braving the Elements," appeared, in 1972, Helen Vendler's review in the *Times* struck early what has since come to be the dominant note in appraisals of Merrill: "The time eventually comes, in a good poet's career, when readers actively long for his books: to know that someone out there is writing down your century, your generation, your language, your life—under whatever terms of difference—makes you wish for news of yourself, for those authentic tidings of invisible things, as Wordsworth called them, that only come in the interpretation of life voiced by poetry."

For Merrill's funeral service, in Stonington, Connecticut, on a raw February afternoon, the little village church—its whitewashed interior suddenly looking rather Greek—was filled. A piping soprano sang "Bist du bei mir" to the plaintive accompaniment of a virginal, and Merrill's good friend the novelist Allan Gurganus delivered a brief eulogy. "Some people contain their grace," he said. "James dispersed his. It was a molecular nimbus he lived within, and he seemed, after nearly seven decades in there, largely unaware of its effervescent impact on the rest of us." Later, at the cemetery, where a mossy oblong of sod lay beside a tiny grave, friend after friend sprinkled a handful of dirt over the poet's ashes. One young poet, when it

First published in *The New Yorker* 71 (27 March 1995), 49–61. Reprinted by permission of J. D. McClatchy.

was his turn, also dropped into the grave a dime-store marble painted to resemble the globe.

For Merrill's friends, the shock has slowly subsided into the dull realization that there will be no more of his witty company. Yes, he was a great poet and knew he was meant to end up as books on a shelf. Those books—the last one, "A Scattering of Salts," is, as it happens, to be published this week—have long since confirmed his mastery: he knew more about the language of poetry than anyone else since Auden and used it to make poems that will remain part of anyone's definition of the art. But so, too, his conversation. He liked, as he once said, "English in its billiard-table sense— words that have been set spinning against their own gravity." At a large dinner party or on a casual stroll with an old acquaintance or a perfect stranger, he had an uncanny, almost anarchic habit of turning everything upside down. By his slight adjustment of perspective or realignment of a syllable, the dire became droll. He rarely relaxed his instinctive habit of reversing a truth or upending the mawkish, and his face loved to anticipate— with its pursed smile and arched brow—the pleasure his remark was about to give.

Last season, for instance, at a Met performance of "Otello," the Desdemona was in trouble long before her tragic end. Carol Vaness became ill during the opera and decided to withdraw. Her Russian cover, hastily done up in such a way as to make her quite a different woman from Vaness, took over the last act. After the performance, Merrill, ambling up the aisle, turned to a friend and shook his head with a rueful giddiness: "Poor Desdemona! She changed the color of her hair, but it didn't save her marriage."

The crack is characteristic in more ways than one. To begin with, he was at the opera, and nothing over the years had given him more pleasure or, at the start, had taught him more. He began going to the Met when he was eleven, and one of his best-known poems, "Matinees," describes its effect: "The point thereafter was to arrange for one's / Own chills and fever, passions and betrayals, / Chiefly in order to make song of them." Opera— its ecstasies and deceptions, its transcendent fires and icy grandeurs—is, above all, a stylized dramatization of our inner lives, our forbidden desires and repressed fears. It may seem surprising in a poet like Merrill, whose surfaces can be so elegant and elusive, but center stage in his work is passion. However his words may work to heighten and refine it, the urgency of the heart's desires is his constant subject.

That Merrill would joke not about Desdemona's murder but about her failed marriage also points to a distant event that had come to shape his imagination. At about the time he started going to the opera, his parents separated. A bitter divorce trial followed, and, because Merrill's father was one of the most powerful financiers in America—a co-founder of the great brokerage house of Merrill, Lynch—the story was national news. One tabloid even ran a photograph of young James with the caption "PAWN IN PARENT'S FIGHT." Again and again in the course of his career, Merrill revisited the scene, and nowhere more memorably than in his sequence of sonnets called "The Broken Home." Thirty years after the fact, the poem manages a knowing shrug: "Always that same old story— / Father Time and Mother Earth, / A marriage on the rocks." But the poem's impulse here to mythologize the trauma is part of a larger scheme. It is as if the divorce represented Merrill's own split personality. As much his father's son as his mother's boy, he had a temperament that by turns revealed what we may as well call paternal and maternal sides. He was drawn equally to the rational and the fanciful, the passionate and the ironic, America and Europe. And, from the very beginning, his ambition as a poet was—like the child attempting to reconcile his warring parents—to harmonize those two sides of his life. More often than not, he preferred to remain of two minds about all matters. And the energy spent exploring these divisions and doublings, all the obsessions and inventions of his work, from the delicacies of metaphor on to the creation of an entire cosmogony, fuelled a career as remarkable as any in American literary history.

As children, most of us fantasize a glamorous alternative: our parents are royal and rich, we live in a palace, we are adored and powerful. But if those happen to be the *facts* of your life instead of your fantasies? Merrill's parents had a brownstone on West Eleventh Street and a stately Stanford White pile in Southampton—The Orchard—with a dozen bedrooms, with conservatories and rose arbors, cooks and chauffeurs. In his 1957 roman à clef, "The Seraglio," Merrill portrays his father in his later years as a sort of pasha, surrounded by wife, ex-wives, mistresses, nurses, and flatterers—a man who loved his wives deeply but cheerlessly while counting on other women for companionship and fun. He was a man whose face "would have made the fortune of any actor. Frank, earnest, noble in repose, it was kept from plain tiresome fineness by being always on the verge of some unlikely humor, mischief or doltishness or greed." Merrill's mother, Hellen Ingram, was Charles Merrill's second wife, a Jacksonville beauty who had once been a newspaper reporter, and she kept close tabs on her son. It's almost natural that Merrill's childhood fantasies weren't the usual ones. If his ballad "Days of 1935" is a fair account of them, he imagined himself kidnapped, like the Lindbergh baby, and carried off to some shabby hideout by a gangster and his moll, with whose cheap looks—her rosebud chewing gum, his sallow, lantern-jawed menace—he falls in love, and from whose violent ways he longs not to be ransomed.

In a 1982 *Paris Review* interview, he said, "It strikes me now maybe that during much of my childhood I found it difficult to *believe* in the way my parents lived. They seemed so utterly taken up with engagements, obligations, ceremonies—every child must feel that, to some extent, about the grown-ups in his life." In fact, like most childhoods, his was lonely. He craved affection, and spent most of his time with a beloved governess, reading up on the Norse myths or devising plots to present in his marionette theatre. The loneliness—perhaps a necessary condition for any poet's working life—and a need to charm run right through his work. By the time he was eight, he was writing poems. By the time he was at Lawrenceville, he meant to make a career of it and told his father so. Charles Merrill had a volume of the boy's early poems and stories—called "Jim's Book"—privately printed, to the young author's immediate delight and future chagrin. Later, distressed by his son's determination, Charles nonetheless took a business-man's approach. He secretly sent his son's fledgling work to several "experts," including the president of Amherst, and asked for their frank opinion. When they all agreed on a precocious talent, the patriarch was overheard to say proudly that he would rather have a poet for a son than a third-rate polo player.

Recently, Merrill had begun to notice in his shaving mirror each morning how much he had come to resemble his father: "a face no longer / sought in dreams but worn as my own" is how one poem puts it. He had never thought to look for that face earlier, since the young need always to consider themselves unique. In his memoir "A Different Person," published two years ago, he remembers looking at himself in 1950:

> From the mirror stares inquiringly a slim person neither tall nor short, in a made-to-order suit of sandy covert cloth and a bow-tie. My bespectacled face is so young and unstretched that only by concentration do the lips close over two glinting chipmunk teeth. My hair, dark with fair highlights, is close-cropped. I have brown eyes, an unexceptional nose, a good jaw. My brow wrinkles when I am sad or worried, as now. Not that what I see dismays me. Until recently I've been an overweight, untidy adolescent; now my image in the glass is the best I can hope for. Something, however, tells me that time will do little to improve it. The outward bloom of youth upon my features will fade long before the budlike spirit behind them opens—if ever it does. It is inside that I need to change. To this end I hope very diffidently to get away from the kind of poetry I've been writing.

The kind of poetry he was writing then—his "First Poems" appeared in 1951—was very much of its time. The aloof, lapidary glamour of the poems, their dissolves and emblems were meant both to disguise feelings only dimly known and to declare his allegiance to a line of poets that could be traced from Wallace Stevens back to the French Symbolists. But before long he had written a novel and had a couple of plays produced Off Broadway, and from both experiences he had learned to write a more fluent and inflected line, often coaxed by narrative.

In 1954, Merrill decided to abandon New York City. He moved, with his companion, David Jackson, to Stonington, a small coastal village—half fishing fleet, half Yankee clapboard—that a friend had suggested might remind him of a Mediterranean port. He and Jackson bought a house; they had a brass bed, a record player, a rowboat, a table and two chairs to work on, and no telephone. He loved the light glinting on Long Island Sound, and the cozy, settled routines of village life; the town, he said, was "full of clever wrinkled semi-famous people whom by the end of our second season we couldn't live without." In 1959, he and Jackson made another move— to Athens. They soon bought a house there, too, and for the next two decades spent half of each year in Greece.

Both moves were, in a sense, strategic withdrawals. Like his friend Elizabeth Bishop, Merrill did what he could to avoid having to lead a Literary Life. Stonington's bright calm began to give his work a more domestic focus. In the collection named for his address, "Water Street" (1962), there is a poem that speaks of his "dull need to make some kind of house / Out of the life lived, out of the love spent." Always aware that the word "stanza" is Italian for "room," Merrill put together poems that would shelter his memories. Increasingly, his poems were autobiographical, reaching back to his childhood or puzzling over some passing event or involvement. He eventually described his poems as "chronicles of love and loss," and that term aptly stresses his sense of a life lived and understood over time, and links his two recurrent themes. From Merrill's college days on, his favorite writer had been Proust, for whom the only true paradise was a lost paradise. For both writers, love is not fully itself until it is lost, until it becomes memory, becomes art.

If the familiarities of Stonington afforded both distance and security, Greece gave him something else. Here was a landscape of ravishing rugged- ness, a culture of exotic simplicities. Better still, a language—he quickly mastered it—in which his accent wouldn't at once betray his class. He loved the anonymity it gave him; he loved the very sound of it: "kaló-kakó, cockatoo-raucous / Coastline of white printless coves / Already strewn with offbeat echolalia."

The poems set in Greece, vivid with local color, are the highlight of his two subsequent books—"Nights and Days" (1966) and "The Fire Screen" (1969). Landscapes as different as New Mexico, Rome, and Key West would later figure in his work as well. Merrill was a poet who looked out at a scene or around a room for prompting. "I always find when I don't like a poem I'm writing, I don't look any more into the human components," he told an interviewer. "I look more to the *setting*—a room, the objects in it." What was in front of his eyes would reveal what was in his mind. It was a quality he especially admired in the poems of Eugenio Montale—the way their "ladles and love letters, their furniture and pets" led finally deep into a labyrinth of feeling. The rooms of Merrill's Stonington house, which gave the impression of a *boutique fantasque*, were themselves an image of his inner life: a clutter of beloved totems. An immense Victorian mirror would reflect masterpiece and tchotchke, piles of books on the horsehair divan, a glass bowl filled with glass globes, bat-motif wallpaper, a Maxfield Parrish, a Tanagra figurine, a snapshot of his goddaughter, a Mogul miniature, a wooden nickel, cacti and shells, a Meissen plate, a lacquered Japanese travelling box, a windup toy bird, the upheld hand of a Buddha.

A couple of years ago, Allan Gurganus wrote to Merrill urging him to reread Tolstoy's novella "Family Happiness." The poet dutifully looked for it but could find it only in French, in one of the worn Pléïade editions he kept by his bed. When he opened to "Le Bonheur Conjugal," out fluttered a piece of paper on which, twenty years earlier, he had typed a stanza from Byron's poem "Beppo"—lines that he imagined at the time described a person he might grow to resemble:

> Then he was faithful, too, as well as amorous,
>> So that no sort of female could complain,
> Although they're now and then a little clamorous;
>> He never put the pretty souls in pain;
> His heart was one of those which most enamour us,
>> Wax to receive and marble to retain:
> He was a lover of the good old school,
> Who still become more constant as they cool.

Rather like his father, Merrill was a lover of the good old school. He'd found his own *bonheur conjugal* in 1953 with David Jackson. Jackson could play the piano, write a story, dash off a water-color; he was ebullient, daring, funny, irresistible. Over their years together, strains in their relationship were sometimes apparent. But they stayed together—if, lately, at a certain distance from each other. It was as if Merrill were determined to keep for himself the kind of relationship his parents had thrown away. He was constant to his other lovers, as well. He'd had affairs before he met Jackson, and several afterward. (For the last dozen years, he was devoted to a young actor, Peter Hooten.) He had a way of turning each affair not only into an abiding friendship but into poetry. He wrote some of the most beautiful love poems of this century. He relished Borges's description of love as "a religion with a fallible god," and few poets have looked on love with such a vulnerable and wary eye:

> Where I hid my face, your touch, quick, merciful,
> Blindfolded me. A god breathed from my lips.
> If that was illusion, I wanted it to last long;
> To dwell, for its daily pittance, with us there,

Cleaning and watering, sighing with love or pain.
I hoped it would climb when it needed to the heights
Even of degradation, as I for one
Seemed, those days, to be always climbing
Into a world of wild
Flowers, feasting, tears—or was I falling, legs
Buckling, heights, depths,
Into a pool of each night's rain?
But you were everywhere beside me, masked,
As who was not, in laughter, pain, and love.

Merrill's sexuality was like a drop of dye let fall into a glass of water: it is subdued but suffuses everything. He wrote openly and seriously about homosexual love long before that was fashionable. In his memoir he writes, "As in the classic account of Sarah Bernhardt descending a spiral staircase— she stood still and *it* revolved around her—my good fortune was to stay in one place while the closet simply disintegrated."

When I met Merrill, he was forty-six and had earned his first full measure of fame. "Nights and Days" had won the 1967 National Book Award, whose judges (W. H. Auden, James Dickey, and Howard Nemerov) singled out "his insistence on taking the kind of tough, poetic chances which make the difference between esthetic success or failure." And he had just published "Braving the Elements," whose exquisite austerities mark a kind of extreme in his work. Dense and rapturous, the poems are set amid the hazards of history and romance. His narrative skills turn out Chekhovian vignettes like "After the Fire" or "Days of 1971," where the end of an affair helps him to a wistful self-knowledge:

"Proust's Law" (are you listening?) is twofold:
a) What least thing our self-love longs for most
Others instinctively withhold;

b) Only when time has slain desire
Is his wish granted to a smiling ghost
Neither harmed nor warmed, now, by the fire.

When "Braving the Elements" was awarded the 1973 Bollingen Prize, Merrill was the subject of a *Times* editorial attacking those who continue to "reward poetry that is literary, private, traditional." That has been a sentiment, a peculiarly American fear of the Fancy, that other readers have shared. Some early critics condescended to his work by calling it "bejewelled." Ironically, their contemptuous dismissal hinted at a larger truth. From the start, but nowhere more than in this book, Merrill took his bearings from the four elements—earth, air, fire, water—and in many of his poems the jewel is their embodiment. Crystal prism or emerald brooch, waterfall or geode, dragonfly or planet, or whatever other brilliant lens he chose, it was to inspect more carefully the natural world's wonders. He once told a young writer, "It's not the precious but the semi-precious one has to resist." And, like most strong poets, he seemed largely indifferent to his critics. He knew his worth, and disdained the lust for celebrity. "Think what one has to *do* to get a mass audience," he once noted wryly to his friend the critic David Kalstone. "I'd rather have one perfect reader. Why dynamite the pond in order to catch that single silver carp? Better to find a bait that only the carp will take."

He was a poet who trusted language to tell him what anything means. Rhyme, wordplay, paradox only help reveal the hidden wish of words. Indeed, the O.E.D. is the collective unconscious of English speakers, he would say, for all our ideas and feelings are to be found there, in the endless recombinations of our words. He was himself rather shy of ideas in poems. "Shaped by ideas like everyone else, I nevertheless avert my eyes from them," he joked, "as from the sight of a nude grandparent, not presentable, indeed taboo, until robed in images." Those images are an astonishment. He notes a hotel's "strange bed, whose recurrent dream we are," or describes a plot of zinnias as "pine cones in drag," or Kufic script as "all trigger tail and gold vowel-sac." His lines are animated with colloquial idiom and quicksilver wit. Their perfection of tone is made to seem offhanded, their weight of allusion and symbol is deftly balanced. If the surfaces of his poems sometimes seemed difficult, it may have been because for most of his career other poets were loudly trumpeting the virtues of the plain style. For his part, Merrill would say that the natural word order isn't "See Jane run." The more *natural* way to put it is actually more complex: "Where on earth can that child be racing off to? Why, it's little—you know, the neighbor's brat—Jane!" So, too, the syntax of his poems darts and capers. The effect on a reader can be vertiginous. The long feather boa of some intellectually complex sentence may suddenly give way to a tank-top phrase. Merrill would have agreed with George Balanchine, who once said that the true figure for the artist should be the gardener or the chef: you love everything because you need everything.

By the mid-seventies, his poems were growing longer. He attributed that change to "middle-age spread." But even he was surprised by the project that occupied him for seven years, from 1974 until 1980. In fact, it was a project that preëmpted him. Ever since moving to Stonington, he and David Jackson had, on spare evenings, sat down at a homemade Ouija board and chatted with the great dead. No sooner did Merrill write up these encounters, in the volume "Divine Comedies," which won him the 1976 Pulitzer Prize, than the spirits demanded that he attend to more rigorous lessons they would give him. "Don't you think there comes a time when everyone, not just a poet, wants to get beyond the self?" Merrill said in an interview. "To reach, if you like, the 'god' within you? The board, in however clumsy or absurd a way, allows for precisely that. Or if it's still *yourself* that you're drawing upon, then that self is much stranger and freer and more farseeing than the one you thought you knew." Resisting the impulse to be either wholly skeptical or merely credulous, Merrill sat for the lessons. The curriculum ranged from subatomic particles to cosmic forces, and the cast included Akhenaton, Pythagoras, Montezuma, T. S. Eliot, Maria Callas, bats and unicorns, scientists and neighbors, God Biology and Mother Nature. In his epic account of it all, the poet managed to make the otherworldly revelations into a very human drama of acceptance, resistance, and ambivalence. And by the time he had gathered all seventeen thousand lines of his adventure into a single volume, "The Changing Light at Sandover" (1982), he had written what is—with the possible exception of Whitman's "Song of Myself"—the strangest and grandest American poem ever: at once eerie, hilarious, and heartbreaking.

"A Scattering of Salts" (to call it his last book instead of his latest sticks in my throat) is a wonderful anthology of Merrill's characteristic strengths as a poet. There are portraits and elegies, sonnets and free-verse riffs, high style and slang. There are pungent, elliptical little lyrics and the longer, loping narratives that were his specialty. In one he describes "family week" at a dude-ranch rehab center he is visiting to be with a friend, who has sought treatment there. The poet tries to adjust to the New Age therapies:

> This wide-angle moonscape, lawns and pool,
> Patients sharing pain like fudge from home—
> As if these were the essentials,
>
> As if a month at what it invites us to think
> Is little more than a fat farm for Anorexics,
> Substance Abusers, Love & Relationship Addicts
> Could help *you*, light of my life, when even your shrink . . .
>
> The message, then? That costly folderol,
> Underwear made to order in Vienna,
> Who needs it! Let the soul hang out
> At Benetton—stone-washed, one size fits all.

It ends with a haunting, lovelorn speculation that blends the newest jargon with one of poetry's oldest images:

> And if the old patterns recur?
> Ask how the co-dependent moon, another night,
> Feels when the light drains wholly from her face.
> Ask what that cold comfort means to her.

Cozy chats over the Ouija board acknowledge death as an event but not as a fact. They might even be said to represent at some level a denial of death. But the three collections that Merrill published during the past decade take a more realistic look at mortality. This final book has a nearly Yeatsian vigor in the face of the end. What Merrill sees on the microscope slide is everything we dread. "Dread? It crows for joy in the manger. / Joy? The tree sparkles on which it will die."

The earnest young poet I was in 1972 found the James Merrill who had kindly invited me to dinner one spring night dauntingly sophisticated. His features were faintly elfin, and his voice—a soft, cultivated baritone—drew one instinctively toward its flickering brightness. He had read everything (I found out later that in his twenties he had taken one winter to read all of Dickens, another for Balzac) but skated past any ponderous discussion of literature—though he could quote at will whole swatches of Baudelaire or Da Ponte or Cole Porter. He never played The Poet in company but felt himself "more like a doctor at a dinner party, just another guest until his hostess slumps to the floor or his little beeper goes off." He rarely read a newspaper and didn't vote, yet was scornfully eloquent about the technocracy's myopic bureaucrats and "their sad knowledge, their fingertip control." He worked at his desk every day, and, even to the extent that he lived for pleasure, he lived rather simply. If he meant to be a dandy in his dress, the results were more often merely eccentric. Old Auden wore carpet slippers to the opera. You could spot Merrill there in mauve Birkenstocks over lime-green socks, neatly pressed corduroys with a Navajo belt buckle, a shirt from the Gap, a Venetian bow tie, a loden cape, and a baseball cap.

His chief pleasure was friendship. Over the years, his friends ranged from Alice Toklas and Maya Deren to Richard Wilbur and Alison Lurie. To each he was tender and loyal. His friends, in turn, responded in such coin as they happened to have in their pockets. In 1968, when Stephen Yenser sent him a fervently used book—a palm-size, velvet-covered, dog-eared copy of "The Rubáiyat of Omar Khayyám," a poem Merrill adored—the poet responded in kind:

> Fortunate those who back from a brief trip,
> To equinoctial storms and scholarship,
> Unwrap, first thing, a present from a friend,
> And into Omar's honeyed pages dip.

Richard Howard once noted that the art of living was one of Merrill's unrivalled talents. "What one wants in this world," Merrill wrote, "isn't so much to 'live' as to . . . *be* lived, to be used by life for its own purposes. What has one to give but oneself?" It was always to Merrill that his friends turned when they needed advice. Here, for instance, is part of a 1973 letter he sent me from Greece. I seem then to have been in the throes of some now forgotten crisis of the heart. How sweetly he edged up to my worries. He began by describing the crowded summer in Athens, and his being content to stay blithely above it. Then he expanded from details to his theme:

> The iron gates of life have seldom seen such traffic, to judge from the confused rumor that reaches us here in the shade of the pearly ones. The real absurdity, you will say (and I'll agree, it's all so novel), is to feel in one's bones how utterly a boundary has been crossed. Here one is in Later Life, and it's perfectly pleasant really, not for a moment that garden of cactus and sour grapes I'd always assumed it *must* be. Oh dear, this sort of thing is probably just what you mean by my being "recessed" into myself. But it's odd. I mean, the times of greatest recession into the self have always been, for me, times of helpless suffering, such as you're going through; when there's no escape from the self. Perhaps any circumstance, any frame of mind, content, pain, trust, distrust, is a niche that limits visibility—for both the occupant and the onlooker? I read your last letter, in any case, with pangs of recognition. There's no special comfort, is there? in being understood at times like these. One is so mortified by one's predicament, and at the same moment so curiously proud of its ramifications. You won't be ready yet to *like* the fact of belonging to a very large group who've all had—allowing for particular differences— the same general experience. Later on, when your sense of humor and propor- tion returns, that fact ought rather to please you: to have so shared in the— or at least *a*—human condition. Write me as much or as little about it as you see fit. As you say, the particulars should probably be saved for the couch. Don't waste time feeling superior to your doctor. You are no doubt cleverer and more presentable than he is, but (with any luck) he knows his business, and the shoes he is making for you will last and last.

Of course, he gave a great deal more than advice to his friends. He was a soft touch, and had learned the difficult art of giving money away gracefully. By a friend's staggering medical bill or the down payment on a house, appeals from ballet companies or animal shelters, stories of neglected old poets on the skids or a young painter who needed equipment his sympathy was easily sparked. In 1956, he used a portion of his inheritance to establish the Ingram Merrill Foundation, whose board of directors was empowered to award grants to writers and artists. Over the years, hundreds of people were helped. The edge was given to the promising beginner.

What Merrill couldn't give away was the stigma that came with his wealth and privilege. Epicurus famously said that riches don't alleviate, only change, one's troubles. The fortune that gave Merrill the chance both to distance himself from the family who made it and to pursue an odd, intricate career was, I'd guess, a nagging source of embarrassment for him and may have occasioned, in turn, his aversion to grand hotels and restaurants, his recycled razor blades and Spartan diet. He used, long ago, to confuse his companions by declaring, "Thank goodness I come from poor parents." He meant that his parents' values had been formed—by the example of *their* parents, who were hardworking and middle-class—before they had money. In a sense, his own values were old-fashioned. What sustained Merrill was dedication to his calling, a high ambition, and a deeply moral purpose. If we give equal weight to each word, then this definition of a poet he once offered sums him up: "a man choosing the words he lives by."

When Merrill's ashes were sent back to be buried in Stonington, a box of papers came, too. Peter Hooten had gathered up poems and drafts from the poet's desk. Among them was a poem called "Koi." Behind the house he and Hooten had been renting in Tucson for the winter was a small ornamental pool of koi, the Japanese carp. The poem—the last he finished, a couple of weeks before he died—is about those fish and his little Jack Russell terrier, Cosmo. Of course, it wasn't written *as* a last poem, but circumstances give it a special poignancy.

Also sent home was his notebook. It is open now on my desk. He'd kept a series of notebooks over the years, their entries irregular, often fragmentary. Things overheard or undergone. Dreams, lists, lines. An image or anagram. The writing—even the handwriting—is swift and elegant. But the last page of this notebook is nearly indecipherable. Suddenly, at the end, you can *see* the difficulty he was having: the script is blurred, and that may be because he had lost his glasses. His breathing, too, was labored. On Friday, he'd been admitted to the hospital with a bout of acute pancreatitis. I spoke with him by telephone on Sunday, the night before he died, and asked about his breathing. He said that, though he'd been given oxygen, the doctors were not unduly concerned. The rest of the conversation was banter and gossip and plans for the future: a cataract operation, the new "Pelléas" at the Met. But his notebook tells another, more anxious story. The last page is dated "5.ii.95," the day before his death. There are two dozen lines, sketches for a poem to be titled "The Next to Last Scene." Typically, it starts by looking around the hospital room, and opens with what in retrospect seems an eerie line: "A room with every last convenience." It glances at TV set, cassette player, smiling lover. He would often, when drafting a poem, fill out the end of a line, knowing where he wanted to go but not exactly how he would get there. He'd done so here. I can make out "to see the other through." And then, the very last thing he wrote, "To set the other free."

*To see the other through. To set the other free.* Who or what is this "other"? The longer I gaze at the page, the more resonant these phrases become. Is it everything beyond and beloved by the self: the man in his life, the world's abundance, the ideal reader? Or all that burdens the soul, distracts the heart? Perhaps the psyche? Even the imagination? The impulse of Merrill's poems all along was both to brave the elements and to release them. Some poets try a change of style to force a change in their work. Merrill was a poet who instead sought fresh experience—a new landscape, a new lover—in order to abide by unexpected demands. At the same time, he sought to release, as if from a spell, the textures and colors of objects, the inner life of our arrangements, the hidden relationships among motives and emotions, the secrets of childhood and the energies of the unconscious.

It is still intolerable to think that there will be no more of his resplendent, plangent, mercurial, wise poems; that their author is like the mirror ceremonially broken at the end of "Sandover," "giving up its whole / Lifetime of images." James Merrill gave his lifetime to language, and to the way its hard truths and mysterious graces come to constitute our lives. Only a few poets in each generation—and Merrill was preëminent in his—can use language to make a style, and style to make a whole world of flesh and spirit, a world as momentous as the heart's upheavals and heaven's order, or as casual as a dime-store marble.

# Index

Akhenaton (Akhnaton), 53, 239
Alighieri, Dante. See Dante
Allen, Donald, 99; *New American Poetry, The*, 99; *Postmoderns, The*, 99
Antin, David, 100
*Arabian Nights*, 32
Ariel, 121, 169
Ashbery, John, 120, 136
Auden, W. H., 16, 19, 47, 52, 54–55, 73, 169, 192, 194, 215, 221, 231, 232, 237, 240; and Merrill, 116–44; "No, Plato, No," 117; "Ode to Terminus," 121; *Rake's Progress, The*, 198
Augustine, Saint, 192
Austen, Jane, 192

Bachelard, Gaston, 36
Bacon, Francis, 56, 192
Balanchine, George, 238
Balliett, Whitney, 4–5
Balzac, Honoré de, 240
Baro, Gene, 6
Barthes, Roland, 19, 146, 153, 154; *Lover's Discourse*, 153
Baudelaire, Charles, 66, 125, 197, 240
Bawer, Bruce, 14
Beatrice, 191, 194, 222
Bedient, Calvin, 9, 10
Beethoven, Ludwig van, 81
Berger, Charles, 11, 12, 13–14, 15, 19, 178, 180; *James Merrill: Critical Essays*, 11, 12, 13–14, 19
Bergson, Henri, 192

Bernard, Saint, 194, 202
Bernhardt, Sarah, 237
Berryman, John, 32
Bewley, Marius, 52
Bishop, Elizabeth, 40, 64, 73, 106, 130, 132, 133, 141, 231, 235; "Bight, The," 130; "Burglar of Babylon, The," 40; "Visits to St. Elizabeths," 106
Blake, William, 191, 192
Blasing, Mutlu Konuk, 18, 19; "Rethinking Models of Literary Change: The Case of James Merrill," 18, 19
Bloom, Harold, 9, 15, 217, 220–21
Bogan, Louise, 4
Bohr, Niels, 192
Bollingen Prize, 2, 7–8, 237
Borges, Jorge Luis, 236
Breslin, James E. B., 99
Brisman, Leslie, 15
Bromwich, David, 9
Brower, Reuben, 83
Brown, Ashley, 15
Browning, Robert, 78; "Fra Lippo Lippi," 78
Buckley, C. A., 18
Bürger, Peter, 101–2
Byron, George Gordon, Lord, 15, 16, 58, 73, 132, 236; *Beppo*, 236

Cacciaguida, 194, 195, 196, 203
Calderón de la Barca, Pedro, 192; *Autos Sacramentales*, 192

Callas, Maria, 239
Casella, 194
Cavafy, C. P., 35, 47, 66, 94
Cavalcanti, Cavalcante, 207
Chamfort, Sebastien Roch Nicholas, 94
Chekhov, Anton, 237
Chilton, Paul, 182
Church, Eliza, 78
Ciacco, 196
Clemons, Walter, 10
Cocteau, Jean, 56
*Commedia*. See Dante
Crane, Hart, 51, 64
Crane, R. S., 111
Creeley, Robert, 149, 158; *Pieces*, 158; *Words*, 149

da Montefeltro, Bonconte, 194, 202
Da Ponte, Lorenzo, 240
Daniel, Arnaut, 190, 206
Dante, 13, 14, 46–47, 48, 51, 55, 77, 135, 143n25, 190–214, 221, 222, 226, 228
Davison, Peter, 5
de Man, Paul, 104
de' Tolomei, Pia, 204
Debussy, Claude, 242; *Pelléas et Mélisande*, 242
Deren, Maya, 45, 192, 195, 240
Dickens, Charles, 90, 240
Dickey, James, 4, 237
Dickinson, Emily, 177, 179; #1129 ("Tell all the Truth but tell it slant—"), 177
Donaldson, Jeffery, 17, 19
Donne, John, 145
Drayton, Michael, 30; "Since there's no help, come let us kiss and part," 30
Dupee, F. W., 149, 150

Easthope, Anthony, 102
Eaves, Morris, 8
Einstein, Alfred, 183, 192, 200
Eliot, T. S., 102, 106, 116, 145, 150, 192, 193, 199, 219, 221, 222, 239; "Tradition and the Individual Talent," 221, 222; *Waste Land, The*, 193, 219
Emerson, Ralph Waldo, 9, 152, 155, 164; "Experience," 152; "Nominalist and Realist," 155

Epicurus, 241

Fanning, Edmund, 90
Farinata, 195
Fermi, Enrico, 192
Fermi, Laura, 179, 180
Fitzgerald, Edward, 62, 81; *Rubáiyat of Omar Khayyám, The*, 62, 81, 91, 92–93, 240
Flint, R. W., 11
Flower, Dean, 10
Forese, 194
Forster, E. M. 29
Frank, Robert, 103–4; *Line in Postmodern Poetry, The*, 103–4
Fraser, Caroline, 161
French Symbolists, 234
Freud, Sigmund, 12, 16, 45, 166, 180, 216–17, 220
Frost, Robert, 59, 164, 225, "Oven Bird, The," 164

Gardner, Thomas, 17
Gérôme, J.-L, 81
Ginsberg, Allen, 4; *Howl*, 4
Giorgione, 49, 192, 219; "La Tempesta," 49, 219
Graves, Robert, 105–8; *White Goddess, The*, 105–8
Guinizelli, Guido, 190
Gurganus, Allan, 231, 236

Harmon, William, 10
Harrington, Michael, 11
Hartnett, D. W., 15
Hayles, N. Katherine, 186
Heade, Martin Johnson, 64
Hecht, Anthony, 6
Hegel, G. W. F., 77
Herbert, George, 61
Hine, Daryl, 56; *In and Out*, 56
Hollander, John, 7, 10, 12, 56; *Reflections on Espionage*, 56
Homer, 202, 222
Hooten, Peter, 170, 236, 242
Horace, 222
Howard, Richard, 6, 17, 240
Hugo, Victor, 47, 55
Humphries, Jefferson, 17
Humphries, Rolfe, 4
Hutcheon, Linda, 222–23, 224, 225

Impressionists, 192
Ingram, Hellen. See Merrill, Hellen
    Ingram
Ingram Merrill Foundation, 241
Innocent VI, Pope, 134

Jackson, David, 1, 11, 14, 45, 47, 137,
    187, 190, 222, 235, 236, 238
Jacoff, Rachel, 13, 221
James, Henry, 88, 95, 118, 147, 159,
    160, 166, 167; *American, The*, 160;
    "Art of Fiction, The," 160; *Golden
    Bowl, The*, 147
Jarrell, Randall, 51, 101
Johnson, Samuel, 54
Jonson, Ben, 146; "Drink to me only with
    thine eyes," 146
Jung, Carl, 137, 180, 185

Kalaidjian, Walter, 17–18
Kallman, Chester, 52
Kalstone, David, 6, 9, 11–12, 13, 131,
    162, 167, 238; *Five Temperaments*,
    11–12
Karr, Mary, 18
Keats, John, 42, 58, 132, 147, 192; "Ode
    to a Nightingale," 132, 147; "Ode to
    Psyche," 147
Keller, Lynn, 16, 152, 153; *Re-making It
    New*, 16
Kennedy, X. J., 5
Kenner, Hugh, 150
Kermode, Frank, 180–82, 184
Kleo, Kyria, 47, 152, 165
Kristeva, Julia, 19, 146, 151, 152–53,
    158, 159, 161, 166, 168, 170
Kuberski, Philip, 17

Labrie, Ross, 13, 119; *James Merrill*, 13
LANGUAGE poets, 99–101
Larkin, Philip, 102
Lasch, Christopher, 177, 188
Latini, Brunetto, 194, 201
Lehman, David, 11, 12, 13–14, 19; *James
    Merrill: Critical Essays*, 11, 12,
    13–14, 19
Levertov, Denise, 175; "On the Edge of
    Darkness: What Is Political Poetry?,"
    175
Leithauser, Brad, 15
Lodeizen, Hans, 47, 194
Lowell, Robert, 4, 5, 32, 51, 106, 112,

145, 149, 156, 158, 192, 231;
    *Dolphin, The*, 156, 158; *Life Studies*,
    4, 5
Loy, Mina, 158; *Love Songs for Joannes*, 158
Lucan, 222
Lucy, Saint, 195
Lurie, Alison, 19, 240

McClatchy, J. D., 11, 12–13, 13, 16, 18,
    19, 20, 111, 138, 220
Macdonald, D. L., 16
Magowan, Robert, 78
Mallarmé, Stéphane, 127
Manley, Lawrence, 111
Mariani, Andrea, 14, 18
Martin, Robert K., 11
Materer, Timothy, 17, 18
Mazzocco, Robert, 11
Mehlman, Jeffrey, 18
Mendelson, Edward, 120
Meredith, William, 5
Merrill, Charles (brother), 78; *Walled
    Garden, The*, 78
Merrill, Charles E. (father), 1, 18, 47,
    64–66, 78–79, 89, 92, 128–29,
    138, 167–68, 215–18, 220, 226,
    232–34, 236
Merrill, Doris (sister), 78
Merrill, Hellen Ingram (mother), 1, 47,
    78–79, 89, 92, 123, 123–24,
    128–29, 138, 159, 161–62, 165,
    166, 167, 168, 215, 218, 219, 220,
    232–33
Merrill, James: and apocalypse, 181–88;
    and Auden, 116–44; critical
    reputation of, 2–20; and Dante,
    190–214; and Florida, 63–66; life of,
    1–2, 7, 12, 18, 50–51, 78–79, 89,
    91–92, 231–43; literary relations in
    work of, 215–30; as love poet,
    145–74; and musical form, 81; and
    opera, 125–26; paradox in work of,
    129–30; place in contemporary
    American poetry of, 2–4, 99–115,
    116–44; and politics, 113, 175–89;

BOOKS:
*Black Swan, The*, 2, 146; *Braving the
    Elements*, 7–8, 13, 38–43, 122, 128,
    146, 158, 164, 165, 167, 231, 237;
    *Changing Light at Sandover, The*, 2,
    8–11, 13–14, 15, 16, 17–18, 19,

61, 72–73, 77, 78, 90, 92, 93, 95,
106, 119–20, 132, 134–42, 169–70,
175–89, 190–214, 215, 217,
220–25, 228, 238–39, 243; *Country
of a Thousand Years of Peace, The*, 5,
12–13, 27–30, 53–54; *(Diblos)
Notebook, The*, 5–6, 8, 56, 123;
*Different Person, A*, 1, 234; *Divine
Comedies*, 9, 11, 44–49, 78, 122,
131, 146, 190, 199, 238; *Fire Screen,
The*, 6–7, 13, 36–37, 47, 122, 124,
128, 146, 154, 155, 157, 158, 162,
164, 166, 167, 169, 202, 235; *First
Poems*, 4, 39, 47, 53, 234; *From the
First Nine*, 10–11, 78, 146, 155;
*Inner Room, The*, 15–16, 147, 215;
*Jim's Book*, 2, 234; *Late Settings*, 15,
16, 57–69, 170, 176, 178; *Mirabell*,
9–10, 15, 50–56, 134, 135, 136,
178, 179, 180, 183, 186, 187, 191,
199–200; *Nights and Days*, 6, 7,
31–35, 38, 138, 146, 148, 149,
151, 152, 154, 158, 160, 169, 192,
235, 237; *Scattering of Salts, A*, 2, 19,
70–73, 239; *Scripts for the Pageant*, 9,
10, 85, 93, 136, 139, 140, 178,
180, 187, 191, 194, 197, 200;
*Selected Poems*, 11; *Seraglio, The*, 4–5,
49, 79, 123, 233; *Water Street*, 5, 6,
13, 31, 32, 34, 35, 45, 80, 104,
118–19, 148, 235

ESSAY:
"The Beaten Path," 179

PLAYS:
*Bait, The*, 96; "Image Maker, The," 16;
*Immortal Husband, The*, 78

POEMS:
"About the Phoenix," 198; "After the
Fire," 41, 164–165, 201, 237;
"Angel," 196; "Another August,"
157, 167; "Arabian Night," 215–17,
220, 226, 228; "At the Bullfight,"
28, 29–30; "Ballroom at Sandover,
The," 222; "Between Us," 149, 151;
"Black Swan, The," 73; *Book of
Ephraim, The*, 9, 10, 11, 44–49,
51–52, 55, 72, 77, 78, 79, 84,
95–96, 123, 134, 137, 146, 157,
158, 164, 169–70, 175, 178, 179,
180, 183, 185, 186, 190, 191, 193,
194–95, 199, 200, 217, 219–20;
"Broken Bowl, The," 146–48, 167;
"Broken Home, The," 34, 45, 49,
51, 78–79, 107, 138, 175, 177,
217–18, 219, 220, 228, 233;
"Bronze," 17, 60–61, 178, 226, 228;
"Caesarion," 59; "Carpet Not Bought,
A," 35; "Charioteer of Delphi, The,"
28, 29; "Childlessness," 107; "Chimes
for Yahya," 203; "Clearing the Title,"
66, 169–70, 225–26, 228; "Coda:
The Higher Keys," 141, 198, 200;
"Country of a Thousand Years of
Peace, The," 47; "Cruise, The," 29;
"Days of 1935," 40–41, 128–29,
166, 168, 233; "Days of 1941 and
'44," 66–67; "Days of 1964," 35,
151–54, 157, 167; "Days of 1971,"
165, 237; "Doodler, The," 30;
"Dream (Escape from the Sculpture
Museum) and Waking," 30; "Dreams
about Clothes," 39–40; "Dunes,
The," 28; "18 West 11th Street,"
41–42, 94; "Envoys, The," 123, 155;
"Fever, A," 95, 159–60, 164, 165,
170; "Fire Poem," 28, 29; "Five Old
Favorites," 217; Flèche D'Or," 42;
"Flying from Byzantium," 111,
123–24, 155–57, 159, 160, 165,
167; "Friend of the Fourth Decade,
The," 122–23, 125, 131, 157, 196,
217, 218, 228; "From the Cupola,"
4, 32, 35, 38, 51, 90, 96, 150, 151,
153, 169, 187; "From the Cutting
Room Floor," 225; "Grass," 61–62,
176; "Hour Glass II," 85;
"Hourglass," 85; "House Fly,"
67–68, 170; "In Monument Valley,"
127; "In Nine Sleep Valley," 51,
164, 168; "Kimono, The," 195;
"Koi," 242; "Komboloi," 42;
"Laboratory Poem," 29; "Last
Words," 157; "Log," 41, 164, 206;
"Losing the Marbles," 226–28; "Lost
in Translation," 9, 18, 49, 51,
77–98, 133–34, 138, 146, 186,
217, 218–19, 220, 228; "McCane's
Falls," 201; "Mandala," 164;
"Marsyas," 28, 30; "Matinees," 6–7,
81, 125, 154, 156, 162, 167, 232;
"Medusa," 198–99; "Midas among

Goldenrod," 199; "Mirror," 12, 30; "More Enterprise," 123; "Mornings in a New House," 124, 161–62, 164, 165; "Narrow Escape, A," 29; "Next to Last Scene, The," 242–43; "Nightgown," 148, 149; "Nine Lives," 72; "Octopus, The," 28; "Olive Grove," 28; "Opera Company, The," 126; "Overdue Pilgrimage to Nova Scotia," 73; "Page from the Koran," 60; "Palm Beach with Portuguese Man-of-War," 63–66, 67; "Part of the Vigil," 155; "Phoenix, The," 29; "Pier Under Pisces, The," 63–64; "Processional," 20, 96–97; "Radiometer," 178; "Remora," 157, 159; "Renewal, A," 30; "Roger Clay's Proposal," 113; "Room at the Heart of Things, A," 147–48, 170; "Salome," 29; "Samos," 184, 185, 201, 204–5; "Santorini: Stopping the Leak," 57–59, 67; "Scenes of Childhood," 217; "Strato in Plaster," 166; "Summer People, The," 77, 128, 162–64, 166, 167; "Survival, A," 28; "Syrinx," 4, 42–43, 169; "Tenancy, A," 107, 148; "Think Tank," 62–63; "Thousand and Second Night, The," 32–34, 35, 81, 148–49, 151, 156, 167, 192; "Timepiece, A," 30; "To a Butterfly," 118–19, 212n18; "To My Greek," 123, 154–55, 156, 158, 159, 162; "Topics," 59–60; "Under Libra: Weights and Measures," 42, 168; "Up and Down," 38, 39, 45, 168; "Upon a Second Marriage," 30; "Upset, An," 61; "Upward Look, An," 71; "Urban Convalescence, An," 31, 51, 104–10; "Valery: Palme," 85–86; "Verse for Urania," 130–31; "Violent Pastoral," 34, 149; "Voices from the Otherworld," 53–54; "Will, The," 81, 194; "Willowware Cup," 42, 167; "Yánnina," 49, 131–33
Merwin, W. S., 19, 112
Midas, 199
Milton, John, 145, 191, 192, 202
Mitsotáki, Maria, 47, 52, 138, 184, 194, 215, 222
Moffett, Judith, 8, 9, 10, 12, 14–15,

134; *James Merrill: An Introduction to the Poetry*, 14–15
Molesworth, Charles, 10
Montale, Eugenio, 94, 235
Montezuma II, 239
Moore, Marianne, 73, 89, 111, 222; "No Swan So Fine," 73
Morse, Robert, 55, 194, 198
Mouflouzélis, Strato, 47, 67–69, 123, 125, 166, 169
Mozart, Wolfgang Amadeus, 81

Nadel, Alan, 18, 219
National Book Award, 2, 237
Nemerov, Howard, 4, 237
New Critics, 2, 147
Newton, Sir Isaac, 186
Nietzsche, Friedrich, 104, 158
Niobe, 199

O'Hara, Frank, 146; "Having a Coke with You," 146
Olson, Charles, 100
Ovid, 222
*Oxford English Dictionary*, 238

Paglia, Camille, 161
Palmer, Michael, 100–101
Panayioti, 41
Parisi, Joseph, 9
Parrish, Maxfield, 236
Pascal, Blaise, 42
*Penguin Book of Love Poetry, The*, 145
Perkins, David, 16, 169
Perloff, Marjorie, 7, 99, 104
Petrarch, 48
Pettingell, Phoebe, 9, 10, 16
Pevear, Richard, 8
Piccarda, 195
Plath, Sylvia, 19
Plato, 138, 152, 192, 194; *Phaedrus*, 153; *Symposium*, 152
Pointillists, 192
Polhemus, Robert, 162; *Erotic Faith*, 162
Polito, Robert, 19; *Reader's Guide to James Merrill's "The Changing Light at Sandover,"* A, 19
Ponge, Francis, 124; *Things*, 124; *Voice of Things, The*, 124
Pope, Alexander, 15, 49, 68, 73, 111, 222; *Rape of the Lock, The*, 111
Porter, Cole, 240

Poss, Stanley, 9
Pound, Ezra, 52, 54, 87, 99, 100, 102,
    104, 106, 107, 116, 150, 164, 199;
    *Cantos, The*, 54, 87, 106, 107, 183;
    "Hugh Selwyn Mauberley," 164
Presley, Elvis, 225
Pritchard, William, 7
Prospero, 39, 72, 121, 169
Proust, Marcel, 1, 13, 15, 39, 45, 47, 49,
    66, 67, 80, 83, 85, 86–87, 88,
    95–96, 125, 192, 197, 235; *A la
    Recherche du temps perdu*, 80, 83
Pulitzer Prize, 2, 238
Pynchon, Thomas, 186
Pythagoras, 239

Ransom, John Crowe, 2, 29
Reeve, F. D., 7
Rich, Adrienne, 32, 145, 146, 149;
    *Leaflets*, 149
Richardson, James, 11
Rilke, Rainer Maria, 2, 19, 60–61,
    79–80, 81, 82, 83–84, 85, 86, 90,
    93, 94, 95, 96, 133, 197, 218–19;
    "Archaic Torso of Apollo, An,"
    60–61,; *Duino Elegies* (8), 93; *Letters to
    a Young Poet*, 86; "Palme"
    (translation), 79–80, 81, 82, 83–84,
    85, 94, 95, 96, 133, 218–19
Rimbaud, Arthur, 41, 151
Rossini, Giacomo, 192

Sacks, Peter, 14
Sáez, Richard, 8, 14
Salter, Mary Jo, 10
Sampson, Dennis, 15–16
Sartre, Jean Paul, 184; *Nausea*, 183
Sayre, Henry, 103–4; *Line in Postmodern
    Poetry, The*, 103–4
Scheherazade, 32, 35, 129
Schulman, Samuel E., 13, 225
Selinger, Eric Murphy, 19
Sexton, Anne, 106
Shakespeare, William, 145; *As You Like It*,
    149; *Love's Labor's Lost*, 145; *Tempest,
    The*, 40, 72, 121, 169
Shaw, Robert B., 9
Shelley, Percy Bysshe, 59, 150, 192;
    "Mont Blanc," 78
Shetley, Vernon, 10, 15, 18; *After the
    Death of Poetry*, 18

Sidney, Sir Philip, 145, 167; *Astrophil and
    Stella*, 145
Singer, Irving, 153, 154
Sloss, Henry, 11, 12
Socrates, 153
Sontag, Susan, 11, 175
Speke, John Hanning, 90
Spender, Stephen, 8
Spenser, Edmund, 145, 164
Spiegelman, Willard, 9, 11, 14, 17
Spinoza, Baruch (Benedict de), 192
Statius, 222
Stein, Gertrude, 100, 157, 192; *Making of
    Americans, The*, 157
Stendhal, (Marie-Henri Beyle), 163
Stevens, Wallace, 2, 47, 49, 51, 54, 60,
    68, 95, 106, 116, 121, 124, 126,
    127, 131, 136, 137, 139, 150, 154,
    155, 170, 175, 182, 192, 221, 234;
    "Final Soliloquy of the Interior
    Paramour," 154, 170; "Notes toward
    a Supreme Fiction," 175, 182;
    "Sunday Morning," 78
Stitt, Peter, 9–10, 15
Strato. See Mouflouzélis, Strato
Stravinsky, Igor, 192, 198; *Rake's Progress,
    The*, 198
Sword, Helen, 18–19

Theodore, Saint, 219
Thomas Aquinas, Saint, 192
Thomas, Dylan, 227; "Do Not Go Gentle
    Into that Good Night," 227
Tillinghast, Richard, 10
Todorov, Tzvetan, 102–3
Toklas, Alice B., 240
Tolstoy, Leo, 236; *Family Happiness*,
    236
Tynianov, 18, 102–3

Valéry, Paul, 49, 77, 79–80, 83, 85, 90,
    94, 95, 96, 133, 197, 218–19;
    "Palme," 49, 79–80, 83, 85, 94, 95,
    96, 133, 218–19
Van Duyn, Mona, 5, 6, 146
Vaness, Carol, 232
Vassilikós, Vassilis (Vassili Vasilikos;
    Vasíli), 94, 184
Vendler, Helen, 8, 10, 15, 16, 19, 94,
    119, 138, 231
Verdi, Giuseppe, 90, 192; *Otello*, 232
Vernon, John, 8

Virgil, 194, 201, 202, 205, 208, 222
von Hallberg, Robert, 12, 112, 175, 178

Wagner, Richard, 6–7, 192, 197; *Das Rheingold*, 6–7
Weathermen, the, 7, 42
Wellesley, Dorothy, 92
Westover, Jeff, 19
White, Edmund, 12
Whitman, Walt, 17, 64, 78, 103, 155, 225; "To You," 155, 239; *Song of Myself*, 239; "When Lilacs Last in the Dooryard Bloom'd," 78
Wilbur, Richard, 240
Wilde, Oscar, 53
Wilkerson, Cathy, 7
Williams, William Carlos, 54, 100, 106, 116, 145, 225; *Paterson*, 54, 183; "This Is Just to Say," 145
Woolf, Virginia, 116

Wordsworth, William, 53, 231; "Tintern Abbey," 78
Wylie, Elinor, 2

Yeaton, Dana, 10
Yeats, William Butler, 2, 6, 15, 18, 32, 39, 40, 55, 58, 59, 60, 77, 92, 111, 125, 145, 156, 166, 183, 191, 192, 205, 207, 221–22, 225, 240; "Circus Animals' Desertion, The," 156; "News for the Delphic Oracle," 166; "Sailing to Byzantium," 125; "Whence Had They Come," 145
Yenser, Stephen, 8, 9, 12, 14, 16, 19, 150, 161, 162, 164, 175–76, 178, 179, 185, 187, 240; *Consuming Myth: The Work of James Merrill, The*, 16

Zimmer, Heinrich, 47
Zimmerman, Lee, 17
Zogheb, Bernard de, 90–91; *Phaedra*, 90